Women in Civil War Texas

Women in Civil War Texas

Diversity and Dissidence in the Trans-Mississippi

EDITED BY

Deborah M. Liles and Angela Boswell

UNT PRESS

Denton, Texas

10 9 8 7 6 5 4 3 2 1

Permissions:
University of North Texas Press
1155 Union Circle #311336
Denton, TX 76203-5017

The paper used in this book meets the minimum requirements of the American National Standard for Permanence of Paper for Printed Library Materials, z39.48.1984. Binding materials have been chosen for durability.

Library of Congress Cataloging-in-Publication Data

Names: Liles, Debbie M., editor. | Boswell, Angela, 1965- editor.
Title: Women in Civil War Texas : diversity and dissidence in the Trans-Mississippi / edited by Deborah M. Liles and Angela Boswell.
Description: Denton, Texas : University of North Texas Press, [2016] | Includes bibliographical references and index.
Identifiers: LCCN 2016028696| ISBN 9781574416510 (cloth : alk. paper) | ISBN 9781574416602 (ebook)
Subjects: LCSH: Texas--History--Civil War, 1861-1865. | Women--Texas--History--19th century. | United States--History--Civil War, 1861-1865--Women. | Women pioneers--Texas.
Classification: LCC F391 .W78 2016 | DDC 305.409764/09034--dc23
LC record available at https://lccn.loc.gov/2016028696

The electronic edition of this book was made possible by the support of the Vick Family Foundation.

For all of the women in our lives, past, present, and future.

Table of Contents

List of Images

Acknowledgments

This book began as a graduate paper in one of Dr. Elizabeth Turner's classes. During the research process it became obvious that published material acknowledging women's participation during the war in Texas was sorely lacking. *Women in Civil War Texas* hopes to fill that void and serve as a baseline for future research. Immense thanks go to the contributing authors who faced the same lack of published material to produce excellent studies; their persistence, patience, and understanding are appreciated more than can be expressed. Thanks also to Alex Mendoza for creating the maps to fit the text of this book, to Rebecca Sharpless for her generous help with indexing, and to Chase Liles for inspiring the cover design. To Ron Chrisman at the University of North Texas Press, thank you for believing in the project from the word go and supporting us through the process. Thanks also to Rick McCaslin and the Department of History for financial support for illustrations.

Photographs of women in Texas during the war years are not as plentiful as one might hope. Archivists and institutions both in and outside of Texas were extremely helpful and supportive of this project. To Brenda McClurkin and Cathy Spitzenberger at the University of Texas at Arlington's Special Collections, Tara Laver at Louisiana State

University's Hill Memorial Library, Anne Peterson and Terrie Heydari at Southern Methodist University's DeGolyer Library, Carlos Cortez and the University of Texas at San Antonio's Institute of Texan Cultures, the staff at the Bosque County Historical Center, Amy Kelly, Registrar at the Old Jail Art Center in Albany, and Nicole Davis, Photography and Media Archivist at the Austin History Center: your help and contributions were invaluable and appreciated.

We would also like to thank our families, especially Mike Liles and Barb Boswell, who now know far more than they probably ever wanted to know about women and their lives in Texas during the Civil War.

Image 1. Map of Texas in 1860.

1860 Texas

Image 2. Mara Wagner and her children.

DeGolyer Library, Southern Methodist University, Lawrence T. Jones III Texas photograph collection Ag2008.0005.2.1.036.
Posing for a photograph in Galveston, Texas, in 1863.

Introduction

Angela Boswell

"That cause can never perish which is sustained by the smiles and approval of our noble Southern women!"[1] proclaimed a Texas newspaper one month after the state seceded from the Union, joined the newly formed Confederate States of America, and began preparing for a war. As in the other Southern states that seceded, Texas secessionists enlisted the support of women for the cause and to sustain the morale of the men in order to win the war that followed. However, the Texans did not anticipate four long years of war, which would come to require much more of women than merely encouraging men to fight for the cause. The American Civil War transformed life for women in Texas in ways similar to their sisters in other Southern states and in ways unique to the state as well. The chapters in this anthology show that although Texas women's experiences of the war were different from those of women in many other Southern states, the hardships were numerous and their history is interesting and diverse.

Southerners, at first, did not believe the war would significantly affect Southern women and the gender ideals that surrounded them. To them, men were the protectors and women (at least white women) were the protected. Almost all aspects of law and society assumed this was the "natural" order, in which women subordinated themselves to men who could better provide for and protect women's interests. Laws and social dictates assumed that women would marry, and once married a woman's identity would be subsumed under that of her husband. Thus, in law, a married woman could not contract business or file any legal suits without the permission and assistance from her husband. In society women were known and addressed by their husbands' names. Women could be trusted for short periods to take on greater roles such as taking care of a farm or plantation in the temporary absence of a husband or continuing to run farms as widows (with the help of sons and family members), but it was always assumed that men would do better than women. On the Texas frontier, women had to take on "male" tasks more often than their established Southern sisters, but the ideals of Southern women in the state remained that men's protection and guidance were preferred to their own. Thus, the impending war seemed at first an opportunity for a further definition of gender roles, one in which men could prove their manhood by fighting a war to protect their homes, while women supported the men in their sacred duties.

Of course, this major war on American soil that split the American people required significantly more "support" and sacrifices than anyone in 1861 had imagined. The front lines and the home front were indistinct for many Southerners, inspiring early tributes to Southern women's sacrifices and contributions, including Henry Jackson's *Southern Women and the Second American Revolution* (1863), published in the middle of the war and meant to inspire women's support as much as to praise it. In the generations after the war, as Southerners continued to look back nostalgically and revere the Southern cause, the United Daughters of the Confederacy encouraged celebrations of noble deeds during the Civil War, especially of the elite men and women, with hopes of shaping the historical understanding of the war. Their efforts encouraged writers to valorize women's contributions during and after the war, motivating such publications as John Levi Underwood's *Women of the Confederacy* (1906) and Matthew Page Andrews' *The Women of the South in War Times* (1920).[2]

Even as the American Civil War captured the imagination of thousands of writers, from biographers to defenders of the "lost cause" to a wide range of historians, women continued to be uncritically celebrated as heroic but passive supporters of their men. With the growth of the field of women's history in the last decades of the twentieth century, critical analyses of the changes, roles, and contributions of Southern women emerged. Mary Elizabeth Massey paved the way with *Bonnet Brigades* (1966), and others followed, leading to the more comprehensive treatment by George Rable, *Civil Wars: Women and the Crisis of Southern Nationalism* (1989), to the summative narrative treating race and class by Laura Edwards, *Scarlett Doesn't Live Here Anymore: Southern Women in the Civil War Era* (2000), and to many, many more focused on specific women or themes.[3] With that renewed interest in Southern women's lives during the war, there also came a flood of published letters and diaries by women, the most influential of which was C. Vann Woodward's republication and annotation of the diary by a Southern politician's wife, Mary Chesnut.[4]

With all the intense interest in Southern women during the Civil War era, only a few of these works included Texas women in any significant way. Rable discussed Texas as a place to which other Southern women escaped during the war, and the popularity of the Louisiana refugee Kate Stone's published diary reinforced that focus.[5] Drew Gilpin Faust's *Mothers of Invention: Women of the Slaveholding South in the American Civil War* (1996) has been one of the few full-length studies of Confederate women to include Texas women.[6] Since the publication of that book, some personal writings of Texas women have been edited and published, including Grimes County's Elizabeth Scott Neblett's diary and letters (which were featured prominently in Faust's work), Harrison County's Harriet Perry's letters, Corpus Christi's Maria von Blücher's letters, and Brazoria County's Sallie McNeill's diary.[7] Historians have also published articles and chapters specifically on Texas women as well.[8]

The scarcity of studies on women in Civil War-era Texas stems from many reasons. One is that historians of the South often do not think of Texas as "Southern." Another is that Southern women's historians have found the eastern Southern states more interesting topics because invasion by troops, battles, and the violence of war occurred so close to the home front, thrusting women into the center of the war. With very few exceptions, Texas women did not have to deal with battles or occupying troops, leading many at the time and since to assert that the state was spared the hardships of war.

Some Texas women, however, did suffer the attack, invasion, or occupation of their homes and communities like other Southern women. Union forces attacked or threatened attack on Aransas Pass, Port Lavaca, Indianola, Sabine Pass, Matagorda, Laredo, Eagle Pass, and other locations various times. When the Union troops fired on Port Lavaca in October 1863, they allowed women and children time to leave. Indianola was attacked and occupied by Union troops in 1862 and then again in 1863. In addition to recalling the fighting in and near the town, Eudora Moore, a child at the time, remembered Federal soldiers searching her house, using "very rough language" with her mother, and tearing down the houses of Confederates in the area to build barracks for the Union soldiers.[9]

In addition to Indianola, Union troops also captured and occupied for some time during the war Brownsville, Sabine Pass, Matagorda Bay, Galveston, and Corpus Christi, among others. The effect of the Union troops' assault and occupation of Corpus Christi on women has been best preserved by Maria von Blücher's letters. She described the hasty packing and panicked flight of the families in the town. After being given forty-eight hours to evacuate, she notes, for miles "one saw one household after another loaded up." Although unhurt, women were reminded of the dangers they faced being in the path of war. Upon returning to town, they found "a great number of houses were shot through and through; two cows were killed, and a Newfoundland dog had its head torn off by flying shrapnel. People who were near the places where the shells exploded say bits of fence poles, etc., were driving in to house walls with incredible force."[10]

One of the primary targets of Union forces, Galveston, was blockaded, attacked more than once, and in 1862 occupied for several months. Families fled their homes as early as 1861 and churches and businesses closed, severely disrupting life and causing hardships for many women. Women who remained on the island dealt with the same fears and consequences that women throughout the occupied South faced. Even after Confederates reoccupied Galveston, periodic exchanges of fire between blockading Union ships and Confederate defenses kept women on edge. Cecilia Labadie recorded in her diary how the "booming of cannon" sent "women and children flying every which way."[11]

Other than those limited interactions, most of Texas escaped direct conflict with Union forces (although news of the Union's plan for a "Red River invasion" did frighten many). While most Texas women did not have to deal with troops, occupations, or battles, they did share with their Southern sisters many of the other burdens caused by the war. The greatest disruption to women's lives was the separation of their families when men joined the army or traveled for other war-related reasons. Men had regularly left their families at home before the war when they needed to travel, and most women had some experience with running the household for some periods of time. The differences during the war, however, were significant. Men were gone for much longer periods of time, and many, many more men from families and communities were away at the same time. Somewhere between 70,000 and 90,000 Texas men served in the Confederate forces, and thousands of other men were separated from their families in the same period due to business, politics, or other reasons. Letter writing served as a crucial link between husbands and wives, as well as other members of the family, who tried to maintain the bonds of affection through distance by sharing details of their lives with one another.

Letters also served as a means for men to try to continue directing the activities of the household while they were away. Early letters to wives often contained many details about how to manage the family's business transactions and especially decisions about agriculture. In the first years of the war, women solicited and received advice on when and where to plant what crops, whom to hire as overseers, when and where to sell crops, what provisions to buy, and many other related matters. By the time men had been gone for more than a year, however, women grew more confident, and men knew less about what was transpiring at home, limiting the advice needed or given.

The situations that women encountered had become different than their husbands remembered. Women were not only running farms, plantations, and sometimes businesses in their husbands' absences, they were doing so during wartime. Shortages, unreliable currency, and droughts (in two years of the four-year war) all affected decisions that needed to be made immediately. The blockade created shortages of many items that had been imported from outside the state such as coffee, sugar, and cloth—even leather was in short supply. The most bitterly missed items formerly imported from the North were cotton cards, and their absence had profound effects not only on women, but on the entire state's economy. Without the ability to import manufactured cloth, women took up spinning and weaving again and tried to turn the abundant cotton crops into clothing for themselves and their soldiers. However, the shortage of cards to comb the cotton prevented women from making enough cloth to sustain the demand, to a point that Gideon Lincecum of Washington County noted that "people in this country are complaining mightily, and indeed some of them are really frightened at the thought of approaching nakedness."[12]

For women in families who owned slaves, managing slave labor became ever more challenging. There were no confirmed slave revolts and a smaller percentage of slaves in Texas than in other states escaped to Union lines because of the distance. However, the absence of white men on the farm, and the scarcity of white men in the communities generally, decreased the threat of punishment and made it increasingly difficult to force men and women to work, especially as many slaves began hearing rumors of impending freedom.[13]

Slave women, as in other Southern states, might have anticipated freedom, but often found themselves being worked harder than before and suffering the same shortages as free women. Slave women also faced family separations as their husbands or sons accompanied masters to the war or were impressed to work on fortifications for the Confederacy. With no legal recognition of their marriages or families, slaves could do nothing to prevent more permanent separations. Slaveholding families facing economic difficulties during the war also mortgaged or sold slaves for ready cash, separating husbands from wives and parents from children.

Thus, most Texas women shared many of the same circumstances as women in other Southern states during the war. As in other Southern states, women's experiences also varied due to race, class, and community. While not nearly as plentiful as the studies of Confederate elite white women, historians have increased the study of different groups of women in the past twenty years, and this has led to a greater understanding of the diversity of the South as a whole, especially in the Civil War era. Because of its location, Texas offers one of the greatest opportunities to examine the effects that diversity had upon women. Texas was not only one of the few states to avoid large-scale Union forces, but it was also the newest and least-settled state, it shared a border with Mexico, and its western settlements pushed the boundary between Texans and Native Americans.

Because of the remoteness from the fighting, the state attracted hundreds of slaveholding families from other parts of the South that were occupied or in danger of being occupied. These Southerners brought with them approximately 51,000 slaves, hoping to prevent the slaves from running away to or being freed by Union armies. African Americans forced to relocate in this manner were often separated from families and always separated from the places and communities that they knew. The rapid growth in slave numbers also led to heightened fears of slave revolts, an already growing anxiety among women whose husbands and fathers were away at war. White families accompanying the slaves brought to Texas included hundreds of elite women who often looked down at what they considered to be a primitive society in this new Southern state. The influx of these privileged women and their attitudes disrupted established social orders in communities, causing new sources of anxiety.

While most Texans supported secession and the war, the state's demographics contributed to some significant ambivalence or outright pro-Union sentiment. Even the governor, Sam Houston, had fiercely opposed secession, leading to his removal from office. As one of the most recently settled states, Texas attracted settlers from the North as well as the South and from all over Europe. North Texas had attracted more immigrants from the Northern states before the war, some of whom had strong ties to families, politics, and traditions in the North. The split in the Union led to divided loyalties, sometimes within families. The extent of pro-Union sentiment also triggered a severe reaction from Confederate neighbors, forcing some men to act upon their convictions by joining the Union army, leaving their wives and families behind as targets of community disapproval and harassment. Others stayed behind at great peril to themselves and their families, as Confederate officials and guerillas exacted vengeance on those they perceived to be enemies within.

Some families in the farthest western settlements of Texas opposed secession because they feared war might weaken the army's protection of their homes from Native Americans, a fear that did indeed come true. Women in this "frontier" region actually lived in a borderlands area, their rights to settlement contested by the Native American groups who had lived and controlled the area only years before. Already physically removed from the settled portions of Texas that resembled Southern society, these women tried to replicate Southern ideals in theory while in reality contributing much more work, self-protection, and independence than socially acceptable. Living and working more often in isolation from other families, frontier women often learned to farm, ride, and shoot to help protect their families from the ever-present threat of raids and wild animals. Although women did learn to take care of themselves when their husbands were gone for short periods of time, the advent of the Civil War changed the situation. Not only did men join the army, leaving families for years, but state militias and Confederate troops could not provide the same level of defense after Union troops were forced from the state. As the Confederates became more desperate for soldiers to fight the war, more troops were moved away from frontier defense. At the same time, conscription law had the potential to draft all men between 18 and 35 (a range that eventually expanded to all men between 17 and 50), leaving even more of the families in remote settlements with only women to protect them. Native Americans took advantage of these vulnerabilities to attempt to reverse the encroachments upon their lands by whites in the previous decades. They attacked, harassed, and terrorized settlers, causing ever more discontent with the Confederate cause, and forcing women to take actions to deal with the consequences, whether it be "forting" up with other families or leaving the region altogether.

One of the largest minority populations to settle in Texas before the war consisted of families from German-speaking regions of Europe. Like their Anglo counterparts, women played subordinate roles in German families, and this subordination was reinforced by Texas laws. However, though they were forbidden any formal political role or the vote, German women were expected to be the purveyors of literacy and culture within the family, and thus they were very likely to express political opinions and discuss such with their husbands. Although cultural differences remained in some parts of the state where Germans were the distinct minority, they adapted to the prevailing Southern ideals that were reinforced by law, economics, and custom. These German families were more likely to support secession and the Confederacy, and the women in these counties were just as likely to experience the same deprivations, frustrations, and separations from family in much the same way as their Southern Anglo sisters.[14] However, several counties in central Texas were comprised predominantly of German immigrants, and they maintained much more of their cultural and social heritage. These counties voted overwhelmingly against secession, and many (if not most) of the German Texans remained opposed to the war throughout. As Confederate Texans called upon men and women to visibly support the Confederacy, many German women in all parts of the state, including some in the counties that had voted against secession, expressed their political support by forming clubs to help supply soldiers and care for soldiers' families. Other German women refused to participate, however, highlighting their own and their families' Unionist sentiments. Opposition to the Confederacy remained strong, especially in the central Texas counties, throwing entire communities there under increased suspicion. Families of men who expressed pro-Union sentiment, or who joined the Union armies, led to harassment by Confederate officials and civilians alike. Even when not directly physically harmed, the intimidation and murders of pro-Union German Texan men had profound effects on women who tried to protect them and their families. With the passage of conscription, German women suffered the added burdens of absent family members who joined the army, who fled the state to avoid joining the army, or who hid from conscription, relying upon women to help them remain undetected.

Above all, Texas was unique in that it was the only Southern state to share a border with a foreign country. Texans used this border to smuggle cotton out of the state and past the Union blockade. Freighters competed with each other and outlaws tried to avoid Confederate regulations and impressments, leading to violent confrontations. Even before the war, Texans and Mexicans had attacked and raided each other's ranches and settlements across the border, and the retaliations for these attacks continued through the war. Women living along the border feared this constant violence that could not be controlled by thinly spread militias and Confederate forces. Most importantly, along the border was a large population of Mexicans and Mexican Americans, at least some of whom had no strong loyalty to the Confederate cause. Suspicions of disloyalty led to the draft being implemented in these areas in draconian fashion.

Tejanas thus had a very different experience of the war than other Southern and even other Texas women.

This volume explores these many and varied themes, highlighting women who shared many of their experiences with other Southern women and women whose circumstances varied significantly. These essays develop the historical understanding of what it meant to be a Texas woman during the Civil War and also contribute to a deeper understanding of the complexity of the war and its effects.

The first chapter of the volume begins at the beginning, as Vicki Betts finds significant vocal support among Texas women for secession and war. In chapter 2 Dorothy Ewing examines how one elite, white, Confederate woman, Caroline Sedberry, coped with her husband's absence, carrying on the business of the plantation in wartime circumstances while her husband served in the legislature. Beverly Rowe demonstrates in chapter 3 the importance of letter writing as a means of connecting families, especially husbands and wives, when men left their homes for the battlefields. Brittany Bounds in chapter 4 demonstrates how white women attempted to continue life as normally as possible while supporting the war effort through various means of entertainment and activities.

Chapters 5 and 6 describe African American women's experience in Texas during the Civil War, with Bruce Glasrud delving into slave life and Linda Hudson exploring court cases regarding African American women. The next two chapters analyze the effects of ethnicity on women's experiences of the war, as Jerry Thompson and Elizabeth Mata explore the impact of the war on Tejanas in chapter 7 and Judith Dykes-Hoffman examines German Texas women in chapter 8. Both the Tejanas and German Texas women dealt with the consequences of suspected or actual disloyalty to the Confederate cause in their communities and families. In chapter 9 Rebecca Sharpless reveals how pro-Union sentiment caused serious difficulties for women throughout the state.

The last two chapters explore two final unique factors in Texas that shaped women's experiences. Large numbers of refugee women in east

Texas during the war led to unusual and often unfriendly interactions between the established communities and visiting women, as addressed by Candice Shockley in chapter 10. In the final chapter, volume co-editor Deborah Liles analyzes the dangers to and resiliency of women on the western frontier during the Civil War.

Several important conclusions can be drawn from the experiences of the women represented in the essays in this collection. First, the war was not solely conducted by armies on faraway battlefields. It required the commitment, sacrifice, and contributions of women who guided families in the absence of husbands; who sustained the morale of men, women, and children; who banded together to supply soldiers whether they were family or strangers; who carried on the work and business of farms and plantations; and who kept the Southern economy from completely crumbling. Texas women made their contributions to these causes as much as their Southern sisters. Second, women in Texas also faced economic disruptions, the scarcity of foods and supplies, and the loss of land and labor that other Southern women faced. Third, although fewer Texas women suffered Union invasion and occupation than women in other states, they equally faced fear of violence from guerilla forces on both sides and fear of slave rebellions. Additionally, Texas women feared different kinds of threats due to hostile Native Americans in the west and renegades and bandits along the foreign border. Finally, while the war caused similar hardships for Texas women as it did for women in other places in the South, the diversity of geography and population in the state created some very different experiences for women. Only through exploring these can historians begin to arrive at a thorough understanding of the impact and importance of the American Civil War.

Notes

1. *Colorado [County] Citizen*, March 2, 1861, p. 2.
2. Henry Jackson, *Southern Women and the Second American Revolution* (Atlanta, GA: Intelligencer Steam Powered Press, 1863); John Levi Underwood, *Women of the Confederacy* (New York: Neale Publishing, 1906); Matthew Page Andrews, *The Women of the South in War Times* (Baltimore: Norman Remington Co., 1920). Even popular ladies' magazines participated in these paeans; see Mrs. Thaddeus Horton, "Story of the Nancy Harts," *Ladies Home Journal* 21 (November 1904): 14. For more, also see the excellent annotated bibliography, Theresa McDevitt, *Women and the American Civil War: An Annotated Bibliography* (Westport, CT.: Praeger, 2003).

Mary Elizabeth Massey, Bonnet Brigades: American Women and the Civil War (New York: Alfred Knopf, 1966); George Rable, Civil Wars: Women and the Crisis of Southern Nationalism (Urbana: University of Illinois Press, 1989); Laura F. Edwards, Scarlett Doesn't Live Here Anymore: Southern Women in the Civil War Era (Urbana: University of Illinois Press, 2000). See also Bell Irvin Wiley, Confederate Women (Wesport, CT: Greenwood Press, 1975); LeeAnn Whites and Alecia P. Long, Occupied Women: Gender, Military Occupation, and the American Civil War (Baton Rouge: Louisiana State University Press, 2009); Victoria E. Ott, Confederate Daughters: Coming of Age during the Civil War (Carbondale: Southern Illinois University Press, 2008); and Lisa Tendrich Frank, Women in the American Civil War, 2 vols. (Santa Barbara: ABC-CLIO, 2008); Kimberly Harrison, The Rhetoric of Rebel Women: Civil War Diaries and Confederate Persuasion (Carbondale: Southern Illinois University Press, 2013). The emergence of gender studies also inspired studies that shed more light on women's lives, such as LeeAnn Whites, Gender Matters: Civil War, Reconstruction, and the Making of the New South (New York: Palgrave Macmillan, 2005) and Stephanie McCurry, Confederate Reckoning: Power and Politics in the Civil War South (Cambridge: Harvard University Press, 2010).

1. C. Vann Woodward, ed., *Mary Chesnut's Civil War* (New Haven, CT: Yale University Press, 1981).
2. Sarah Katherine Stone, *Brokenburn: The Journal of Kate Stone, 1861–1868*, ed. John Q. Anderson (Baton Rouge: Louisiana State University, 1955).
3. Drew Gilpin Faust, *Mothers of Invention: Women of the Slaveholding South in the American Civil War* (Chapel Hill: University of North Carolina Press, 1996).
4. Elizabeth Scott Neblett, *A Rebel Wife in Texas: The Diary and Letters of Elizabeth Scott Neblett, 1852–1864*, ed. Erika L. Murr (Baton Rouge: Louisiana State University Press, 2001); M. Jane Johansson, ed., *Widows by the Thousand: the Civil War Letters of Theophilus and Harriet Perry, 1862-1864* (Fayetteville: University of Arkansas Press, 2000); Maria von Blücher, *Maria von Blücher's Corpus Christi: Letters from the South Texas Frontier, 1849-1879*, ed. Bruce S. Cheeseman (College Station: Texas A&M University Press, 2002). See also Eliza Ripley, *From Flag to Flag: A Woman's Adventures and Experiences in the South during the War, in Mexico, and in Cuba*, (New York: D. Appleton and Company, 1889); Orange Cicero Perry and Mary America Aikin Perry, *Dear America: Some Letters of Orange Cicero Perry and Mary America (Aikin) Connor*, ed. Seymour V. Connor (Austin: Jenkins Publishing Company, 1971); Camilla Davis Trammell, ed., *Seven Pines: Its Occupants and Their Letters, 1825-1872* (Dallas: Southern Methodist University Press, 1986) and Vicki Adams Tongate, *Another Year Finds Me in Texas: The Civil War Diary of Lucy Pier Stevens* (Austin: University of Texas Press, 2016).
5. Paul A. Levengood, "In the Absence of Scarcity: the Civil War Prosperity of Houston, Texas," *Southwestern Historical Quarterly* 101 (April 1998): 400-426; Randolph B. Campbell and Donald K. Pickens, "'My Dear Husband': A Texas Slave's Love Letter, 1862," *The Journal of Negro History* 65 (Autumn, 1980): 361-364; Chapter 4 of Angela Boswell, *Her Act and Deed: Women's Lives in a Rural Southern County, 1837-1873* (College Station: Texas A&M University Press, 2001); Drew Gilpin Faust, "Trying to Do a Man's Business: Gender, Violence, and Slave Management in Civil War Texas," *Southern Stories: Slaveholders in Peace and War* (Columbia: University of Missouri Press, 1992); Angela Boswell, "Harriet Perry: A Woman's Life in Civil War Texas," *Texas Women: Their Histories, Their Lives*, eds. Elizabeth Hayes

Turner, Stephanie Cole, and Rebecca Sharpless (Athens: University of Georgia Press, 2015); Vicki Betts, "'A Sacred Charge upon Our Hands': Assisting the Families of Confederate Soldiers in Texas, 1861-1865," *The Seventh Star of the Confederacy: Texas during the Civil War,* ed. by Kenneth W. Howell (Denton: University of North Texas Press, 2009), among many others. Also, Vicki Betts maintains an extensive web page with sources on east Texas women during the Civil War era: http://libguides.uttyler.edu/c.php?g=357604&p=2413869.

6. Eudora Moore in *Texas Tears and Texas Sunshine: Voices of Frontier Women,* ed. by Jo Ella Powell Exley (College Station: Texas A&M University Press, 1985), 142-53.
7. Blücher, *Maria von Blücher's Corpus Christi,* 130-31.
8. Ceclia Labadie Diary, 1863, Folder 94-0004, Galveston and Texas History Center, Rosenberg Library, Galveston, Texas. See also James M. Schmidt, *Galveston and the Civil War: An Island City in the Maelstrom* (Charleston, SC: History Press, 2012) and Ralph Wooster, *Civil War Texas: A History and Guide* (Austin: Texas State Historical Association, 1999).
9. Jerry Bryan Lincecum, Edward Hake Phillips, and Peggy A. Redshaw, eds. *Gideon Lincecum's Sword: Civil War Letters from the Texas Home Front* (Denton: University of North Texas Press, 2001), 195.
10. Faust, "Trying to Do a Man's Business," 174-91.
11. Angela Boswell, *Her Act and Deed: Women's Public Lives in a Rural Southern County 1837-1873* (College Station: Texas A&M University Press, 2001), 9-10, 93-94. See also Glen E. Lich, *The German Texans* (San Antonio: University of Texas Institute of Texan Cultures, 1981); Rudolph Leopold Biesele, *The History of the German Settlements in Texas, 1831-1861* (Austin, TX: Press of Von Boeckmann-Jones, 1930); Terry G. Jordan, *German Seed in Texas Soil: Immigrant Farmers in Nineteenth-Century Texas* (Austin and London: University of Texas Press, 1966).

Image 3. Eudora Caroline Perry or Minerva Van Zandt.

Courtesy *Fort Worth Star-Telegram* Collection, Special Collections, The University of Texas at Arlington Libraries, Arlington, Texas.

This photograph is believed to be either Eudora Caroline Perry or Minerva Van Zandt.

Chapter 1

"Everyone Has the War Fever"

Anglo-Texan Women Prepare for Secession and War

Vicki Betts

Starting with the presidential election of 1860, many Anglo-Texan women involved themselves in the politics of secession and supported the war through the early months of the following year. Pro-secession newspaper editors published women's letters and heralded their efforts in the first months of the war, balancing their public portrayal both as delicate symbols of hearth and home, worthy of defense, and as steadfast inheritors of their Revolutionary War grandmothers' strength and honor. These newspapers recorded the activities of many women who marched in parades, wrote to newspapers, attended political gatherings, pledged boycotts, presented flags, gathered to sew clothing and tents, raised funds, and urged enlistment. Flag presentation speeches, usually delivered by county belles, displayed the passion of women, many of whom appear to have been well educated, while the formation of women's "militias" demonstrated that Texas women and girls were not afraid to pick up a rifle. It all seemed so glorious before the summer battles of Manassas and Wilson's Creek, when the war began to bring on "days of weariness and nights of sorrow."[1]

American women were still sixty years away from national suffrage, but a substantial number were interested in the political issues of the day, even in the more conservative South.[2] During the presidential election of 1860, both Texas Democrats and Constitutional Unionists called upon the ladies to attend political barbecues, the first in Dallas and the latter in San Antonio.[3] At a Huntsville barbecue on November 3, 1860, the ladies presented a transparency with the inscription "We had rather be the widows of State Right patriots than the wives of submissionists."[4] After Lincoln's election, Anglo-Texas women became even more public in their support of a political cause: secession.

In anticipation of upcoming struggles, citizens of Independence, including almost 100 women, held a large political meeting on November 17, 1860, and raised the "Lone Star Banner" in the center of the public square. Young ladies of the local Baylor University also unfurled a lone star flag from their boarding house.[5] The *Bellville Countryman* noted that concerned women were in attendance at another town meeting the following day, and that they were as patriotic as women in the American Revolution.[6] The women of Indianola presented a "Lone Star Flag" to a pro-secession procession that marched to the "largest and most enthusiastic meeting ever held in Calhoun County."[7] And in Corsicana, Mrs. Emily Middleton noted in her November 24 diary entry that she had visited a friend who was making cockades for "a company of young gentlemen." The ladies had presented the cockades along with a flag "given . . . as a testimonial of their approbation of their course in the political movement of secession occasioned by Lincoln's election." She noted that she was not a politician but that "it seems absolutely necessary that action must be taken in the case, and some measures taken to preserve the rights of the South. May the Ruler of the world guide those to whom the direction of our affairs is given, and a peaceable adjustment be made."[8] These actions and concerns show how many Texas women avidly followed the rapidly developing political situation in the South, indicating with their presence and their handiwork that they stood beside their menfolk in the steps they were taking toward independence.

Women's support of the war, either for the North or for the South, could be seen in various activities in the late months of 1860. In a rare flag face off in late November, the Unionists of Kaufman rang the bells of both churches and the hotel, and then a procession of ladies marched to the Methodist church "bearing a handsomely wrought flag, the workmanship of their own hands." In support of their connection to the anti-secession cause, they had made "a Union Flag—the star spangled banner—the stars and stripes, or National Flag." Miss Kate Parsons addressed the district judge "with much grace and elegance," but he, in turn, lectured her and the others on the proper relationship between the federal union and the states, suggesting that it was the North that had disrespected the once glorious flag that "under its broad stripes and bright stars we have our rights under the Constitution, or die in the defense of them." The Unionist crowd took their flag to a nearby store where it was "thrown to the breeze." The next day the bells rang again, and this time Miss Sallie Gibbs presented the community with a blue flag with fifteen white stars, one larger than the others, representing the Southern states and Texas. After an appropriate response, the flag was taken to the top framework of the incomplete new courthouse "and streamed away to the north under the pressure of a brisk wind, ominous of the defiant attitude of our people."[9]

Further north in Dallas, which had partially burned in August, and whose conservative leaders at the time had blamed abolitionists for the destruction, another parade took place. On December 1 fifteen young girls, who were proclaimed to be as "innocent and pure as the early spring flowers of our prairies," led a procession from the Dallas Hotel to the county courthouse as they each held a banner with the name of a Southern state. A large crowd of "ladies and gentlemen" followed behind as local families, including wives and daughters, witnessed the event.[10] One month later Austin followed with a similar demonstration. Behind the chief marshal, his assistant, and a musical band were "beautiful young ladies bearing the glorious insignia of so many [fifteen] gallant States, riding their spirited and beautiful steeds with ease and grace, and accompanied by their stalwart and chivalrous companions, presented a soul-stirring sight of youth, beauty and courage, animated by the noblest patriotism." They were followed by women on horseback, with and without flags. When they arrived at the site of the Old Capitol they raised a flag sewn by Mrs. Andrew N. Hopkins with the Lone Star of Texas surrounded by smaller stars up the 130-foot-tall flagstaff.[11]

An anonymous Texas woman, assuming the pseudonym "Volumnia," wrote to the *Austin State Gazette* the day before the South Carolina convention commenced. She challenged the men of Texas to once again raise the Lone Star flag that had flown during the struggle for independence from Mexico when Texians had fought for "freedom without control." She asserted that Texas women, too, love their country and their homes, and they would love the men who would protect them. Volumnia saw the hand of Northern fanatics in the Indian raids and the slave insurrection panic just a few months previous and urged the Unionists of the state "to look upon these things as they really exist." If they did so, she knew they would support the cause of secession. During an era and in a region in which women seldom wrote politically, Volumnia spoke out forcefully in print, challenging men to do their duty as men and as Texans.[12]

When necessary, the state's women could also take the political floor. In Crescent, Refugio County, no male leader volunteered at a secession meeting "when all at once, the banner of San Jacinto unfurled in her hand, appeared Miss Adams," who told the group:

> Sons of Texas, it is not in the sphere of a lady to address a political assembly; but when the honor of her sex and the freedom of her country are at stake; when men are either deterred by danger, or slumber in indifference, it is her duty to raise her voice . . . Sons of Texas, in the name of my sex, for the freedom of the South, I

> present you the coat of arms of Texas; protect it, we shall stand by your side!

Clearly many Texas women, while acknowledging the traditional separate spheres of men in politics and women at home, were finding it extremely difficult to stand on the sidelines, particularly if the men around them hesitated.[13]

Women demonstrated their determination to support the Confederacy with their actions. When someone cut down the Lone Star flag in La Grange, the "patriotic town Ladies" immediately made another that was reportedly "made by fair hands, raised by patriots, is appreciated by true hearts, and shall be defended by freemen."[14] On February 23, the day of the popular vote, the tableau of fifteen young ladies representing the fifteen Southern states was repeated in San Augustine, where Miss Martha Anderson gave a patriotic speech and presented a flag to the Red Land Minute Company.[15] As this was taking place, in Port Sullivan, Milam County, those in favor of secession hosted a fine barbecue, attended by both ladies and gentlemen. Henry Pendarvis reported that he was "more impressed than ever with the firmness and patriotism of Texan ladies . . . Capt. [Conway O.] Barton called on all the ladies in favor of secession to make it known by rising to their feet. To see who should be first on their feet was the greater struggle, for in an instant every lady, even down to the girls of 8 or 10 years, were up; not one kept her seat; they were all united."[16]

As the new symbol of fifteen pure young sister states of the South emerged, Southern women searched for their historic potential to contribute to a cause. As early as 1767, before the American Revolution, the production and wearing of homespun clothing demonstrated women's commitment to home industry, simplicity, and democracy. An observant editor of the time wrote how "The industry and frugality of the American ladies much exalt their character in the eyes of the World and serve to show how greatly they are contributing to bring about the political salvation of a whole Continent."[17] Symbolic homespun revived again with the Embargo Act of 1807, and then during the Nullification Crisis in the 1830s where the target was New England's textiles. At the beginning of the 1860s, New England textiles again became the focus of scorn as the South headed toward secession and war. The *Crockett Printer* reported that Ellis County women imitated "their grandmothers in days of yore, when oppression forced us from beneath the British yoke of bondage, almost as degrading as that of the servile masters of the North at present." It touted how they had formed "home spun societies," vowing to "wear and use all such articles of Southern make as they can possible [*sic*] obtain, in prefence [*sic*] to the Northern articles."[18] An Alexandria, Louisiana, newspaper quoted a Texan as saying "This is a commendable spirit at any time, and particularly now in these decidedly revolutionary times, when each separate sovereignty [illegible] that it must look to its own resources, that we must depend upon our own looms and discard as far as possible all foreign fabrics."[19] In the spring of 1861, homespun might have been the fashion, but within a few years it would become a necessity for many.[20]

The final political measures were taken to separate Texas from the federal Union and join it to the Confederacy in February and March. Military companies started forming, and each community seemed compelled to present a flag as part of a civic commitment ceremony between the men and their families and friends they were swearing to protect. Accounts of these ceremonies, many in great detail, filled the newspapers for months. One of the first was for the flag of the Clarksville Red River Rangers on February 22, which was described as an "Independence Flag" with a "solitary star" prepared by the ladies. Miss Margaret Anderson, age twenty-one, a teacher and daughter of Rev. John Anderson, the head of the Clarksville Male and Female Academy, spoke on behalf of the community. As she assured the men that the local citizens were behind their men, she recalled the proud history of the Texas Revolution and asserted that with the election of Lincoln "the South has no other honorable course to pursue, than to withdraw from a compact into which she entered, or submit to the trampling under foot of her dearest rights."

She told the men, "If the frenzy of the North shall compel you to take up arms to fight for heaven-born liberty, and your sacred rights, you will be engaged in a noble and glorious cause. . . . if fight you must, remember! [T]here is much at stake, and much will be required of you. Remember you will be accompanied by the prayers and best wishes of innumerable friends and kindred."[21]

In late April, the W. P. Lane Rangers had assembled in Marshall before riding toward the western frontier. The local ladies had sewn a banner that displayed the Confederate national flag with eight stars on one side and a lone star flag on the reverse. On one of the sides was painted "'Semper Paratus,' W.P. Lane Rangers, by the ladies of Marshall. April 20th 1861." As in Clarksville the women exhibited their support for their men and the cause when Miss Sallie O. Smith delivered her speech from atop an elegant white horse. She lauded the young men assembled as "the gallant inheritors of the renown and valor of the Alamo and San Jacinto." She told them that although the women they left behind would wield no sword or rifle, "be assured that in our bosoms burns a patriotism as lofty—a courage, in our appropriate sphere, as daring—and a heroism as chivalric, as that which nerves the brawniest arm which wields the battle-axe, and cleaves down the foe upon the field of carnage." Yet, if the need arose, she advised the "Lincolns and Sewards and Garrisons of the day hear it and tremble—then some Southern Penthesilia, some Joan—not of Arc, but of Texas; some Boadices, burning with Southern fire, shall leap from her retirement, and full panoplied, like Pallas from the head of Jupiter, shall brandish her sabre and call, like avenging spirits from the deep, another hundred thousand heroines to avenge the wrongs of their brothers and their country."[22] Such stirring rhetoric both supplied the needed moral support for the men as they rode off into unknown circumstances and suggested the frustration of women left behind to wait and watch. If needed, as Miss Smith proclaimed, the women of Texas were willing to take up the legendary mantles of the heroines of history and mythology and strike for their menfolk and the Confederacy.

Image 4. Third Texas Cavalry and Flag of the Texas Hunters and Marshall Guards.

Courtesy *Fort Worth Star-Telegram* Collection, Special Collections, The University of Texas at Arlington Libraries, Arlington, Texas.
One side of this handmade silk flag has golden letters and a scene of a successful deer hunt; the other has the first national flag of the Confederacy with thirteen stars, known as the "Stars and Bars." Presented to the Texas Hunters by Eudora Perry (see Image 3) in May 1861.

A May Day party at Jonesville, in eastern Harrison County, became the site of the flag presentation to the Texas Hunters, later a company of the Third Texas Cavalry. The Marshall *Texas Republican* reported how twenty-two-year-old Miss Eudora Perry, the daughter of a local physician and planter, delivered a speech with "many eloquent passages, and combined appropriateness of thought, felicity of expression, and purity of diction."[23] The flag, made by the ladies, was emblazoned with "Texas Hunters" in gold and the scene of a successful stag hunt, with huntsmen admiring the kill, attended by their hounds. The reverse side was a national Confederate flag with thirteen white stars.[24] While these unique company flags were usually soon sent home in favor of regimental standards, the Texas Hunters' was reportedly the first Confederate flag to fly over Springfield, Missouri, later that summer.[25]

In another ceremony a courageous Eleanor Gregg, daughter of Episcopal Bishop Alexander Gregg, and a mere seventeen years old, presented a national Confederate flag to the Tom Green Rifles, later Company B, Fourth Texas Infantry in the Army of Northern Virginia. She spoke in the chamber of the House of Representatives in the state capitol, perhaps the first woman to do so, and told the assembled crowd that the soldiers of Texas had a special heritage to defend, proudly won again and again since the fight for Texas independence. She challenged them to "fight for your cherished rights, fight for your own holy institutions. Yes, fight for your homes and firesides, for all the South holds dear." The prayers of their loved ones, particularly their mothers, wives and sisters would follow them, their new country would bless them, and God would sustain them to the end. With such moral support, how could they not succeed?[26]

Soldiers needed more than flags to be able to defend their homes and firesides—they needed uniforms, tents, other equipment, and medical supplies. Prior to secession, Texas women had honed their fundraising skills by organizing fairs, suppers, and concerts to build churches, support schools, and aid the needy at home and on the frontier.[27] By April of 1861, after the war began at Fort Sumter, their attention turned to the military companies being raised in every county and to the Confederate government in general. They joined concerts at the Masonic Female Institute at Marshall to benefit the Marshall Guards. That same month Miss M. E. Hopkins of Galveston became the first subscriber to the Confederate loan by taking six hundred dollars in bonds for the local Baptist Sewing Society. Other Galvestonian ladies raised more than two thousand dollars with a fair. Women in Austin, Bellville, and Caldwell County also contributed funds. After equipping three of her own sons for the service, Martha M. Meriwether, a widow in Guadalupe County, promised to gather and donate her entire cotton crop to the Confederate cause.[28]

As Confederate military companies formed, women organized societies to offer their more traditional skills such as sewing and fabricating uniforms and tents well before quartermasters' departments geared up production. The *Dallas Herald* proclaimed "Hurrah for the Ladies!" who were making lint for bandages, while others "were busy with the needle, day and night, fitting out the volunteers for the campaign. May the married ladies receive their husbands back, safe and sound; and the young girls win a gallant soldier for a partner in life. God bless the ladies of Dallas." The *Trinity Advocate* in Palestine noted that "The ladies, may Heaven's choicest blessings rest upon them, enrolled themselves into a Dorcas sewing society, and have labored incessantly for more than a week past in preparing the clothes and tents for their defenders." In early June fifty or sixty ladies met in the courthouse in Marshall to prepare lint and bandages, while the Ladies' Needle Battalion organized in Austin to sew uniforms at the capitol. Letitia Walton wrote to her mother back in Mississippi to tell her that she had finished making her first dress coat and was very pleased with the results.[29] Ellen Porter Phelps in LaGrange wrote in her diary that she basted seams for another woman to complete on her sewing machine. She added that "Some of the ladies are about as patriotic as the men. Mrs. Sharp, an old lady of 79 years, wished St. Louis might be laid in ashes if it offered any resistance to Secession, said she had fitted out companies for five 'wars' and wished she had 40 sons for the Southern Confederacy."[30] Fifty or sixty ladies in Clarksville, with "sundry sewing machines" worked for several days making up clothing and tents for John C. Burks' company, destined for the Eleventh Texas Cavalry. More than forty women set up shop sewing tents and uniforms in a Corsicana church, some staying five days. Houston women took over a room above the office of the *Houston Telegraph*, accumulated sewing machines and made uniforms from cloth supplied by the state penitentiary, "each company in a particular color." In Marshall fabric for coats, pants, drawers, and shirts was purchased and cut by a tailor, with the pieces to be distributed over the entire county for sewing "so that every lady may do something."[31] These women rallied and supported their men and country with their contributions of time and effort, preparing these needed supplies before the Confederate government was able to assume a greater proportion of the responsibility.

At the same time other women in Texas assumed the vow to protect the hearth and home front. In mid-May the ladies of Centerville organized a military company of their own and practiced target shooting with rifles and pistols to prepare for an invasion by "Lincolnites," or raids by Indians. In Rusk County the young ladies chose an effigy of Abraham Lincoln for a target, "which they completely riddled with bullets." The local newspaper remarked, "Talk about wiping out a people whose women and children are expert rifle and pistol shooters! The idea is absurd."[32] The *Goliad Messenger* noted that their women were also target shooting and called Lincoln "a gone sucker."[33] The *Bellville Countryman* praised the movement, adding "Instances were common in our early history of the daring deeds performed by women, the heroic mothers of liberty. Though there may be no necessity the experiment can do no harm."[34] These women were far from the portrayal of the helpless Southern woman. While largely a symbolic gesture, target shooting perhaps also served as a release for the frustrations of feeling useless in a period that called for male action and heroism.

Although "P." in Dallas declared that "Everyone has the war fever," and in Lancaster, Nannie Snead wrote that "War, war, war, is the daily conversation of every lady and gentleman that I meet," by the end of the summer of 1861, in some areas of the state, recruitment had begun to lag. Women, particularly young women, started using their considerable powers of persuasion to aid enlistment. In the Mill Creek area of Austin County, the *Bellville Countryman* reported that "Madam Rumor says that the ladies of this neighborhood are going to form a company for the protection of such young men as will not volunteer to assist their country in gaining its independence."[35] To the north Dr. William E. Oakes of Waco reported that "the young ladies have entered into an agreement to refuse associating with or countenancing any unmarried man who does not volunteer in the war."[36] In Austin Amelia Barr met two crying girls whose brothers had just marched off in a local company. In her memoirs she recollected:

> [T]hey had driven them into it, and they were now crying because they had succeeded in doing so. "What unreasonable creatures women are!" I thought. However, in a great many cases, it was the women of a family who compelled the men to enlist as soldiers, by a course of moral suasion no man with any feeling could endure. They would not eat with them, speak to them, or listen if spoken to. They ignored all their personal necessities, or met them with constant tears and voiceless reproaches, and what man could bear his family weeping over him, as if he was already dead to their love and respect?[37]

With the first major battles, Bull Run or Manassas on July 21 and Wilson's Creek or Oak Hills on August 10, the war fever phase of the young Confederate nation began to come to a close. While the ladies of Lancaster could still lead an impromptu victory celebration complete with cannons, drums, and a parade, other women, often older, faced the reality of war much more soberly.[38] One unnamed Texas mother wrote to her sister in Atlanta, Georgia, in late August of 1861 about the enlistment of her four sons. She had given them up to the Confederacy due to patriotism, but acknowledged that she felt no joy in it, "the light will have gone out of my house forever when they leave it." She blamed her loss on the North who had forced "this unnatural war." Her boys must fight for "their rights and honor" and without that she had rather see them dead. For her, all that was left was "days of weariness and nights of sorrow." War held no glory for her.[39]

Sixty to seventy thousand Texas men left their homes to serve in the Confederate Army, leaving wives, mothers, and sweethearts behind to manage as best they could.[40] What began for many Anglo-Texas women with a thrill of enthusiasm, dragged through four years of new challenges, deprivation, and grief. The nation they hoped to assist in creating did not survive. Their menfolk did not march back victorious, with banners flying, as had been predicted in 1861. Despite their losses, however, in years to come these women would take justifiable pride in their efforts to sustain their families, their state, and their region.

NOTES

1. "A Lady with the Right Spirit," *Southern Confederacy* (Atlanta, GA), August 10, 1861. For a good general look at the importance of women as icons and actors in the Confederacy, see Nina Silber, *Gender and the Sectional Conflict* (Chapel Hill: University of North Carolina Press, 2008).
2. Mary P. Ryan, *Women in Public: Between Banners and Ballots, 1825-1880* (Baltimore: Johns Hopkins University Press, 1990), 135; Rosemarie Zagarri, *Revolutionary Backlash: Women and Politics in the Early American Republic* (Philadelphia: University of Pennsylvania Press, 2007), 163; Laura F. Edwards, *Scarlett Doesn't Live Here Anymore: Southern Women in the Civil War Era* (Urbana: University of Illinois Press, 2000), 17; Adrienne Caughfield, *True Women and Westward Expansion* (College Station: Texas A&M University Press, 2005), 138; "Washington County Politics," *Weekly Journal* (Galveston, TX), September 24, 1852; "Presentation of the Ladies Flag," *Texas State Gazette*, July 4, 1857. See also Elizabeth R. Varon, "Tippecanoe and the Ladies, Too: White Women and Party Politics in Antebellum Virginia," *Journal of American History* 82, no. 2 (Sept. 1995): 494-521.
3. "State Barbecue! Grand Democratic Mass Meeting!! The Northern Prairies of Texas in a Blaze! The Fire of Democracy Lighted on Every Hill and Plain!!" *Standard* (Clarksville, TX), September 22, 1860; "The Barbecue at the San Pedro Springs," *Standard*, October 27, 1860.
4. *Texas Republican* (Marshall, TX), November 24, 1860. For the significance of women at political barbecues in another state, see Christopher J. Olsen, *Political Culture and Secession in Mississippi: Masculinity, Honor and the Antiparty Tradition, 1830-1860* (New York: Oxford University Press, 2000), 104-105.
5. Achille to Dear Ma, Independence, [Texas], November 17, 1860. Lavinia Ferris correspondence, George A. Ferris Family Papers, folder 4, Texas State Library and Archives, Austin, TX. Robert Maberry, Jr., in *Texas Flags* (College Station: Texas A&M University Press, 2001), 57, identifies the secession era "Lone Star flag" not as the 1839 Republic

of Texas flag/current state flag, but as any flag with a prominent five pointed star.

6. *Bellville* [TX] *Countryman,* November 21, 1860.
7. "Grand Mass Meeting!!! The Sovereigns in Council! The Voice of Calhoun!! The Lone Star Flag again Unfurled!!! The People Rally Around it Without Distinction of Party!" *Indianola* [TX] *Courier,* November 24, 1860.
8. Emily Milner Van Hook Middleton, *Diary of Mrs. Emily Milner Van Hook Middleton, 1856 May 2-1898 October 23,* ed. Tia Templeton Atwood and Edna Hawkins, photocopy of transcribed diary, Historical Manuscripts Collection, Special Collections, University of Texas at Arlington Libraries. For the use of political cockades in the early Republic, see Simon P. Newman, *Parades and the Politics of the Street: Festive Culture in the Early American Republic* (Philadelphia: University of Pennsylvania Press, 1997), 154-156.
9. "Court Week in Kaufman," *Dallas Herald,* November 28, 1860. While the cult of true womanhood encouraged women to remain silent and keep to hearth and home, increasing educational opportunities for girls often included requiring them to speak in front of mixed groups at year-end ceremonies. See Mary Kelley, *Learning to Stand and Speak: Women, Education, and Public Life in America's Republic* (Williamsburg, VA and Chapel Hill, NC: Published for the Omohundro Institute of Early American History and Culture by the University of North Carolina Press, 2006) and Christie Ann Farnham, *The Education of the Southern Belle: Higher Education and Student Socialization in the Antebellum South* (New York: New York University Press, 1994).
10. "Enthusiastic Meeting at Dallas. Glorious Demonstration!" *Dallas Herald,* December 5, 1860. The earlier use of street politics and celebration to build nationalism is explored in David Waldstreicher, *In the Midst of Perpetual Fetes: The Making of American Nationalism, 1776-1820* (Williamsburg, VA and Chapel Hill, NC: Published for the Omohundro Institute of Early American History and Culture by the University of North Carolina Press, 1997).
11. "Hang the Banner Upon the Outer Wall," *Austin State Gazette,* January 5, 1861; "A Magnificent Tribute to the Honor and Liberties of Texas! The Lone Star Unfurled from a Lofty Flag-Staff, Planted Upon the

Site of the Old Capitol, Hallowed by Glorious Memories!" *Austin State Gazette*, January 12, 1861.

12. Volumnia to Editor Gazette, December 16, [1860], *Austin State Gazette*, December 29, 1860. Volumnia wrote another letter on December 30, in which she challenged the men of Texas: "You will come; you must come to your country's standard. It has been raised in other States. You have here men, mothers and kindred that call upon you. Will you stand still and let the clouds and gloom of night surround them? There will be no gloom, there will be no night, if the men of the South do their duty."

13. "A Lady Leader," *Galveston Weekly News*, February 12, 1861. For more on the relationship of gender and secession, see Drew Gilpin Faust, *Mothers of Invention: Women of the Slaveholding South in the American Civil War* (Chapel Hill: University of North Carolina Press, 1996), 9-12, 59 and Stephanie McCurry, "Citizens, Soldiers' Wives, and 'Hiley Hope Up' Slaves: The Problem of Political Obligation in the Civil War South" in *Gender and the Southern Body Politic*, ed. by Nancy Bercaw (Jackson: University Press of Mississippi, 2000), 95-129. For more on how Southern newspaper editors promoted the public role of women during the war, see Mary M. Cronin, "Patriotic Ladies and Gallant Heroines: Images of Confederate Women in Southern Newspapers, 1861-65," *Journalism History* 36, no. 3 (Fall 2010): 138-149.

14. LaGrange, [TX] *State Rights Democrat*, February 21, 1861.

15. Margaret Swett Henson and Deolece Parmelee, *The Cartwrights of San Augustine: Three Generations of Agricultural Entrepreneurs in Nineteenth-Century Texas* (Austin: Texas State Historical Association, 1993), 199.

16. "From Port Sullivan," Henry Pendarvis to Editor Gazette, February 24, 1861, *Austin State Gazette*, March 9, 1861.

17. Catherine Clinton, *The Other Civil War: American Women in the Nineteenth Century*, rev. ed. (New York: Farrar, Straus & Giroux, 1984), 13.

18. "Woman at Work," *Crockett Printer* quoted in *Dallas Herald*, February 27, 1861. The *Dallas Herald* had perhaps inspired the Ellis County women with an article on Virginia "Homespun Parties," published in their February 8, 1861, issue.

19. *The Constitutional* (Alexandria, LA), May 25, 1861.

20. For more information on patriotic homespun in the South, see Vicki Betts, "'They Call It Patriotism': Homespun as Politics in the South, 1860-1861," accessed December 19, 2013, http://www.uttyler.edu/vbetts/homespun%20patriotism.htm. For more on Texas home textile production, see Paula Mitchell Marks, *Hands to the Spindle: Texas Women and Home Textile Production, 1822-1880* (College Station: Texas A&M University Press, 1996).

21. "Address of Miss M. B. Anderson, Presenting a Flag to the Red River Rangers," *Standard*, March 9, 1861; "Clarksville Male and Female Academy," *Handbook of Texas Online*, accessed December 27, 2013, http://www.tshaonline.org/handbook/online/articles/kbc27; Eighth Census of the United States, Red River County, Texas, Schedule 1 (Free Population). For more on women's activities across the South during the spring and summer of 1861, see Stephanie McCurry, *Confederate Reckoning: Power and Politics in the Civil War South* (Cambridge, MA: Harvard University Press, 2010), 89-94. For more on flag presentations, see Wayne K. Durrill, "Ritual, Community and War: Local Flag Presentation Ceremonies and Disunity in the Early Confederacy," *Journal of Social History* 39, no. 4 (Summer 2006): 1105-1122. For more on the use of the Texas Revolution as inspiration for secession, see Andrew F. Lang, "'Victory Is Our Only Road to Peace': Texas Wartime Morale, and Confederate Nationalism, 1860-1865" (Master's thesis, University of North Texas, 2008), 17-18.

22. "Organization and Departure of the W. P. Rangers," (Marshall) *Texas Republican*, April 27, 1861; W. W. Heartsill, *Fourteen Hundred and 91 Days in the Confederate Army*, ed. by Bell Irvin Wiley (Jackson, TN: McCowat-Mercer Press, 1954), 4. "Semper paratus" is Latin for "always ready." For more on the significance of flags to the Confederate people, see Robert E. Bonner, *Colors and Blood: Flag Passions of the Confederate South* (Princeton, NJ: Princeton University Press, 2002).

23. "Trip to Jonesville," (Marshall) *Texas Republican*, May 4, 1861.

24. Max S. Lale, "The Boy-Bugler of the Third Texas Cavalry: The A. B. Blocker Narrative, Part 1," *Military History of Texas and the Southwest* 14, no. 2 (1979), 73; Randolph B. Campbell, *A Southern Community in Crisis: Harrison County, Texas, 1850-1880* (Austin: Texas State Historical Association, 1983), 201.

25. "What the Ladies of Marshall Did," (Marshall) *Texas Republican*, September 21, 1861.

26. "Miss Gregg's Address," *Austin State Gazette*, July 29, 1861. Other presentation speeches include: *Galveston Weekly News*, February 19, 1861; "Hurrah for San Augustine," *Austin State Gazette*, March 16, 1861; "Cameron," *Austin State Gazette*, April 20, 1861; *Dallas Herald*, May 8, 1861; "A Flag," *Standard*, May 11, 1861; "Presentation of Banner," *Austin State Gazette*, May 11, 1861; "Letter from Dallas," *Texas Republican*, May 18, 1861; "For the Dallas Herald," *Dallas Herald*, May 22, 1861; "A Trip to the West," *Texas Republican*, May 25, 1861; *Standard*, May 25, 1861; "The Home Guard," *Standard*, May 25, 1861; Fred Tarpley, *Jefferson: Riverport to the Southwest* (Austin: Eakin Press, 1983), 85; "Departure of the Marshall Guards," *Texas Republican*, June 1, 1861; Harold B. Simpson, *Hood's Texas Brigade: Lee's Grenadier Guard* (Fort Worth: Landmark Publishing, 1999), 28; "The Boys Moving," *Bellville Countryman*, June 5, 1861; *Standard*, June 8, 1861; Mollie E. Moore, "Address Delivered Upon the Presentation of a Banner to the Smith County Artillery Company on Their Departure on the 10th inst.," Mary Evelyn Davis Scrapbook, Briscoe Center for American History, University of Texas at Austin; Robert C. Cotner, *James Stephen Hogg: A Biography* (Austin: University of Texas Press, 1959), 3; S. B. Barron, *The Lone Star Defenders: A Chronicle of the Third Texas Cavalry, Ross' Brigade* (New York: Neale Publishing Co., 1908), 20; "Flag Presentation," *The Ranchero* (Brownsville, TX), June 15, 1861; *Standard*, June 22, 1861; "Flag Presentation," *Dallas Herald*, June 26, 1861; "For the Dallas Herald," *Dallas Herald*, June 26, 1861; *Standard*, June 29, 1861; J. J. Faulk, *History of Henderson County* (Athens, TX: Athens Review Printing Co., 1929), 129; *Austin State Gazette*, July 13, 1861; Mollie McDowall, *Memoirs of Mollie McDowall (Mary Ann Nicholson) 1843-1931*, ed. by Ethel Mary Franklin Smith (Austin: National Society of the Colonial Dames of America in the State of Texas, 1978), 47; "The 'Davis Guards,'" (Marshall) *Texas Republican*, July 13, 1861; *Standard*, July 13, 1861; *Bellville Countryman*, July 17, 1861; "The Regimental Flag," *Dallas Herald*, July 24, 1861; (Marshall) *Texas Republican*, July 27, 1861; "Banner Presentation at Pittsville," *Bellville Countryman* July 31, 1861; *Dallas Herald*, August 7, 1861; "Address of Mrs. E. F. Gibson," *Dallas Herald*, August 14, 1861; *Dallas Herald*, August 21, 1861.

27. *The* (Brownsville) *Ranchero*, October 6, 1860; "The Ladies' Supper," (San Antonio) *Alamo Express*, October 15, 1860; "Ladies' Fair," Marshall *Harrison Flag*, December 8, 1860; "Supper and Fair," (Marshall, Texas) *Harrison Flag*, December 29, 1860; *Galveston Weekly News*, February 5, 1861.

28. (Marshall) *Texas Republican*, April 27, 1861; *Austin State Gazette*, April 27, 1861; *Austin State Gazette*, June 8, 1861; *Austin State Gazette*, June 8, 1861; *Bellville Countryman*, July 27, 1861; *Austin State Gazette*, July 27, 1861; *San Antonio Ledger*, July 11, 1861, quoted in the *Memphis Daily Appeal*, August 3, 1861. For the significance of Confederate women's organizations and of those organizations to women, see Faust, *Mothers of Invention*, 22-27.

29. "Hurrah for the Ladies!" *Dallas Herald*, May 8, 1861; "Patriotism," *Austin State Gazette*, May 18, 1861; (Marshall) *Texas Republican*, June 8, 1861; *Austin State Gazette*, June 15, 1861; Letitia Walton to Mary Watkins, April 24, 1861, Austin, Texas, *Letters from Forest Place: A Plantation Family's Correspondence, 1846-1881*, E. Grey Dimond and Herman Hattaway, eds., (Jackson: University Press of Mississippi, 1993), 234.

30. Ellen Porter Phelps Diaries, 1861-1866, Mary Ellen Phelps Family Papers, 1861-1870s, Texas State Library and Archives, Austin, 27.

31. "Assembly of Notables," *Standard*, June 22, 1861; Alva Taylor, "The Diary of Jacob Eliot," *Navarro County Scroll* (Corsicana, TX: Navarro County Historical Society, 1965), 83; *Austin State Gazette*, July 6, 1861; "To the Ladies of Harrison," (Marshall) *Texas Republican*, August 17, 1861.

32. (Marshall) *Texas Republican*, May 18, 1861; *Dallas Herald*, May 22, 1861.

33. *Bellville Countryman*, May 22, 1861.

34. *Bellville Countryman*, June 12, 1861. For more on Confederate "women's militias" see Mary M. Cronin, "Daughters of the New Revolutionary War: Representations of Confederate Women and Gun Culture in the Confederate Press, 1861-1864," *American Journalism* 28, no. 4 (Fall 2011): 55-80.

35. (Marshall) *Texas Republican*, May 18, 1861; "Letter from Dallas County," *Bellville Countryman*, August 21, 1861.

36. "Mill Creek Neighborhood," *Bellville Countryman*, July 31, 1861; *Austin State Gazette*, July 27, 1861.
37. Amelia Edith Huddleston Barr, *All the Days of My Life: An Autobiography: The Red Leaves of a Human Heart* (New York: D. Appleton, 1913), 229.
38. "Letter from Dallas County," *Bellville Countryman*, August 21, 1861.
39. "A Lady with the Right Spirit," (Atlanta, Georgia) *Southern Confederacy*, August 10, 1861.
40. Ralph A. Wooster, "Introduction," *Lone Star Blue and Gray: Essays on Texas in the Civil War*, ed. Ralph A. Wooster (Austin: Texas State Historical Association, 1995), viii.

Image 5. Caroline Sedberry.

Courtesy of the Bosque County Collection, Bosque County Historical Commission, Meridian, Texas.

This photograph of Caroline Sedberry was taken several years after the war.

Chapter 2

Caroline Sedberry, Politician's Wife

An Ordinary Woman in Extraordinary Times

Dorothy Ewing

On December 20, 1860, the legislature of South Carolina voted to secede from the Union, beginning a wave of secessions throughout the South. On February 23, 1861, voters in Bosque County elected 223 to 79 to secede. A mass meeting to organize a Committee of Public Safety was held at Meridian on March 17, with Chief Justice William Rush Sedberry, husband of Caroline Sedberry, presiding. As the nation prepared for a civil war, the life of Caroline Sedberry and thousands of other Southern women began to change dramatically.[1]

Southern women were overwhelmingly in favor of secession and expected to make sacrifices for the cause that they supported. As the war progressed, they were forced by necessity to take on more work and responsibility. By the war's end, many had undertaken jobs they had never expected to perform and did them well. Caroline was one of those women. Like most women on the Texas frontier, she was accustomed to her husband's absences; however, the Civil War presented extended absences that left her in total control of the farm. Except for William's brief visits home and limited, unpredictable correspondence during the war years, Caroline made decisions about planting, sowing, harvesting, and selling farm products, as well as other business matters. Her letters reflect her early insecurity and uncertainty about making decisions alone. As William's absence grew longer, Caroline accepted and grew more comfortable in her unexpected leadership role. Her story is representative of many women who adapted during the war years from one dependent on her husband's authority and guidance to a woman who was competent, successful, and willing to perform duties commonly attributed to men before the war.

Caroline Huntley Alexander Sedberry was born in Tennessee, and on January 26, 1843, married William Rush Sedberry in Maury, Tennessee. William and Caroline moved to Texas in the fall/winter of 1852-53 and brought their slaves with them. William and Caroline had eleven children, six boys and five girls, although one son and one daughter died in early childhood. In December 1855, William purchased 500 acres on the Bosque River near the town of Meridian in Bosque County, Texas, for $800 plus a promissory note for $450.[2]

William was a descendant of Benjamin Rush, a signer of the American Declaration of Independence. He, along with other pioneers, organized Bosque County in 1854. He was the second county judge in 1858. In a proclamation published June 13, 1861, William announced his candidacy for the Sixtieth Representative District, promising to be a good representative of the people. His proclamation reads in part, "We are threatened with a protracted and bloody war. But we are in the right; our cause is just...." He was elected a member of the Texas State Legislature in 1861. William went to Austin as a member of the Texas House of Representatives to help with the incorporation of Texas into the Confederacy. While attending the legislative session in Austin during the winter of 1861-62, William wrote to Caroline about his disgust with the boring buncombe speeches, with the women who fawned over the legislators, and about his frustration with the governor's veto of the per diem bill that had been passed by both houses. He also wrote that he would definitely be on one of the Standing Committees and had been told he would be on others. In November of 1861 he wrote, "Tell John Locker I introduced a Sabbath law and I think I will get it through as good luck would have it the day after I introduced my bill there came in a petition from the Methodist Conference to the Legislature to pass a Sunday law, and it and my bill were refered [*sic*] to the judiciary committee and they reported back my bill and recommended its passage. So I think I will get it through quite easy." However, his letters also contained directions to Caroline about running the farm, including one in which he drew a sketch describing the location where the wheat should be planted.[3]

Along with his written instructions to Caroline from Austin during the first year of the war, William included descriptions of his living arrangements and roommates. One letter described some of the capital's social activities: "I was at the Governor's Grand Levee last night and it was the finest thing in the way of parties I ever witnessed. I never saw a better display in my life. Some 600 persons were present. The Governor is a model little fellow, plain sociable and clever and his wife is the best fellow of the two."[4]

After he completed his work in the legislature in early 1862, William, along with two of his sons, Summerfield (Summer) and Merritt, joined the Confederate Army. Caroline was left to manage the farm with the help of their slaves and her other children. Fourteen-year-old Annette, the oldest at home, was soon sent to boarding school. Twelve-year-old Rush was the oldest son at home. None of Caroline's remaining children had the maturity or the knowledge to help with decision-making and planning. Of the seven slaves they owned, three were children below the age of fourteen.[5]

Image 6. Caroline Sedberry's region of Texas during the Civil War.

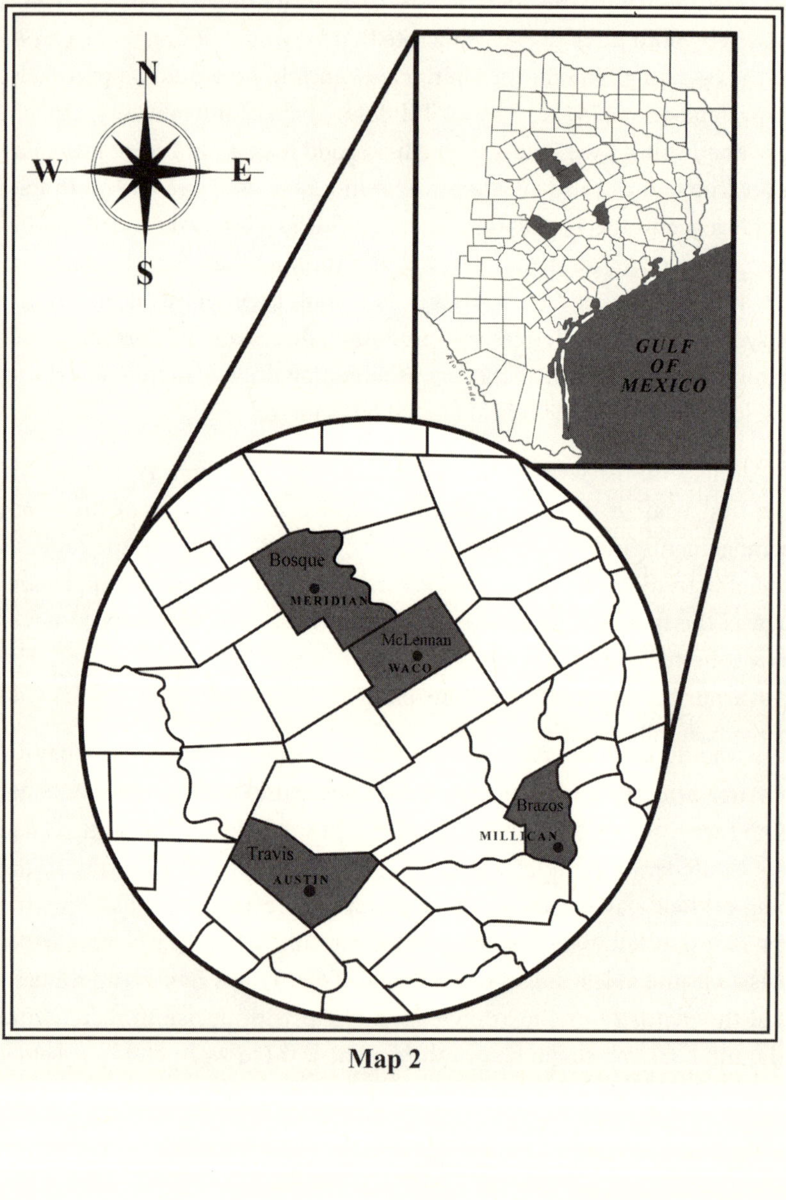

Map 2

Although Caroline obviously was accustomed, as most frontier women were, to overseeing the farm and business matters in the sometimes lengthy absence of her husband, her early letters to William while he served the Texas government in Austin show her insecurity in assuming complete responsibility. Although William expected the legislature to be in session only a short time, the weeks stretched out and work on the farm required decision-making. Caroline at this point expressed her uncertainty by writing "I wish you would write to me when to commence planting...." Although in January 1862 William was still in Austin, by April of that year he was stationed at Camp Speight in Brazos County near Millican, Texas (see Map 2). In the same letter in which Caroline lamented "really I am not capable of attending to any business but I will do the best I can," she wrote that she "never saw anything to equal [the rye], I don't recon. You know you did not think it would make much. Well, the greater portion of it is waist high." And May 15, 1862, she reported that she was getting along well with farming, had cut ten acres of wheat, was plowing corn the second time, and that the wheat, rye, and barley looked fine. As the spring passed, she fretted about continued rains ruining the crops, but by June she had harvested all but two acres of rye and oats. Her letters also mentioned planting vegetables such as turnips, beets, and potatoes. Although she was unexpectedly thrust into the traditional male role, she appeared to be able to manage the day-to-day running of the farm fairly well, although in at least one letter she expressed the wish that he were home to superintend the work and in all letters wrote that she longed for his return. William often encouraged her, writing "You must do the best you can and trust all to God. He will bring us all home safe if you will but trust him, yet if necessary we must be offered up for our country and liberty. ...I still love you more and more every day."[6]

Her letters reflect the emotional rollercoaster she was on as she stepped into an unfamiliar role. Her confidence grew as she made more initial decisions and asserted her opinions more readily. Certainly she reached the point of making suggestions, which exhibited her possible newfound knowledge of crop rotation. This can be seen when she suggested that perhaps William wanted the barley planted the same as the previous year, but thought possibly that area might be better for corn and up near the stables a good place for the barley.[7] Despite revealing that she was capable of dealing with these issues, Caroline's letters to her husband often reflected her feelings of inadequacy and despair. She talked about feelings of "utter helplessness" and lived with the constant fear that he would not return. Her writing tells how she was often depressed and had trouble sleeping.[8]

Raising crops was one thing; making decisions about when and for how much to sell them was quite another. Although Caroline had some definite ideas about what her farm products should be worth, she often found herself being manipulated not only by entrepreneurs but sometimes by her neighbors and fellow townspeople. One of the townspeople, "Old Wilbur," had asked for seven bushels for seed and agreed to pay the going price. When the time came to purchase the seed, he offered her less and said she had agreed to that price, which she disputed. In her letter to William she called him "an old Abolition scamp" and regretted selling him any seed.[9]

In another instance Caroline called on a man named Bob Earle to collect a debt for William. Earle claimed to have lost the note, stating that he owed Sedberry $143 and wasn't sure of the date of the note to determine interest due. Caroline later challenged him to admit that the note was actually for $150 plus interest. Concerned about her assertiveness, she wrote to William, "I was afraid I was doing wrong. Did I do right?" Although she was obviously holding her own in attending to business and farm matters, this anxious query suggests she was still not totally comfortable in her new management role. When a Dr. Willingham wanted to buy her wheat at two dollars per bushel, she refused. In a diatribe to William she stated she was entitled to get more money if she could, as she was alone with no help and had to pay dearly for all she purchased. By getting the best price she could, she wrote, surely no "reasonable man would think hard of me." In another letter she complained that the provost marshal was setting prices for wheat and flour, and that entrepreneurs were able to sell elsewhere for more and then send money to Bosque County to buy for less. She was outraged at the inequities that the war brought, particularly to women struggling to take care of their families and homes.[10]

William had apparently told Caroline what notes to pay and what to collect, and she tried to follow his instructions. Unfortunately, she often ran into problems when untrustworthy people tried to take advantage of her status as a woman alone. A Mr. Johnson, who had given a branding iron to William, demanded that she pay for it, although it was supposed to have been in exchange for a favor. Johnson also convinced her son Merritt that William owed him ten dollars, which Merritt then gave to him; Caroline felt they owed no such debt. Another man sold her wormy bacon after assuring her he would not. In another case, she attempted to settle a debt by deducting money owed to her husband for colts he had previously sold, but the patron, Mr. Corum, denied owing for the colts. She firmly stood her ground, told him her husband had left the account with her, and she would not pay the debt until William had authorized the payment. Another man tried to fool her into believing grain was down to $1.50 instead of $2, but she knew better. She wrote to William that "he thought I was a fool and didn't know any better. I didn't let on." This same man also tried to purchase a loom she had commissioned from a carpenter by going to the carpenter behind her back to purchase it. She wrote, "[I] didn't tell you how he done me about my loom. It was a little thing but it shows that he would take the advantage if he had the chance." These attempts to cheat her left her frustrated and angry. In one letter she said, "I think a man that will try to tak [*sic*] the advantage of a woman in a settlement is meaner than a dog."[11]

Although Caroline had doubts about her ability to make decisions, William expressed nothing but confidence in her skills. In one letter, after advising her about collecting and paying some debts, he wrote, "do the thing you think best about these things, exercise your own judgment, and do the best you can." To further reassure her of his confidence in her he wrote, "I only make these suggestions to assist you in the exercise of your judgment. I want you if you think different from the way I advise you, you must do the way you think best for I can't tell how everything is and you know circumstances always alter cases so do the best you can."[12]

By August 1862 Caroline's assurance in her ability to manage was stronger. She informed William that she would keep the rye for them to eat and sell the wheat because it was selling for $2.25 a bushel in Waco. She also planned to sell the mules for a good price. She then bartered with a builder to construct a house to store her wheat, exchanging the services of one of their slaves for some of the cost. In October she reported that she had sold 307 bushels of wheat for $3 per bushel, used part of the money to pay a note due Bill Jones for $350 plus interest of $8.60, and was relieved to have this debt paid.[13]

In October 1862 she wrote "We haven't commenced sowing wheat yet. I had the ploughs fixed last week...." She described the army worms that were devastating some of the neighbors' crops and reported that she was waiting for the cold weather to check the worms and for the ground to dry out so that she could have the crops planted. Caroline planned and prepared for the work needed to insure that the farm would flourish. She sometimes complained about the hard work she endured. She recorded "I have to neglect so many things I hardly take time to make up my bed." The long hours overseeing the farm, tending to her children, and nursing those who were ailing was taking its toll on her.[14]

In addition to running the farm, Caroline assumed the role of doctor and nurse for her children, who were frequently ill. Merritt was sent home from the army to recover from measles and a bad cough. Annette came down with measles and Caroline worried that the other children would catch them. Her letters were interspersed with frequent references to the illness of one or another of the children, ailing neighbors, and some of her own aches and pains. In June she wrote that Merritt was still sick, coughed a lot, and had severe pain in his shoulder. In the same letter she reported that Willie was sick all week and the children all had bad colds. In August 1862 she even took on the tending of a sick neighbor, "Mr. Jacob," at night. In September she wrote that Will was sick and had broken out in the measles.[15]

Even as she dealt with the many illnesses of her family, she fretted about the health of William and her sons. The excessive amount of sickness in the Sedberry household was mirrored and exceeded by the army camps of sons and husbands. The lack of personal cleanliness, improperly handled food, the inadequate number of doctors, and camps poorly located where mosquitoes and other insects thrived caused disease to be widespread among the soldiers. William's letters to his wife often referred to camp illnesses. In June 1862 he mentioned measles and fever in Camp Speight as well as some deaths. From Camp Nelson near Austin, Arkansas, he wrote that venereal disease was rampant and that there was a great deal of other sickness such as pneumonia. He stated that they were burying twenty to thirty men every day because they were not used to the climate, had little medicine, lacked hospitals, and were exposed to the elements. Her son Summer wrote in July 1862 that because of sickness his regiment of 7,000 men had only about 200 who were ready for duty.[16]

As shortages became widespread and cloth became increasingly difficult to obtain, Caroline by necessity added weaving and sewing to her tasks. The shortage of leather and cloth was widespread in Texas. Maria von Blücher of Corpus Christi wrote to her parents in Germany about the difficulty of keeping her family in clothes and shoes. In October 1862 she complained, "Shoes are there none at all, and it was good fortune that I had two hides of good leather from which I myself prepare shoes for our family." She reported that clothes could only be purchased in Mexico with silver, and that fabric was very expensive. Other women in Texas and the South turned to similar tasks for which they were untrained. They carded cotton, spun thread, and knitted. They wore homemade shoes and made clothes out of such unexpected things as the parlor table cover and cast-off clothing from the Yankees, which they re-dyed.[17]

Caroline attempted to buy wool to make uniforms for her husband and sons, but could not find any. Some of the thread she bought was rotten. She made clothes for her younger son out of William's jacket and bartered to get calico to make dresses for Annette. She carded wool, and then after finally gaining access to a loom, spent many hours weaving wool for uniforms. Because of the many demands on her time, she hired someone else to do some of the sewing. She worried that she would be unable to get uniforms made before winter set in and expressed a particular concern to William that their son Summer was "barefooted...and was very needy for clothes." She wrote, "I am so much afraid he will suffer before his [clothing] gets to him." Summer was not the only one who was barefoot. Shoes and boots became a commodity in short supply as the war went on and the Northern blockade became more effective. Caroline managed to buy shoes for Rush and for all the slaves except Sam, and to have a pair made for Annette. She herself, however, was "in a manner barefooted," as were her small children.[18]

By the fall of 1862, Caroline had made an unwanted discovery: she was pregnant. She told William in a letter, as she complained about how tired she was and about her frequent headaches: "I recon [*sic*] it happened the last time you were at home. I try to bear it the best I can." She advised him that she would not be confined until April. The prospect of having another baby, when she was already pushed to the limit with the never-ending chores, caused her to ask plaintively in her letter to William, "Don't you feel sorry for me?"[19]

Not all Southern women, particularly yeomen women, were educated; Caroline, however, was. Her letters show her to be quite literate. She may have been less well trained in mathematics, as she was reluctant to settle a note with interest calculations until the amount was verified by a man she could trust. She worried about her son Rush, who became a doctor after the war, not getting an education, but knew that she was unable to manage without him. Although some children during this century did not receive an education because they were needed to work on the farms, the 1860 census shows that the Sedberrys' three school-age sons who were still at home and their daughter, Annette, all attended school. Annette was sent to boarding school in August 1862. Caroline was not happy with the school and wanted to change, but knew she would not be able to travel much longer because of her pregnancy. She asked William to write to Annette and advise her. Caroline eventually made a trip to visit Annette and moved her because "I wouldn't care anything about the rough fare if they would keep clean beds and be nice about their cooking." She also expressed concern about how long she would be able to continue to keep Annette in the boarding school because of the cost.[20]

As did other Southern women, Caroline felt very strongly about those serving in the Confederate Army. Her disdain for those who only joined after conscription became law was evident in one of her letters. Unswerving patriotism was predominantly the norm for Southern women in the early stages of the war. The Confederate government used the American Revolution as a comparison with the Confederate cause, using the stereotypical dependent Southern female for appeal but adding determination and self-sacrifice to their description. Many of these women were accustomed to self-denial and ministering to the needs of others; this was a part of the symbolism of femininity for them. They also were used to being "protected" by the men in their lives. Whatever the new demands placed on women by the war, most Southern women staunchly supported the Confederate cause and held in contempt those men who were unwilling to serve. Mary Chesnut of South Carolina even lost patience with her own husband for what she perceived as his indifference to the war effort when he seemed unable to decide whether to join the army or run for public office. She vowed, "If I had been a man in this great revolution—I should have either been killed at once or made a name and done some good for my country."[21]

The Confederate government exhorted women to help maintain morale and to keep their men willing to serve, and especially to refrain from writing depressing letters to their men in the army. As the war dragged on, the women of the Confederacy became disillusioned about the cause and became less willing to sacrifice their loved ones, particularly when their feminine role of being protected was being swept away by invading Northern armies.[22]

Caroline, the Confederate government notwithstanding, had no reservations about sharing her ills, complaints, and miseries with her husband, regardless of the effect on his morale. Her letters are full of her trials, her inability to sleep because of the pressure on her, her weariness, and her physical ills. She often told him when she wrote that she had a bad headache or some other ailment and mentioned how much work there was to do. She told him that weaving was hard and that she was not used to such work. In one letter, for example, she complained that someone was stealing corn out of the crib, that the hogs were a lot of trouble, that she could not find the mares, and that half the people left behind were rogues who "would steal the last mouthful out of our mouths."[23]

During the time of the correspondence with her husband, Caroline still had the use of several slaves. Even with their help and that of the children at home, she was overwhelmed by the unending tasks confronting her. Other well-to-do women of the South, who were accustomed to having slaves for drudgery and for distasteful jobs, found it difficult to adapt without slaves. When their slaves left as freemen, these women were left with cooking and laundry chores for which they had no experience. Martha F. Horne of Missouri reminisced, "I had never cooked a meal when the [N]egro women left, and had a hard time learning." Maria von Blücher wrote to her parents, "We wash, iron, dye, cook soap, etc., also have ourselves made indigo from the shrub..." Unaccustomed as some of these women were to basic chores, they nevertheless overcame their aversion to them and did whatever was required of them. As did other women, Caroline planted vegetables, carded wool, sewed, nursed, and mothered her children, all while overseeing the business end of the farm.[24]

In spite of their support of the Confederacy and the war effort, both Caroline and William frequently expressed in their letters, not only their longing for William's return, but their devotion to one another and their strong wish that the war would be over soon. In June 1862 Caroline wrote, "Oh my dearest one. You don't know how anxious I am for you to come home for life is almost a perfect blank without you. It seems that it has been a year since I got a letter from you." She also told him that if something happened to him she wouldn't want to live any longer, although she knew that was wrong since she should want to live for her children. In another letter she lamented, "Oh this cruel war, will it ever end. I almost get out of heart sometimes. I can't think of anything, only you and the children. I dreamed last night you were dead, and Oh, if I have to realize it what will become of poor me. God forbid it." William wrote, "Oh, this cruel war is breaking and bleeding the hearts of many thousands; it is tearing asunder husbands and wives and relatives and friends of all kinds. O, that it would end and we can be permitted to embrace each other to remain together during life." In a letter to William, Caroline wrote, "I have dreamed about you often lately and I can't keep those little lines out of my head that says:

> 'One minutes dream about thee
> Were worth a long and endless year
> Of waking bliss without thee
> My own love, my only dear.'"[25]

Caroline's letters continually reflected her longing to see her husband again and her fear that he would not return. In May 1862 she wrote, "...I will pray for you continually as long as life shall last. If it were not for the hope that I have I don't think I could survive...." The news Caroline Sedberry dreaded most was sent to her mother-in-law, Nancy. A letter dated January 2, 1863, informed William's mother that he had died of illness. The letter had been sent to Nancy, "at the request of Summer and

[N]oing [*sic*] the conditions at cousin Caroline's we thought it best to rite [*sic*] to you first and let you send word on this letter up to her as soon as you get these few lines," taking care that Caroline be told the news gently. William's son, Summer, was with his father when he died and took care of the burial arrangements in Little Rock, Arkansas. One can only imagine the devastating effect this news had on Caroline, then in her fifth or sixth month of pregnancy.[26]

William acknowledged his confidence in his wife's ability by appointing "my dear and beloved wife Caroline H. Sedberry my first executrix to be assisted by J. S. and Merritt A. Sedberry." In addition to the farm in Bosque County, he owned 570 acres in San Augustine County, nine slaves, and various livestock. Two slaves were considered William's separate property, but the balance of the estate, valued at $24,386, was considered common property. William's will also contained a provision that as their children became of age, that Caroline "give and dispose to them as she may deem just and right, giveing [*sic*] to each the same in value as they come of age..."[27]

After the war Caroline raised her family and continued to farm the family property. The 1870 census listed seven of her children residing in her household, including the seven-year-old daughter with whom she was pregnant at the time of William's death, as well as 25-year-old Merritt, who had lost an arm in the war. A history of Bosque County reports, "Caroline made regular trips by horse-and-buggy into Clifton and Meridian to shop and to sell her produce."

Despite Caroline's efforts, the postwar years were difficult, and by 1870 the estate had dwindled to $4,500, according to census records. This did not necessarily reflect bad management on Caroline's part. Of the $24,836 shown as the value of William's estate in the probate documents, $7,300 was designated as the value of his slaves. In 1864 Bosque County tax records valued the slaves at $8,500. The 500 acres was valued at $3,500 at the time of William's death and was down to $1,500 in 1864. By 1870 the land showed an increase in value to $2,500, but the value of livestock and other personal property had declined to $439. The total assessed value in 1864 without the value of the slaves would have been only $1,820, whereas the assessed value in 1870 was $2,939. Although assessed values are not necessarily market value, these figures show that even in the midst of Reconstruction Caroline managed to maintain control of the farm. [28]

In 1871, nine years after William Sedberry's death, Caroline married John Stith. In the years following, she deeded acreage from the Sedberry farm to three of her sons in accordance with what she considered William's wishes. In 1890 Stith filed a description of a plot of land 16 feet by 16 feet overlooking the Bosque Valley "to have and to hold inviolate forever for a final resting place for my old worn out boddy [*sic*] when I go out of it." Caroline, who died in 1895 before Stith, is buried in the Sedberry family plot in the Clifton, Texas, cemetery. She is identified by her maiden name on her tombstone, "C. H. Alexander, Wife of William R. Sedberry." Strangely, no mention is made of the man to whom she had been married for the last twenty-four years.[29]

Women of Caroline Sedberry's class were driven by necessity to perform tasks they had never done before and to accept challenges they had never expected to meet. They persevered against overwhelming odds, often grimly, but did what they had to do in order to help their families survive. Caroline, whose letters early on reflected her insecurity, grew so bold as to write to her husband, "I have a notion to sell out pretty close, for if the Indians come in as some think they will and we have to leave our homes I am afraid I will lose a heap. That pesters me nearly to death." This from a woman who less than a year earlier wrote that she was not capable of attending to any business.[30]

NOTES

1. Richard H. Sewell, *A House Divided: Sectionalism and Civil War, 1848-1865* (Baltimore: The Johns Hopkins University Press, 1988), 80; William C. Pool, *Bosque County, Texas* (San Marcos: San Marcos Record Press, 1954), 18-29.
2. Pool, *Bosque County,* 18-29; John H. Herndon through his attorney J. N. Mabray to William R. Sedberry, Volume B, 396-397, Bosque County Deed Records, Bosque County Courthouse, Meridian, Texas; The Bosque County History Book Committee, *A History of Bosque County, Texas* (Dallas: Curtis Media Corporation, 1986), 664-668.
3. *A History of Bosque County, Texas,* 664-668; Sedberry Papers, Dan E. Kilgore Collection 7, Special Collections and Archives, Mary and Jeff Bell Library (Corpus Christi: Texas A&M University-Corpus Christi), William R. Sedberry to Caroline H. Sedberry, November 1,1861, through January 1, 1862, May 13, 1862, August 9, 1862, October 30, 1862. Letters from William and Caroline will hereafter be referenced as WRS and CHS and are found in Folders 1.5 through 1.26 and Folder 1.36; undated fragments are identified by Folder numbers. Proclamation by William Sedberry dated June 13, 1861, is located in Folder Oversize 2.1. "Buncombe" is defined as nonsense, ostentatious talking, from Buncombe, North Carolina, whose member made an irrelevant speech in Congress, circa 1820, simply to impress his constituents. Common usage today is spelled "bunkum" (Shorter Oxford English Dictionary, Fifth Edition).
4. WRS to CHS, November 27, 1861.
5. Eighth Census of the United States (1860), Bosque County, Texas, Schedule 1 (Free Population, and Schedule 2 (Slave Population); Special Collections and Archives, Texas A&M University-Corpus Christi.
6. A number of historians have written on gender issues in Texas and the frontier. Sandra L. Myres' *Westering Women and the Frontier Experience,* Mark Carroll's *Homesteads Ungovernable,* and Angela Boswell's *Her Act and Deed: Women's Lives in a Rural Southern County, 1837-1873,* and others effectively describe gender relations and women's percep-

tions of their roles during this period. CHS to WRS, November 17, 1862, May 6, 1862 through June 17, 1862, undated fragment; WRS to CHS, May 8, 1862.

7. CHS to WRS, undated fragment Folder 1.24.
8. CHS to WRS, May 6 and 18, 1862, June 17, 1862, August 7, 1862, September 1, 1862.
9. CHS to WRS, undated fragment Folder 1.24.
10. CHS to WRS, June 18, 1862, and September 4, 1862.
11. CHS to WRS, undated fragment Folder 1.24; August 1, 1862.
12. WRS to CHS, undated fragment, Folder 1.36.
13. CHS to WRS, August 22, 1862 and October 2, 1862.
14. CHS to WRS, October 18, 1862.
15. CHS to WRS, June 17 and 21, 1862, July 25, 1862, August 29, 1862, September 1 and 25, 1862, October 10, 1862, November 17, 1861, undated fragment, Folder 1.24.
16. Ralph A. Wooster and Robert Wooster, "'Rarin' for a Fight': Texans in the Confederate Army," *Southwestern Historical Quarterly* 84 (April 1981): 423-25; WRS to CHS, April 28, 1862, June 12, 1862, August 9, 1862, October 30, 1862 and November 9, 1862; John Summerfield Sedberry to Caroline H. Sedberry, July 20,1862, Sedberry Papers; CHS to WRS, August 1, 1862.
17. Bruce S. Cheeseman, ed., *Maria von Blücher's Corpus Christi: Letters from the South Texas Frontier, 1849-1879* (College Station: Texas A&M University Press, 2002), 129; Blücher Collection, Special Collections and Archives, Texas A&M University-Corpus Christi.
18. CHS to WRS, August 1, 1862, August 7, 1862, August 15, 1862, September 25, 1862, October 23, 1862, undated fragment, Folder 1.24.
19. CHS to WRS, October 23, 1862.
20. CHS to WRS, August 29, 1862, September 21, 1862, November 7, 1862, and November 21, 1862, undated fragment, Folder 1.24.
21. CHS to WRS, undated fragment Folder 1.24; George C. Rable, *Civil Wars: Women and the Crisis of Southern Nationalism* (Urbana: University of Illinois Press, 1989), 153; C. Vann Woodward and Elisabeth

Muhlenfeld, *The Private Mary Chesnut: The Unpublished Civil War Diaries* (New York: Oxford University Press, 1984), 179-180.

22. Catherine Clinton and Nina Silver, eds., *Divided Houses: Gender and the Civil War* (New York: Oxford University Press, 1992), 179-180, 198-199.
23. CHS to WRS, August 7 and 17, 1862, September 1, 1862, October 10, 1862.
24. Suzanne Lebsock, *The Free Women of Petersburg* (New York: W. W. Norton & Company, 1985), 146, 158-9; United Daughters of the Confederacy, Missouri Division, *Reminiscences of the Women of Missouri During the '60s*, 43; Texas A&M University-Corpus Christi, Mary and Jeff Bell Library, microfilm, Reel 864, No. 7077; Cheeseman, *Maria von Blücher*; Maria von Blücher to parents October 29, 1863, Blücher Collection.
25. CHS to WRS, June 17, 1862, October 18, 1862, November 10, 1861.
26. CHS to WRS, May 6, 1962; M. L. Alexander to Mrs. Nancy Sedberry, January 2, 1863; Sedberry Papers.
27. Bosque County, Texas, *Bosque County Probate Minutes*, 1863, Volume D1, pages 345-48.
28. Ninth Census of the United States (1870), Bosque County, Texas, La Retama Central Library, Corpus Christi, Texas; "Texas, County Tax Rolls, 1846-1910," database with images, *FamilySearch*, accessed 10 July 2015, https://familysearch.org/ark:/61902/1:1; C. H. Sedberry, 1870, citing Bosque County, Texas, United States, State Archives, Austin; FHL microfilm 2,282,104.
29. Ninth Census of the United States; *History of Bosque County*; Bosque County Marriage Records 1860-75, Volume B, p. 233; Bosque County Deed Records, Volume 16, pp. 190-191; Volume 3, pp. 209-211; Volume N, pp. 8-10; Volume N, pp. 518-521, Bosque County Court House, Meridian, Texas.
30. CHS to WRS, September 4, 1862.

Image 7. Louisa Van Zandt Clough.

Courtesy Jeremiah Morrill Clough Papers, Special Collections, The University of Texas at Arlington Libraries, Arlington, Texas.

Louisa and other family members were often at the home of Minerva Van Zandt during the war.

Chapter 3

He Said, She Said

Gendered Correspondence among Texans

Beverly Rowe

The impact of the Civil War can be seen in what soldiers wrote about camp life, and how their wives, mothers, and sisters described life at home without the men they depended upon. It can be seen in what soldiers wrote about the institution of slavery, the concept of emancipation, in what women wrote about being without the help of their slaves and their perceptions of slaves' disloyalty to their masters' families. And finally, it can be seen through the men's and women's changing viewpoints as the duration of the war extended from months to years. The letters of Mary Jones, George Ingram, Martha Ingram, Isaiah Harlan, Douglas J. Cater, Khleber Miller Van Zandt, and John W. Watkins allow the reader to see the everyday effects experienced by a few men and women in Texas.[1]

In the early days of the war, men enlisted with high spirits, looking forward to their first battles. It was a "Glorious Cause" and they believed that God was on their side. Their letters show how high hopes and excitement rapidly deteriorated when the reality of day-to-day soldiering became clear to them. The stark differences between camp and civilian life were the first realities they faced. Many men, such as Khleber Miller Van Zandt, learned new skills—skills they once thought of as "women's work." He bragged that he had learned to be a good cook who made "mighty fine biscuits," and that it would "amuse you to see me down on my knees, with a tray of flour before me on the ground, hard at work kneading dough and then making them into biscuits." As a drill officer for his company in Chalybeat Springs in mid-July, 1861, he observed that he thought he could "get my company pretty proficient in the manual of arms and in Company drill," as men were anxious to learn and he thought he had the skills to teach them.[2]

Camp life was vastly different from the life they had known as civilians. In October, 1861, Van Zandt wrote to his wife, Minerva, from Shreveport, Louisiana, that the men in his company were all being subordinate, were trying to do their duty, and that he was proud of his group's orderliness and behavior in light of what he saw from other groups stationed near them. In November 1861, Douglas Cater wrote to his Cousin Em from Osage Springs, Arkansas, that his regiment was camped in the "roughest, rockiest, poorest country he had ever seen" near the Missouri-Arkansas state line. He also mentioned that the men were all homesick and asking for furloughs to go home. John W. Watkins wrote his wife Irene that "nearly all the boys have gone to town today and camp is quite dull." Isaiah Harlan wrote his mother that his regiment's tents were "good, large enough and comfortable," even though they were on the ground, and he did not know how long they would be forced to endure the dampness, which he believed was the cause of his persistent cough. Harlan described his duties of daily drills and guard duty, and his fears: "If I live, I'll make a soldier yet. I hope I'll not turn out to be a coward." Harlan also noted that, "It seems to be the settled policy of those in authority to keep us entirely in the dark as to the movements of our troops." These comments by the soldiers to their relatives showed their disillusionment with the glorious cause, camp life, and their fellow soldiers. [3]

Most soldiers expressed frustration with the lack of supplies and how difficult they were to obtain. Van Zandt told his wife that the men in his mess had to buy their rations and that they were fishing for buffalo fish to acquire a source of meat. Harlan addressed the quality of the food when he wrote that, "We are fed altogether on bacon and bread, at times a little Arkansas beef, worse than the meanest beef we got at Virginia Point last winter," and that "most of the boys think that they would starve almost if they could not get something more and have accordingly turned out to pillaging the surrounding country. They take everything they can get hold of. Cows, hogs, sheep, poultry, nothing escapes them." He did not approve of the Confederate Army taking needed supplies from loyal Southern citizens. Additionally, Harlan told his mother that his company had not yet drawn their arms and "Lord only knows when we will. We committed a great error in sending those back we had; but we were told that we would draw them."[4]

Clothing was also a constant need and in short supply. Harlan bemoaned that clothing would need to be provided by friends and family, as it was believed it would not be supplied for his department. Friends and neighbors at home did, in fact, supply many goods for their soldiers. Mary Jones wrote to her son Charles, "I sent down by Mrs. Allen your cloak, a pillow and some towels. She promised to see what you needed & furnish you with the same for instance a comfort or a mattress or both." However, there was much frustration because of this additional burden on the women at home. Martha Ingram's letter to her husband, George, supports Harlan's lament: "I received a letter from Kenon yesterday. He wishes me to send him some cloaths which is all moste an impossibility. The people hear had supposed that the government would supply the men with cloaths and had not prepared to make there cloaths. I canot wride about to hunt up cloaths. If I was a man perhaps I might but as it is it will be a poore show."[5]

Sickness, lack of health care, and death seemed to be uppermost on soldiers' minds when writing home. Van Zandt noted the emergence of measles in his camp in November of 1861, and Harlan wrote of "a great deal of sickness in his camp near Little Rock. Not more than one third of the regiment is able to do duty. We have about 25 or thirty in our company, the rest are sick or unwell. Measles is the prevailing disease. Three of our company have died." Van Zandt expressed concern for the lack of sanitary precautions taken by enlisted men stating that "a majority of them take no care of themselves in camp; they lie down with impunity on wet blankets and damp straw, they eat their food half cooked. They are careless and unconcerned about the cleanliness of their persons or their clothing." He also questioned the qualifications of responding doctors and blamed their lack of ability on authorities who made such callous decisions. Women left at home worried about their soldiers' access to health care, reflecting a clear understanding of their men's plight. Mary Jones wrote, "I have no confidence that you will receive any attention but on the contrary will be expected to do duty unless you are very sick." Battle fatigue and weariness with the deaths of soldiers caused Isaiah Harlan to write his sister, "I have seen dead men enough. I never want to witness such a scene again as I did on the battle ground of Chickamauga."[6] One can only imagine the impact such letters had on the women.

Soldiers were often greeted by beautiful, flirtatious women as they marched through various towns on their way to the next battle, and many letters contained information about these women. Van Zandt wrote that as his company marched through Minden, Louisiana, pretty women waving handkerchiefs and flags wished them "God Speed," and that "As I was walking along by a fine dwelling a very pretty young lady was standing by the fence, and calling to me, asked me to accept a small Confederate flag made of paper of red, white and blue and which was attached to a sprig of Cape Jessamine with a beautiful flower at the end." The men who mentioned women flirting with them, admonished their wives not to be jealous, as the women's attention was directed at a "soldier," rather than at him specifically. He also wrote about how soldiers treated women in the areas the army passed through: "The boys of the 3rd Texas tell some hard tales on each other in regards to their conduct with the women up in Tennessee. Dick says that Nath was as bad as any of them." Apparently, the lack of morals extended to the commanders, as well. In February of 1863, Van Zandt wrote his wife, "When officers do not act the part of gentlemen, they can not expect their men to do so." He wrote that a certain general died as a result of stab wounds inflicted by a jealous husband when he was found in bed with the other man's wife. It is uncertain how women reacted to these stories, but some were undoubtedly concerned about their men's fidelity.[7]

Soldiers observed and wrote about shortcomings of fellow soldiers, both as military men and as moral men. With regard to new recruits, Van Zandt wrote, "New recruits are having trouble adjusting to camp life. One jumped into the river and tried to drown himself. He was saved, but died a few days later – scared to death by enemy shelling." His frustration with older men who enlisted is evident when he wrote that "In all the companies are old men, who have more patriotism than judgment, more infirmities than prowess. They all should have staid at home and the colony of Graves which now rise up on the bossom of Kentucky's soil as one of the dire evils of this war, and the ocean of tears which have fallen from the faces of their mothers, sisters, wives and daughters all might have been spared."[8]

As the war progressed the men's letters reflected the lack of enthusiasm that often led to desertion. George Ingram commented, "The boys are very impatient and in great suspense. They have their heads set homewards and many are determined to go orders or no orders." Isaiah Harlan commented that fifty-eight men in his regiment had been arrested for mutiny. Van Zandt informed his wife that, "nearly all of our boys who were captured and paroled have run away and gone home without reporting to the proper authorities." Those who were caught deserting were dealt with severely. Harlan somberly informed his mother, "Notwithstanding yesterday was such an unpleasant day [as] our division was called out to witness the execution of a deserter. He was a native at least a citizen of Arkansas, had deserted and gone over to the enemy and I suppose was taken with them, was Court Martialed and sentenced to be shot to death with musketry. I was not close enough to see how he took it. He was not killed at the first fire, a very painful occurrence. I believe he was fired upon three times before he was pronounced dead."[9] Surely other women heard about such horrors perpetrated on the men and worried that their own soldiers could be subjected to such terrible endings for trying to return home.

Isaiah Harlan's letters reflect the feeling of helplessness and concern with everyday life in their absence. He wrote to his mother requesting his brother, Alpheus, "take care of my papers. See that my [N]egroes are clothed &c. Keep an account of all expenses incurred on my account and when I return if I every do, we'll have a settlement and I'd satisfy him." And later, in May 1862: "I am very anxious to know what is going on at home and especially whether E. [Eliphalet] and A. [Alpheus] are still at home." Harlan advised his brother Eliphalet to purchase property with the proceeds of the cotton crop because he rightly believed that Confederate money would decline in value over time, while the value of property would remain stable. He tried to send as much of his pay home so his brother could convert his pay in Confederate dollars into property or gold. His ongoing concern with the decrease in value, and the possibility that he may not return, is evident in a subsequent letter from Arkansas Post in December 1862: "I think you had better dispose of every dollar that you do not absolutely need in the purchase of property. We can divide it when I return if I every do. If I do not, I'll not need my share."[10]

An important element contributing to Southern success during the war was the continued production of crops and livestock. Martha Ingram's letter to her husband reflects her efforts: "There is nine young colts and I [think] this is all that wee will have. The horses are fat and slick now. They look almoste as large again now as they did when you was hear. There is won [one] deepe bay almoste black. I think if he was broke we could get two Hundred dollars for him. I wishe we had some of them broke and up there now whil the boys have there pockits full of money." Just a few months later she wrote, "There is a greate deel of corn made hear. Ma made 52 bushels of wheat. She did not make no grass nor Barley though if the Stock does not distroy her corn she will make corn enough to do her two years." Isaiah Harlan responded to a letter he had received from his brother, saying that he was pleased their farm had produced one hundred bales of cotton in wartime even though that was a little more than half of what they previously produced. However, he expressed concern over missing hogs and advised his brother to look for them down in the area between the Little Brazos and Sandy Rivers.[11]

Mail service proved to be one of the biggest frustrations for soldiers in camp. Letters from home were precious. George Ingram wrote, "If you could see my trembling hand when I open your letters and see my eyes fill with tears as I trace the lines you would not then ask me if I were tired of your scribbling." Isaiah Harlan's comment that "Soldiering is a melancholy business at least it is to me and I think a little news from home at intervals along would do me good," speaks to the importance of letters from home. Almost a year later, a letter to his mother shows that things had not improved: "I do not suppose from what Margaret says that more than half of them [letters] get there atal . . . Generally I get them at from twelve to twenty days from the time when they are written or about half the time that it takes mine to get home to you." Mail service was not much better on the home front. Mary Jones wrote, "Mr. Bush the Mail Carrier has promised to bring my Mail Matter down once a week & send it to the school house so I will get my papers & letters more regular hereafter." Martha Ingram wrote George, "In yore last letter you said you had not heard from me since you parted with me. It is strange that you do not get my letters. I write nearly every weeke." Toward the end of the war, mail service was so irregular that regiments were allowed to elect one member each to go home, carry mail from soldiers, pick up mail from home, and meet with families to give them whatever news they had.[12]

Women left at home faced uncertainty, hardships, and difficult decision-making. Minerva Van Zandt complained that she was having to handle affairs that her husband normally took care of, such as renting out their home and selling horses. Khleber answered, "I am sorry that affairs at home are giving you so much anxiety and trouble." However, he told her that he was turning matters on the home front over to her because he had no time to even think about them. Martha Ingram made a decision she later regretted: "I am sorry that I let Mr. Steel have the Pony and if I can get him back I will do so. . . . It greaves me when I know that I have don anything that is not in accordance with your notions."[13] Her disappointment in her actions when she was trying to do her best during her husband's absence was surely difficult for both of them.

Having access to money was vital to both soldiers and the women at home. Mary Jones wrote to her son, "I have heard that you all had been paid off. I hope so as you need some money to purchase little necessaries, medicine &&. Do take care of your money and don't get out if possible. You need not send me any of it, that is if you can take care of it yourself, but should you send any I will *keep* it for *you* as I can get along with what little I have." She also wrote that she was making up for money shortages by housing refugees: "Mrs. Winnie of Galveston is here with family occupying the log cabin & dining room. They of course cook & eat to themselves. I furnish her with firewood, potatoes, meal & the rent of the rooms and all these things you know will be quite a little income for me these hard times." Martha Ingram wrote to her husband, "I got fifty dollars by Doctor McKiney which you said would pay for the cloaths that I sent you. I was in hopes that you would receive them as a present from yore best friends. I am very thankful for the money and will do the best with the money that I can." Van Zandt tried to send money to his wife by mail and by way of other soldiers returning to their home county with mixed results. In April of 1863, he sent her one hundred dollars to pay taxes, and then worried about whether she would actually receive the money. George Ingram wrote that he was sending his wife Martha seven hundred dollars by way of two men who had been furloughed.[14]

Women frequently mentioned the slaves they owned to the soldiers in their letters. Mary Jones wrote that slaves Sarah, Mary, and Julia had taken turns with some illness and as one got better, another one became sick, and that "Crumwell keeps well and is the *man* of *all business* on the place." When the Negroes were getting the corn crop in, Jerry and Willis would pull it down and Mary and Crum would haul it in. The mystery illness might have been malaria, because Mary said one of the slaves was out of quinine and Mary would have to get some by a returning steamboat if it could get through. Martha Ingram wrote that she would need to hire a woman the next year to help her spin because she did not have time to get the work done by herself. It was later disclosed that Martha was pregnant. Commenting on disciplining bondsmen and changing patterns of deference, Martha wrote, "Mr. Wade under took to whip Tup not long since when Tup turnd the joke and whipped Wade. Tup struck at Wade with a stick and Wade saved himself by running up to Tup causing him to hit so far over that the end of the stick struck Wade in the back. Wade has bin lade up ever since and is not able to work yet. Mr. Cole and Mr. Glen whipped Tup. Gave him three hundred. The Negroes are almoste free hear."[15]

As late as mid-1863, Southern men and Southern women were still buying slaves. In May 1863, Martha Ingram wrote that two men she knew had gone to Arkansas to buy themselves some Negroes, but she hoped they would get a load of spun thread instead, as that would be of more help to her. Ingram said that an "old Man Mitchel" was at "Unkle Ervins" place with a large gang of Negroes and noted that they were "two mutch on the high feluting order for this contry. I hope there will not be any more Negroes braught hear." In August 1863 Isaiah Harlan wrote his brother Eliphalet, "Sell by all means if you can do so advantageously and buy negroes, land, or stock unless you can sell for specie. If I had a pile of gold I might be tempted to dig a hole and put it away until the war ends. Sheep would be a good investment if they could be cared for, also good mares or [N]egroes." Other owners planned for the continuation of chattel labor by pairing their male and female slaves. Isaiah Harlan instructed his brother:

> I don't know what to say about those [N]egroes. Jenny and Sam are no doubt both anxious to get rid of each other. Sam and Mat [a woman] might be as much so in less than six months. You may do as you please about it. You may put Mat to any keen active [N]egro boy that you please. You may put her to Jess if you want to or to Sam. I object to Jake. . . . Let them suit themselves. If you can consistently do so. You can't allow them too many privileges in that respect. If you do they will be running every where. Get them together agreeable if you can and then make them stick.[16]

From the comments in these letters, it appears that these Southerners thought they would win the war and life would return to the way it used to be.

The women were stunned by the escalation of commodity prices as the war progressed. Martha Ingram's letters to George demonstrate the continued worry and frustration she endured at a time when enlisted men were paid but twelve dollars per month. In December 1862: "Corn is selling hear at three dollars per bushel and down in Falls, co., where Unkle Ervin lives two dollars. Three year old beafes are selling at thirty dollars. Pork selling twenty-five cents per pound. I think I will buy some pork and make but little meate do." And, "it seames to me that helf of the people have gon wilde after money. It would astonish you if you could be hear and hear the prises of things. Every thing is going up and every boddy is trying to get the biggest prise. It is a shame to see how they act." In May 1863: "If I get the money that you spoke of sending me I think I will send to Brownsvill for some Calico and domestick. We can get Calico [at some cent] per yard for gold and you can get won dollar of gold for three dollars of Confederate money. Calico is selling at three dollars per yard and domesticks the same. These prises will do for some folks to pay but I think I will ware patches first."[17] As the war progressed and prices continued to rise, her frustration and anxiety would have undoubtedly escalated.

In camp the men also faced commodity hardships. Isaiah Harlan wrote to his mother that while he was a prisoner at Camp Model-Farm near Petersburg, Virginia, his group could not get enough to eat because Virginia "has been the center of war so long that edibles of all sorts are nearly exhausted. Those that have money can get little messes of fish, greens, pies, etc. that help the cause a little, but they have to pay the most outrageous prices that you ever heard of." Harlan wrote his brother Eliphalet that "Prices are strictly on the increase here as they are I suppose everywhere else in the [C]onfederacy for example sweet potatoes sell at twelve dollars per bushel, [I]rish to, price of hen eggs one dollar per dozen. I gave four dollars yesterday for a pair of cotton socks. I was almost barefotted or I should not have don it. If we could get into the country far enough we might get things cheaper."[18]

The impact of the Civil War evoked different responses from men and women throughout the war years. In the early years of the war, 1861 and 1862, people believed that the war would be of short duration. In October 1861 Khleber Van Zandt complained to his wife, "When will Lincoln cease this wicked, fratercidal war, and let parted loved ones be united?" And later, in January 1862, "I am in hopes this unholy war will not last more than a year longer, if that." Isaiah Harlan missed his mother, "Ma, I must state that it seems to me that I never knew your worth so well or thought so much of you as I have since I have been in the army." Mary Jones told her sister Florence, "Mr. Lincon seems every way disposed to make peace, all though he was elected by the *Black Republicans,* they cannot rule him altogether, now that he is placed at the head of Government he will be obliged to rule and go according to the laws and the Constitution if he does not, there is plenty of outsiders that will keep him strait." Isaiah Harlan told his brother, "It begins to look as though the war would wear us all out and we had as well resign all hopes of ever getting home again. Lincoln has always been determined to prosecute it to the bitter end and I am afraid that a few successes will unite the whole north in his support. If so God only knows when or where it will end."[19]

By 1862 and 1863 some of the men had been captured and taken to prisoner of war camps in the North. Isaiah Harlan wrote his mother, "We had a very serious time of it after we were captured, especially on the way to Camp Douglas. We suffered horribly. We were almost starved and frozen to death." Van Zandt was captured in February 1862, then freed in September of that same year. He told his wife that after release he was being sent from Vicksburg, Mississippi, to Clinton, Mississippi, and that while he was in prison he lost a lot of weight and had had the mumps. While in prison he was sometimes treated like a gentleman and sometimes like a dog.[20]

Confusion, anxiety, and frustration peppered the letters in 1863. Van Zandt wrote, "I certainly think that when everyone at the North is so loud mouthed about peace, that it can not be kept off a long while." The following month he noted, "The enemy are not making the same efforts and displaying the same energy that they did this time last year. It is thought by some that they will not desert or attempt to fight any more large battles, but that their policy will be to occupy as much of our country as possible and prevent the planting and raising bread stuffs and thus 'starve us out.'"[21]

As the war progressed into its final stages, the overall tone of letters and diary entries were decidedly despondent. Isaiah Harlan wrote, "Vicksburg has fallen. . . Joe Johnston is falling back before Grant. . . . Things look Gloomy but I hope all will turn out well at last." By January 1864 he believed that should the war continue, as he thought it would, the South would "not be worth a farthing." He was convinced that the South would lose as confidence and determination was lacking in both regular citizens and in the army due in part to "bad generalship and short-sighted legislation [that] brought us to the very brink of destruction, and negligence and corruption in officials and greed in the masses are working to the same end." He was also leery that new taxes from the Confederate Congress would "have the tendency to transfer a great deal of property from present owners to stockjobbers, speculators &c. those who have been enabled to mass large sums of Confederate money." As Harlan worried about pecuniary matters, Martha Ingram fretted about her family life, "Will this war ever close and you be at Home to help train our little boys and make our fireside bright for now that you are away there is a continual gloom pervade the hold place. May God bless you and hasten the time of peace."[22]

Two of the men mentioned in the letters did not come home from war at all. Isaiah Harlan was killed in Georgia sometime after April 25, 1864. Mary Jones' son was killed somewhere in Kentucky in 1862. She wrote, "James Hageman returned home the 21st of July and from him I learned that it was the opinion our dear Charlie was no more, tho no one saw him die. . . ." Mary said that because no sign of Charlie had been found and that he was only presumed dead, she would not give up hope of seeing him again.[23]

Southerners, both men and women, wrote how the Civil War changed their lives and those of their neighbors and families. The soldiers documented the rumors, troop movements, incompetent officers, and deprivations they faced. They documented their dead comrades and tried to get word home to tell families of their losses. Women at home wrote about their feelings of abandonment, their reluctance to pick up duties usually assigned to the men of the south, and their worries about the future of their families. By the end of the war, they all seemed to recognize that there could be no return to life as it once was.

NOTES

1. Mary Jones Collection, Willis Library, University of North Texas, Denton, Texas. Mary Jones was originally from Lawrence County, Arkansas, and was the widow of Hugh McCrory, a soldier with Felix Huston's volunteers. She married Anson Jones who served as President of the Republic of Texas from 1844 to 1846. At the time of the Civil War, Mary lived in Harris County, Texas, and had been widowed a second time. The letters in this collection were written to her son, C. Anson Jones; Henry L. Ingram, comp., *Civil War Letters of George W. and Martha F. Ingram, 1861-1865*, Cushing Library, Texas A&M University, College Station, Texas. George W. Ingram enlisted in the 12th Texas Cavalry from Hillsboro, Texas, and served as an officer in Company A. This letter collection contains correspondence between George and his wife, Martha; Harlan, Isaiah, Isaiah Harlan's Civil War Letters, Company G., 10th Texas Infantry Regiment File, Confederate Research Center, Harold B. Simpson Hill College History Complex, Hillsboro, Texas. Isaiah Harlan enlisted in Captain Lauderdale's Company from Washington County, Texas. This collection contains letters Isaiah wrote to his mother, his brother Alpheus, his brother Eliphalet and his sister Margaret; Douglas J. Cater, "Civil War Letters to 'Dear Cousin Em', 1861-1865," SMF311, Southwest Arkansas Regional Archives, Washington, Arkansas. Douglas J. Cater enlisted in the 19th Louisiana Volunteers and most of his letters were written to his cousin, Em, who lived near New Salem, Texas; Khleber Miller Van Zandt, Van Zandt Collection, 7th Texas Infantry File, Confederate Research Center, Harold B. Simpson Hill College History Complex, Hill College, Hillsboro, Texas. Khleber Miller Van Zandt, a lawyer, helped organize Company D., 7th Texas Infantry, from Marshall, Harrison County, Texas, and saw action in Mississippi and Tennessee. He wrote most of his letters to his wife, Minerva; Watkins, John W., Watkins Letter Collection, 5th Texas Regiment File, Confederate Research Center, Harold B. Simpson Hill College History Complex, Hillsboro, Texas. John W. Watkins wrote his letters to his wife Irene, at home in Marlin, Texas. Watkins enlisted in the 5th Texas Regiment and served mostly in Louisiana. Excerpts from letters include original spelling and grammar.

2. Van Zandt, October 20, 1861, July 19, 1861.
3. Van Zandt, October 12, 1861; Cater, November 24, 1861; Watkins, October 1, 1862; Harlan, November 10, 1861; Harlan, August 8, 1863.
4. Van Zandt, April 3, 1863; Harlan, June 8, 1862, November 15, 1863, November 24, 1861.
5. Harlan, August 13, 1862; Jones, September 18, 1861; Martha Ingram, August 30, 1863.
6. Van Zandt, November 26, 1861; Harlan, July 17, 1862; Van Zandt, January 12, 1862; Jones, October 12, 1861; Harlan, October 19, 1863.
7. Van Zandt, October 16, 1863, July 16, 1863, February 28, 1863, May 10, 1863.
8. Van Zandt, April 26, 1863, January 12, 1862.
9. Ingram, September 3, 1863; Harlan, July 18, 1862; Van Zandt, July 29, 1863; Harlan, March 23, 1864.
10. Harlan, November 10, 1861, May 11, 1862, September 28, 1862, November 2, 1862, December 3, 1862.
11. Martha Ingram, May 30, 1863, July 27, 1863; Harlan, December 15, 1861.
12. Ingram, January 2, 1863; Harlan, November 10, 1861, November 2, 1862; Jones, September 18, 1861; Martha Ingram, June 25, 1862; Harlan, March 5, 1864.
13. Van Zandt, January 12, 1862; Martha Ingram, December 25, 1862.
14. Jones, December 9, 1861, October 28, 1861; Martha Ingram, December 25, 1862; Van Zandt, April 3, 1863, July 29, 1863, April 3, 1863; Ingram, June 17, 1863; Minerva Van Zandt, July 16, 1863.
15. Jones, September 18, 1861; Martha Ingram, June 25, 1862, January 2, 1863.
16. Martha Ingram, May 30, 1863, August 30, 1863; Harlan, August 3, 1863, July 18, 1862.
17. Martha Ingram, December 25, 1862, May 30, 1863.
18. Harlan, April 26, 1863, November 15, 1863.
19. Van Zandt, October 25, 1861, January 12, 1862; Harlan, November 1862; Jones, March 11, 1861; Harlan, July 13, 1863.

20. Harlan, April 26, 1863; Van Zandt, September 17, 1862.
21. Van Zandt, February 28, 1863, April 3, 1863.
22. Harlan, July 13, 1863, January 13, 1864, March 3, 1864; Martha Ingram, February 29, 1864.
23. Jones, August 2, 1862.

Image 8. Josie Scott.

DeGolyer Library, Southern Methodist University, Lawrence T. Jones III Texas photograph collection Ag2008.0005.1.03.02

Josie Scott is holding a portrait of her husband, Lt. John G. Scott, C.S.A. Photograph taken in Palestine, Anderson County, Texas, in 1863.

Chapter 4

Finding Joy through Hard Times

Texas Women's Activities during the Civil War

Brittany Bounds

In December 1861 at the beginning of the Civil War, a group of women in Houston gave a performance for the Twelfth Texas Cavalry. Several young ladies representing each Confederate state carried a small white banner with the state's painting onto the stage, facing thousands of spectators and the lined-up infantry. Yet dark clouds had begun to form, and they released a downpour of rain upon the participants before the speaker was able to address the gathering. Sadly, the women had to flee to save their fine bonnets in advance of their recognition.[1]

Like the rain on such a joyous day, the Civil War moved into the Confederate South, dimming spirits and forcing southern women to act to maintain control over their situation. The war disrupted normal life for the residents of Texas, but the women who remained in the state found ways to stay entertained and preoccupied, both in helping the war effort and maintaining normal relationships in social settings. Ladies provided highly advertised social events for the soldiers both as encouragement of the men's enlistment and relief from their own household duties. Some regular tasks such as reading books and newspapers, visiting neighbors, holidays, and musical concerts continued, even if altered from their normal state. Whereas material items and appearances were important before the war, many women realized the important immaterial necessities were religion, news, and family. Women clung to the things in life that were irreplaceable and fulfilling. Through war contributions, social interactions, and news, Texan women were able to stay preoccupied throughout the war. In effect these activities helped avoid the severe depression that many Confederate women in other parts of the South endured when their conspicuous consumerism dramatically declined, and helped Texans find a glimmer of joy through the hard times of war. In this way, activities with hospitals and church and through collecting news gave these women a sense of control during a trying period in their lives and in the country's history.

While some of the activities that women performed during the Civil War remained within traditional gender and class roles, others clearly overstepped those boundaries. Women had normally been expected to provide clothing for their family, and they still continued this perfunctory provision. However, they also were requested to expand their efforts to provide tents and other materials for the soldiers when the Confederate Army ran short in supply. Additionally, they also began to make their own homespun material for clothing, which many elite husbands considered below their wives' stature and a job for female slaves.[2] Further, in dealing with their slaves, many plantation wives assumed the master's role as overseer. While some slipped into this role easily, others were bound by their gender and encountered difficulties with managing male slaves. Yet the expansion of the planter lady's role from "mother" of the slaves into the male realm of power as "father" over the slaves also reflected their desire to be "full-fledged members of their class."[3] Whereas manufacturing clothes and managing slaves kept a Texas planter-class woman at home, service as a nurse provided a lady an independence not afforded her under the normal patriarchal control of the plantation.[4] The new, if temporary, positions and duties the war demanded of women gave them new opportunities for control over their own domain, and allowed them to act outside of the prescribed gender roles of the time.

Texan women were inspired and required to help in the war effort as a means to have power over sickness and death. At the start of the Civil War, women immediately began forming Aid Societies, considered loyal and patriotic, all over the state of Texas.[5] Even the girls at Bellville Academy followed their mothers' example by spending their extra time spinning wool to knit socks for the soldiers.[6] Women frequently planned highly advertised social gatherings for soldiers to provide encouragement and important funds to Soldier's Homes. The ladies of Clarksville, San Antonio, Galveston, Hempstead, and especially Houston, frequently held dinners, concerts, and tableaux – picturesque representations of stories – to raise funds for the sick and wounded Texas soldiers or their families. The Soldiers' Aid Society of Henderson, Texas, charged a dollar for admittance to a "Tableaux Vivants, Acting Charades, selections from Shakespeare, vocal and instrumental music" in December 1863.[7] One evening of entertainment consisting of tableaux and concert at the Casino in San Antonio fetched a handsome sum of $500, all of which was donated to care for sick Texan soldiers.[8] Even African Americans in Houston volunteered to hold Grand Balls during the war "for the benefit of sick soldiers," raising more than $80 for two events in 1862 and $123 in December 1863 and prompting the editor in the *Tri-Weekly Telegraph* to comment, "Put that in your pipe, Old Abe."[9] The women of the Hospital Fund Association of San Antonio performed a tableau in March 1863, then sent their $1,100 of raised funds to the Texas Hospital in Virginia to support the state's soldiers as they fought so far from home.[10] Incredibly, in April 1863, the women in Hempstead held a fair that brought in $10,000, an unprecedented sum yet raised for the troops in Texas.[11] Towards the end of the war, women also helped to organize Soldier's Homes to provide a refuge for returning soldiers, including food, lodging, and medical attendance. In 1864 the citizens of Austin,

San Antonio, Fairfield and Rutler in Freestone County, Springfield in Limestone County, Palestine, and Houston organized their homes to provide quarters for their returning soldiers.[12]

To display their Confederate pride, women sewed flags and banners for their local regiments and presented them with the patriotism and loveliness a woman was expected to possess. The ladies of Marshall presented their company of Rangers a "splendid flag" as "the love and beauty of woman have always been intimately associated with the valor of the soldier and the sanctity of his cause."[13] In May 1861 Miss Belle Gordon from Clarkesville, bestowing her pride, presented a flag to the Red River Home Guard while saying, "With the most intense feelings of diffidence and pride, I appear this day before you, on behalf of the ladies, who have prepared this flag for your acceptance."[14] In June 1861 Mrs. Spotswood presented a flag to the Red River Dragoons with much "sympathy and patriotism," offering the womanly "religion of her love and prayers."[15] The ladies of Marshall were alternately eager to present flags, as they did thrice in July 1861.[16]

Yet women gave more than flags and prepared themselves and their husbands for fighting. One gentleman in Dallas observed the ladies there not only fitted their regiment with flags and clothing, but also bullets.[17] The women in Houston also stayed busy "making cartridges."[18] The *Bellville Countryman* commended women for drilling and practicing the use of firearms to protect their homes from Indians or abolitionists, calling their actions "PURE patriotism."[19]

Young ladies away at schools and colleges also participated in the war effort. In 1863 the young women of the East Texas Female College gave a performance "consisting of tableaux, farces, plays, &c., for the benefit of our grave yard" to properly bury the soldiers that died in the war.[20] In the same way the ladies at Rutersville Female College also raised funds by giving a tableau and concert at the Texas Military Institute, raising $175 for the Texas Rangers.[21] Mrs. Halsey and her pupils at the Halsey Academy in Bovine Bend, Austin County raised $326 with a supper and tableaux to benefit the sick soldiers of Galveston.[22] The young ladies at Halsey Academy in Bellville followed suit by giving a dinner and tableaux in May 1863 to aid the General Hospital at Galveston.[23] Women of all ages participated in the war effort to show their support of the soldiers, proving the extent of the war's impact.

Women were requested to provide items to assist the wounded from areas across the state. Three women of Clarksville provided a "box of well-prepared lint" and "a roll of soft linen for dressings," items that proved "indispensable" to the Twenty-Ninth Regiment at Camp Lee.[24] W.P. Riddell, Surgeon at the Galveston General Hospital, publicly thanked eight women for their contributions of supplies and food to the hospital.[25] William Robinson, also a surgeon at Galveston, thanked the ladies of Courtney, Hempstead, and Huntsville for a wide assortment of donations to the hospital. The Israelite ladies of Houston forwarded $131 to the hospital in Houston to assist with the needs of the sick soldiers.[26] The ladies of Marshall also answered the call for lint and bandages for the impending troop deployment.[27] As military supplies to state hospitals were in short supply, these women's donations were highly valued, publicly acknowledged, and further requested.

Physicians at the hospitals were grateful for the donated money and medical supplies, but were even more grateful for help caring for the sick and wounded. M. C. K. of Tyler thanked the women of the area "for their kind and faithful attendance upon the hospital" after it opened in June 1862.[28] Some ladies helped the sick in the Texas hospitals, yet not to the same degree that ladies in other southern states affected by the war, as the lack of fighting in the state did not produce as great of a need. George Ingram credited the women who helped in the hospitals, expressing their importance, as a friend had received "attention from members of our company and especially from the Ladies of Hempsted [*sic*] and all the inmates of the hospital share the kind hospitalities of that place."[29] Further South, the Post Hospital in Corpus Christi in December 1862 became "almost destitute of every comfort suitable for the sick," requesting the residents of the area to contribute bedding and clothes.[30] By January the hospital had received many donations, but additionally requested a female cook.[31] The hospital in Galveston also requested "Cooks, Washerwomen and Nurses," whom they would pay a "liberal price."[32] The ladies of Harrison County established Wayside Hospital in July 1863, and those in Rusk County established a Way Side Hospital in August 1863.[33] The ladies of Orange received hearty thanks from William Madison, the surgeon in charge at a field hospital, as their efforts to soothe the sick soldiers resulted in many smiles and, more importantly, hope.[34] Other women selflessly cared for the sick with risk to their own lives. Miss Eva Harris was memorialized in print in July 1862 after her generous care for ailing soldiers at the Houston hospital led to her contracting a disease that killed her.[35] Outside of the hospital, women in La Grange established a diner to provide free food for soldiers passing through, a commendable activity on which the editor of the *State Gazette* commented.[36] The Ladies' Aid Society in Marshall also belatedly organized a Soldier's Home from a renovated hotel in Marshall in January 1865 to provide food and lodging to soldiers returning from the war.[37]

Out of patriotism, women both wealthy and poor were expected to make uniforms for the soldiers from the start of the war. One lady who organized a Ladies' Aid Society in Bellville implored the local women to join her in making clothing and tents for the soldiers. She argued it was women's "bounden duty" to provide for volunteers who did not have a uniform, for God had "wisely" denied the female sex "the privilege of bearing arms and mixing in the turmoil of battle strife." They could instead overcome their deficiency by furnishing the soldiering men with battle necessities.[38] The *Clarksville Standard* reported in June 1861 that fifty to sixty ladies with their sewing machines completed "every required kind of clothing, and tents, for the company," after which they were considered "well provided for."[39] W. I. Cocke, the surgeon of the Sixteenth Regiment, requested that the ladies of Austin provide tents to replace the ones they needed to turn into administration due to rapid troop movements, as another command had already acquired them.[40]

Newspapers conveyed a sense of urgency and desperation in the provision for soldiers. Although the *Galveston Weekly News* commended the local ladies for providing enough socks for the soldiers through the winter of 1861, they implored them to "do all that love, patriotism and duty require" by knitting even more for the upcoming winter.[41] At the end of October 1862, the same newspaper encouraged both black and white women to be "kept constantly employed" at their spinning wheels and hand looms to produce the cloth needed to provide for soldiers' clothing, as "future generations are now dependent on the soldiers who are fighting the battles of our country."[42] Even though each loom could only produce a few yards of cloth, if the thousands of black and white women in Texas could spin the raw wool and cotton, they could together clothe the whole army.[43]

Newspapers freely granted thankfulness to the women who provided so much to the soldiers. In a *Galveston Weekly News* article titled "The Gentler but More Heroic Sex," the author bestowed much gratitude on the ladies of Texas. He recognized that women's sphere of action had greatly enlarged since the beginning of the war, displaying women's "true worth and beauty of character." Ladies had exhibited a new "courage and firmness" through extending moral support to the Confederate cause and material aid through providing clothing for the soldiers. The article further asserted, "It would be difficult to name any department of the social economy which is not honored by their heroic presence and supported by their daring energy."[44]

While many women were engaged in noble ways, other women found entertainment and financial support for themselves by servicing soldiers through "street walking." Prostitution flourished in Texas as elsewhere during the war years. Accused of being Yankees, La Grange's Mrs. Swine and her prostitute Tillie were removed from the town's hotel, but other women still used private residences.[45] A respectable lady from Houston named Lucia submitted an editorial to the newspaper expressing her outrage at the activities of these women, suggesting that these questionable women be "placed out of town," rather than on the same street as upright people. She explained her annoyance at having someone she knew arrive at her house, mistaking it for a house he wished to visit; the newspaper editor supported her encouragement of decency.[46]

Although some events did change, many social activities and holidays remained the same across the state. Some regular tasks, such as reading books and newspapers, visiting neighbors, hunting, fishing, barbeques, and musical concerts continued throughout the state. The Fourth of July was only celebrated in some locales, such as Corpus Christi in 1861 and 1863, as the city congratulated the South on maintaining independence with a Sunday school celebration at the Court House through social amusements and a dinner.[47] Ironically, many cities did not have the financial means to celebrate the nation's birthday with pomp during a war that tore the nation apart.

Christmas was still celebrated, although the quantity of gifts was reduced. The *Texas Republican* out of Marshall commented on the first Christmas of the war as "serious and solemn, but not altogether gloomy," as the local residents were able to bear sacrifices "with a spirit of emulation."[48] Yet Marshall's second Christmas passed "with more than the usual amount of gaiety," attested by the large number of parties given in the town.[49] Some ladies in Houston instead spent their Christmas in 1862 providing a dinner for the patients at the Houston hospital.[50] Martha Ingram admitted to her husband that her holiday was not as bright, writing, "This is Christmas night and I am all alone and lonely. Ma and the Little boys have gon [*sic*] to bed and the Negroes have gone in search of some amusement.... I would claim yore [*sic*] Christmas gift and I would tell you what it must bee [*sic*] —won kiss imprinted from yore lips on mine."[51] Adversely, Parilee Daniels, a slave in Red River County, remembered great festivities, explaining, "On Christmas morning we all was happy the men drinking egg nog and the women making them and helping drink them." Her mistress "would set a great long table with nearly everything that was good to eat, with Mistress at front of the table and Maser by her side, then we would all eat and by the time we got everything cleaned up it would be night." Both white and black got together to "play and begin their music, the young white children and old, also were in there dancing and last all night long."[52] Not everyone was as fortunate or optimistic, as recorded by a six-year-old in San Antonio, who "in speaking of Christmas the other day remarked that he did not expect to get any thing [*sic*] this time, as he reckoned *Old Santa Claus was a Conscript* and had been sent to the wars."[53]

Church activities also continued, although some Sunday services, camp meetings, revivals, and associational meetings were limited due to lack of male leadership. In Marshall a cumulative Sunday School Celebration and Dinner was held May 7, 1862, at the Methodist Church.[54] Even the free blacks in Houston found church a priority during their traditional day off, as the "African church" on a Sunday would fill past its capacity.[55] While some slaves sang and prayed for a release from slavery, others prayed for their deployed masters. Andrew Goodman, a slave in Tyler, was not informed of the purpose for the war, and thus he and his fellow slaves prayed for his master's protection.[56]

Religion held an extreme importance with both soldiers and their families as a way to try to control God through their increasingly blighted circumstances. Both personal letters and diaries consistently referred to God and church throughout the length of the war. Like the Union forces, Texans prayed for protection and confession. This provided a sense of solace that no matter what happened, God would keep them in his will. Confederate families believed that God was on their side in the war and would ultimately allow them to defeat the Union, a belief the North held as well. For many evangelicals, the Old Testament idea of national sin helped explain Southern troubles even if it did not make them more endurable. "Pridefulness... ingratitude, violence, profaneness, blasphemy and oppression reign in our Midst," Cornelia Noble wailed, sounding the proper note of lamentation.[57]

Correspondence revealed the strong nature of Texans' spiritual beliefs. Lizzie Scott Neblett asked her husband Will to "write soon, [and] often, and May the Good Lord bless, confess, and protect you, is [and] will be the constant prayer of one who would freely lay down his life to save yours."[58] Joseph Oden's wife, Salle, wrote him, "And let me know whether you have any hope of heaven, if you get killed if not I want you to pray for it & you may rest assured that you have a wife that will pray in your behalf & has for a long time...."[59] Martha Ingram wrote to George, "I am truly glad that you have so much confidence in yore commander thoug[h] I think it would be well for you to trust moste [*sic*] in God for he rules all things."[60] Theophilus Perry remarked to his father in his letter, "I feel thankful to High Heaven that I have been so cheerful and healthy, and pray God to prepare with his Grace to submit with Christian resignation to the fortunes of war."[61]

Military chaplains encouraged the distribution of Bibles to keep morale high. A chaplain from the army asked the women of Houston to provide Bibles and organize a "Confederate States Soldiers' Tract Society."[62] Chaplain L. H. Baldwin acknowledged the receipt of $800 from the citizens of Houston to buy Bibles for the soldiers, which assisted in the revival in Galveston leading to "eighty conversions, with sixty-five accessions to the Camp Church, which is composed of each Evangelical denomination of Christians."[63]

Women also went to church during the war, some to seek solace from their loneliness through the social gathering. Popular churches in Texas during the war were Presbyterian, Methodist, and to a lesser degree, Baptist. Generally, churches held separate services for the different races, or placed the blacks in a rear location. Harriet Perry told her husband, "I have been to church every Sunday, except the one I was at your Fathers [*sic*]—I take Rufus [their slave] with me—It is great consolation to me—I go to prayer meeting too."[64] For white women, church provided a sense of comfort and a method of control over their circumstances, as they could ask God for protection over their husbands and sons and help at home.

Church also provided control over racial relations, as some slaves went to church during the war as well. Parilee Daniels remembered, "No we did not have a church on our plantation, but the white people did in the center of the small settlement and they had room built to one side where they carried us to church. Old Bro. Berry preached to us there and everybody just loved that man of God."[65] Normally barefoot, Lucy Lewis was only able to wear shoes when she "used to sing an' pray in church," where the "preacher wah a nigger slave."[66] After services, white preachers would baptize slaves while white people sang on the banks of the river. As Daniels recognized, "The white people was proud to see us join the church cause [*sic*] that would make better slaves out of us, we minded our Masers better, work better and everything."[67] Millie Forward of Jasper recalled, "In slav'ry days, de w'ite folks didn' read de Bible to us, and dey go to church at Col' Springs and Magnolia Springs, and leabe de chillen at home." Millie was glad to "jine de Mef'dis Church at Col' Springs under Rev. Payne."[68] Churches were segregated, slaves were not allowed to read the Bible themselves, and Christianizing them would make them more submissive. Yet churches played an important role in the continuance of social activities that allowed for a sense of normalcy and control in an uncertain environment.

Along with war contributions and social activities, a third matter of importance was the value of receiving news. During the war, Texan women made a hobby out of garnering news from the front to be in command of information. Women wrote to their husbands both requesting reports they had as well as informing them of the news they had heard at home from friends or increasingly scarce newspapers. At the beginning of the war, the *Standard* out of Clarksville encouraged men to let women read news to "qualify her for conversation" on the present world, including "the mental, political, and religious improvements of our time." They underestimated the level of involvement women would have with newspapers during the war.[69] Some women even stepped up during the war to fill men's positions in literary circles, as Mrs. Lancaster took command as editor of the *Texas Ranger* while her husband was fighting in the war.[70]

Texas newspapers did not circulate in the same frequency as other southern states or as compared to previous circulation during the war due to the decreasing availability and rising cost of paper. In 1862 the cost of paper and ink, which would normally cost $200, cost the *Texas Republican* $800. Paper before the war cost $3 per ream; in 1863 it increased from $14 per ream to $50 per ream, a 1500 percent increase.[71] By the end of 1863, a ream of paper cost $2500 and ink $150 in Shreveport, Louisiana, and in Texas. Costs were 18 to 25 cents above Louisiana prices.[72] Many papers in Texas were required to either reduce their size or quit publishing altogether; prices for subscriptions inevitably increased to cover the rising prices.[73] In April 1861, the *Tyler Reporter* charged $2.50 per year for a weekly issue; by November 1864, a six-month subscription was $25.[74] The *Texas Republican* was required to increase subscription rates to $5 per year in July 1863. However, the newspaper went out of publication shortly after until September; when it resumed, it asked its readers to pay the same rates as Shreveport's newspaper, which was also $25 for six months.[75] To alleviate the financial burden of purchasing newspapers, Houston opened a reading room to allow the public to read the news from different newspapers at no charge.[76] This helped women stay informed, even if they could not afford to purchase the newspapers.

Women craved the news of the war as its developments affected their lives. One wealthy refugee in Tyler, Kate Stone, listed in her diary the publications they received at their new home. This showed not only her attachment to the news, but also her way of controlling information by recording it in her diary. Historian Kelly McMichael explained that women wrote in the plural first person in their letters and diaries as "we" and "us" in references to battles and at home to link themselves to the battlefield.[77] Newspapers held vital information on troop locations, movements, and battle outcomes that most women wanted to know and share. Dishearteningly, some newspapers exaggerated battle successes by the Confederacy or outright lied about them. These reports served to decrease women's morale when finding out the truth.[78]

Some women even wrote editorials to their local newspapers to request information, supplies, or companionship. One month after the war started, two single ladies in Clarksville submitted a poem to attract two bachelors with "the courage to propose." They promised "unsullied virtue," no gossip, and to "wash, brew or bake, small splutter we make, for 'Quiet and Thrift' is the motto we take."[79] Matilda Smith, after losing her property in Springfield, Missouri, to jayhawkers, moved to Texas in search of her brother and published a plea for information in Honey Grove.[80] A lady in Houston sent a request to the *Tri-Weekly Telegraph* to find out any news from her two sons, for if she "could only hear from them it would be such a source of gratification to my feelings." She did not regret encouraging her sons to join the army as they were "calculated to make good soldiers," but she felt sorry she could offer "no more to brave the conflict."[81] Other women like Grandma Matlock in Crockett denounced deserters in an editorial by encouraging the local women to make the deserters petticoats to save their nation from shame and reproach.[82]

Women shared news with each other as well, hearing tidbits of information from husbands and brothers in other states and news at home on the frontier. Martha Ingram explained to her husband George that her friend was "big on news, and shares 'rumors' about Vicksburg, Helena, and Neworleans [*sic*]."[83] Louisa Perry wrote to her brother Theophilus to pass on news from her cousin Tempie. Tempie had received a letter from their cousin Sid, who had been in three battles and was expecting another. As McMichael stated, Louisa placed the emphasis on the collective "we" as she wrote about Sid's experiences: "he says our loss was heavy but we just finished up the [Y]ankees."[84] Theophilus, in turn, was disappointed that he did not have any news to provide to his wife from Shreveport in 1862, although he did offer what he could: "There is no news here from the seat of war any where [*sic*]. It is believed that Price will soon cross the Mississippi."[85] Rumors about those back home made their way into wives' letters as well, indulging their husbands on the affairs in their hometown while they continued to spread the news.[86]

Letters from men served a vital purpose in reassuring wives not only that their husbands and sons were still alive, but also that they still loved them. Martha Ingram exclaimed to her husband, "Oh what a pleasure it is to reade [*sic*] yore interesting letters. It is nearly all the pleasure that I have. You say you do not think the war will last many months longer. I hope this is true for I am tiard [*sic*] of war and war news and long for time to com [*sic*] when wee [*sic*] will have peace."[87] Women were disappointed and often resentful when they did not receive letters from the front, taking it personally that their husbands had not written to them. Many of them simply did not realize that their men were busy on the field and could not write more often.

Conversely, men needed the comforts of home they received through their wives' letters. According to historian George Rable, women dealt with the daily challenges of discipline, traditionally the man's sphere, instead of discussing them with their husbands. Instead, they filled their letters with the "homey tidbits that men savored: the appearance of baby teeth, the cute way a little girl's mouth looked saying *papa*, the distress of a son learning that his father had no little boys to hug in camp." On the down side, many of these stories undoubtedly made some men's desire to return home stronger than ever, while others may have seen that their wives were only putting up a cheerful front.[88] Historian Drew Gilpin Faust argues that letter writing encouraged "a new frankness, a new emotional accessibility, and a new intensity of feeling between husbands and wives."[89] Letters undoubtedly helped both husband and wife overcome the distances placed between them by the war.

In coping with the effects of the Civil War on home life, Texan women found three main ways to stay preoccupied and maintain control through a turbulent time. They assisted the Confederate war effort by providing supplies, funds, and manpower to the wounded. Ladies also turned towards social activities and church for spiritual solace and continued to celebrate holidays through social gatherings. Lastly, Texan women, like their contemporaries throughout the South, followed news of the war through family, friends, and newspapers for more than mere hobby. They engaged in all these activities to maintain a semblance of control over their lives.

NOTES

1. Letter from George Ingram to Martha Ingram, Dec. 13, 1861, compiled by Henry L. Ingram. Introd. by Charles R. Schultz, *Civil War Letters of George and Martha Ingram* (College Station: Texas A&M University, 1973), 14.
2. George C. Rable, *Civil Wars: Women and the Crisis of Southern Nationalism* (Urbana: University of Illinois Press, 1991), 62.
3. Leann Whites, "The Civil War as a Crisis in Gender," *Divided Houses: Gender and the Civil War*, Catherine Clinton and Nina Silber, eds., (New York: Oxford University Press, 1992), 6-8.
4. Cheryl A. Wells, "Battle Time: Gender, Modernity, and Confederate Hospitals," *Journal of Social History* 35, no. 2 (Winter 2001), 409.
5. In many cities and counties (for example, Bellville, Austin, Galveston, Houston, Danville, San Antonio, Richmond, Polk County, Harrison County, Montgomery County), women formed associations to raise money or provide supplies to the soldiers. *Bellville Countryman*, July 17, 1861, July 24, 1861, May 24, 1862; *Galveston Weekly News*, August 17, 1861, April 15, 1862, May 13, 1862, July 2, 1862, December 3, 1862; *Texas Republican*, November 16, 1861, February 5, 1863; *Tri-Weekly Telegraph*, April 4, 1862; *San Antonio Herald*, January 22, 1862.
6. *Bellville Countryman*, October 16, 1861.
7. Newspapers were abundant with announcements of tableaux, balls, and concerts given in support of the soldiers in Clarksville, Galveston, Houston, Marshall, Waco, and Henderson. Quotation is from the *Henderson Times*, December 12, 1863. Clarksville *Standard*, June 16, 1863; *Galveston Weekly News*, January 14, 1862, September 10, 1862, December 17, 1862, June 24, 1863; *San Antonio Herald*, January 4, 1862; *Texas Republican*, January 3, 1863; *Tri-Weekly Telegraph*, December 5, 1863, *Henderson Times*, December 12, 1863, December 17, 1864; *Tri-Weekly Telegraph*, November 1, 1861, January 13, 1862, January 30, 1862, February 14, 1862, March 4, 1862, April 16, 1862, April 28, 1862, September 26, 1862, October 15, 1862, December 8, 1862, January 30, 1863, February 13, 1863, May 18, 1863, June 18, 1863, August 10, 1863, August 20, 1863, December 26, 1864.

8. A sum of $500 in 1862 would amount to approximately $12,000 in 2014. *San Antonio Herald,* January 22, 1862.
9. *Tri-Weekly Telegraph,* July 30, 1862, December 8, 1863.
10. *San Antonio Herald,* March 21, 1863.
11. *Galveston Weekly News,* April 29, 1863.
12. Ibid., December 19, 1864, December 30, 1864.
13. *Texas Republican,* April 20, 1861.
14. *Clarksville Standard,* May 18, 1861.
15. Ibid., June 8, 1861.
16. *Texas Republican,* July 13, 1861, July 20, 1861, July 27, 1861.
17. Ibid., May 18, 1861.
18. *Tri-Weekly Telegraph,* June 6, 1862.
19. *Bellville Countryman,* June 12, 1861.
20. *Tyler Reporter,* April 16, 1863.
21. *Tri-Weekly Telegraph,* January 30, 1863.
22. *Tri-Weekly Telegraph,* June 2, 1863.
23. *Bellville Countryman,* May 16, 1863.
24. *Clarksville Standard,* February 14, 1863.
25. *Galveston Weekly News,* January 14, 1862.
26. *Tri-Weekly Telegraph,* March 26, 1862.
27. *Texas Republican,* June 8, 1861.
28. *Tyler Reporter,* June 19, 1862.
29. George Ingram, November 6, 1861, Ingram, 8.
30. *Ranchero,* December 11, 1862.
31. *Ranchero,* January 1, 1863.
32. *Tri-Weekly Telegraph,* March 30, 1863.
33. *Texas Republican,* July 18, 1863; *Henderson Times,* August 29, 1863.
34. *Tri-Weekly Telegraph,* July 24, 1863.
35. *Tri-Weekly Telegraph,* July 16, 1862.
36. *Texas Republican,* January 13, 1865

37. *Tri-Weekly Telegraph*, October 20, 1863.
38. *Bellville Countryman*, July 24, 1861.
39. *Clarksville Standard*, June 22, 1861.
40. *Bellville Countryman*, October 10, 1863.
41. *Galveston Weekly News*, October 1, 1862.
42. *Galveston Weekly News*, October 15, 1862.
43. *Galveston Weekly News*, October 29, 1862.
44. *Galveston Weekly News*, December 17, 1862.
45. Walter F. Pilcher, "Chicken Ranch," *Handbook of Texas Online*, accessed 5/5/2015, http://www.tshaonline.org/handbook/online .
46. *Tri-Weekly Telegraph*, June 30, 1862.
47. *Ranchero*, June 29, 1861, July 6, 1861.
48. *Texas Republican*, January 4, 1862.
49. *Texas Republican*, January 3, 1863.
50. *Tri-Weekly Telegraph*, December 29, 1862.
51. Letter, Martha Ingram at Hillsborough to George Ingram, December 25, 1862, Ingram, 43-44.
52. George P. Rawick, *The American Slave: A Composite Autobiography* Volume 6: Part 5 (Westport, Conn.: Greenwood Pub. Co., 1972), 1035-1036.
53. *San Antonio Herald*, December 27, 1862.
54. *Texas Republican*, May 17, 1862.
55. *Tri-Weekly Telegraph*, August 13, 1862.
56. George P. Rawick, *The American Slave: A Composite Autobiography*, Volume 5: Part 4. 1526-1527.
57. Rable, *Civil Wars*, 216.
58. Letter, Lizzie Scott Neblett to Will Neblett, April 26, 1863. Lizzie Scott Neblett papers, 1849-1865, Dolph Briscoe Center for American History, The University of Texas at Austin, Box 2F81.
59. Letter, Salle Oden to Joseph Oden, November 16, 1863. Civil War Miscellany Papers, Dolph Briscoe Center for American History, The University of Texas at Austin, Box 2N237.

60. Letter, Martha Ingram to George Ingram, June 19, 1862. Civil War Miscellany Papers, Dolph Briscoe Center for American History, The University of Texas at Austin, Box 2N237.

61. Letter, Theophilus to his father, August 17, 1862. M. Jane Johansson, ed., *Widows by the Thousand: The Civil War Correspondence of Theophilus and Harriet Perry, 1862-1864* (Fayetteville: University of Arkansas Press, 2000), 17-18.

62. *Tri-Weekly Telegraph,* July 15, 1863.

63. *Tri-Weekly Telegraph,* January 26, 1864.

64. Johansson, *Widows by the Thousand,* 13.

65. George P. Rawick, *The American Slave: A Composite Autobiography* Volume 8: Part 6 (Westport, CT: Greenwood Pub. Co., 1972), 1033-1034.

66. George P. Rawick, *The American Slave: A Composite Autobiography* Volume 6: Part 5 (Westport, CT: Greenwood Pub. Co., 1972), 2363.

67. George P. Rawick, *The American Slave: A Composite Autobiography* Volume 8: Part 6 (Westport, CT: Greenwood Pub. Co., 1972), 1033-1034.

68. George P. Rawick, *The American Slave: A Composite Autobiography* Volume 8: Part 7 (Westport, CT: Greenwood Pub. Co., 1972), 1384.

69. *Clarksville Standard,* March 2, 1861.

70. *Galveston Weekly News,* March 25, 1863.

71. *Texas Republican,* November 22, 1862; *Galveston Weekly News,* May 6, 1863; *Tri-Weekly Telegraph,* March 20, 1863.

72. *Tri-Weekly Telegraph,* December 9, 1863.

73. Due to financial difficulties arising from the war, many newspapers in the state either were reduced to a half-sheet, lessened frequency, or forced to stop operations altogether. This applied to the *Galveston News, Texas Christian Advocate, Tri-Weekly Alamo Express, Bellville Countryman, The Matagorda Gazette, Indianola Courier, LaGrange Democrat, Bastrop Advertiser, Liberty Gazette, Lone Star, Brenham Enquirer, Richmond Reporter, Texas Baptist, Central Texan, Rusk Enquirer, Houston Telegraph, Dallas Herald, Nacogdoches Chronicle, Waco Southerner, Crocket Quid Nunc, Texas Republican*; *Clarksville Standard,* July 20, 1861, *Alamo Express,* May 3, 1861; *Bellville Coun-*

tryman, June 12, 1861, July 24, 1861, October 16, 1861; *Texas Republican*, November 16, 1861, November 30, 1861, December 8, 1863; *Tri-Weekly Telegraph*, January 14, 1864.

74. *Tyler Reporter*, April 11, 1861, November 10, 1864.
75. *Bellville Countryman*, January 8, 1862, February 22, 1862; *Texas Republican*, February 8, 1862, July 18, 1863, September 9, 1864.
76. *Texas Baptist*, April 11, 1861.
77. Kelly McMichael, "'Memories Are Short but Monuments Lengthen Remembrances': The United Daughters of the Confederacy and the Power of Civil War Memory," in *Lone Star Pasts: Memory and History in Texas,* Gregg Cantrell and Elizabeth Hayes Turner eds., (College Station: Texas A&M University Press, 2007), 157-166, 177-179.
78. Dana McMichael, *How Confederate Women Created New Self-Identities as the Civil War Progressed: A Study of Their Diaries* (Lewiston, NY: Edwin Mellen Press, 2008), 17.
79. *Clarksville Standard*, May 11, 1861.
80. *Clarksville Standard*, February 8, 1862.
81. *Tri-Weekly Telegraph*, July 7, 1862.
82. *Bellville Countryman*, October 31, 1863.
83. Letter, Martha Ingram to George Ingram, June 19, 1862. Civil War Miscellany Box 2N237,
84. Johansson, *Widows by the Thousand*, 16.
85. Johansson, *Widows by the Thousand*, 5.
86. Drew Gilpin Faust, *Mothers of Invention: Women of the Slaveholding South in the American Civil War* (Chapel Hill: University of North Carolina Press, 1996), 126.
87. Martha Hillsborough, Dec. 25, 1862, Ingram, 43.
88. Rable, *Civil Wars*, 62.
89. Faust, *Mothers of Invention*, 118.

Image 9. Sophia, Lidia, and Maria LaCoste.

Sophia La Coste, [Image 085-0433]. Institute of Texan Cultures, UTSA Libraries, San Antonio, Texas.

This photograph of two young girls and their "nursemaid" was taken at Louis de Plangue's studio in Brownsville, Texas, ca. 1865.

Chapter 5

Black Texas Women and the Freedom War

Bruce A. Glasrud

Born in the 1830s in Alabama, slave Rachel Hamilton was brought by her owner, Andrew Jackson Hamilton, to Travis County, Texas, in 1847. She subsequently married Nathaniel Grumbles, also a slave in Travis County and from that relationship a son, James Grumbles, was born in 1857. In a fortunate circumstance, Rachel Hamilton was freed by her owner, anti-secessionist leader Andrew Jackson Hamilton. Although she was able to secure work as a hired servant in Austin, Texas, law provided that newly freed blacks could not remain in the state without permission of the legislature. She was arrested—her apprehension likely also served as a warning to her former owner about his behavior—and rather than leave her family in the state she chose to re-enslave herself in order to remain in Texas, becoming the caretaker nurse of Maggie, the daughter of her new "guardian," Aaron Burleson. Rachel's son James remained with her.

Rachel Hamilton's life and story tell us much about the precarious and difficult status of black Texas women prior to and during the Civil War. The lives of black Texas women, whether free or slave, were controlled either by white owners or by white law, sometimes both. Rachel Hamilton later left her slave husband, was freed again (along with all other Texas slaves) on June 19, 1865, and in 1870 married Robert Hornsby; they farmed and raised five children. Rachel Hornsby lived until she was seventy-five years of age, not long enough, however, to tell us her story; we know about Rachel Hornsby from her son's 1930s W. P. A. interview.[1]

During the Civil War, or what black Texans referred to as the Freedom War, black Texas women were in an extremely vulnerable and precarious position. Being a slave meant serving under the close scrutiny of sometimes vicious and unscrupulous owners or overseers. On the other hand, black freedwomen too, though not enslaved, endured an insecure status in a region where whites were determined to retain control of black labor and black behavior. The Civil War was fought by Confederate Texans to ensure a subservient labor supply and to continue the white supremacist domination of blacks in Texas. During the war African American slave and free women lived and worked while many white male Texans left the state to fight to retain the twofold prongs of slavery and alleged white superiority.

While a number of studies have been produced that survey the condition and treatment of blacks in Civil War Texas, little scholarly interest has focused on the experiences and needs of black Texas women during those war years. The general status of black Texans in the Civil War period in Texas has been explored by Alwyn Barr, Randolph B. "Mike" Campbell, Bruce Glasrud and Ronald Goodwin, and James Marten.[2] The best and most complete account of black women during slavery, including the war years, is Angela Boswell's perceptive article. Information on black women during these difficult years can also be located in Ruthe Winegarten's two general works on Texas's black women.[3]

Other scholars discuss or mention the topic of black Civil War Texas as well, including the studies of Carl Moneyhon, Elizabeth Silverthorne, and James M. Smallwood. Cecil Earl Harper Jr. covers this era in his study. Two additional historians touched on issues of importance to understanding blacks in Civil War Texas; they are Nancy Cohen-Lack and Drew Gilpin Faust.[4] Two chapters in this current book, *Women in Civil War Texas*, are exceedingly useful in exploring additional avenues of black women's life and work during the war.[5]

In order to understand both the magnitude of African enslavement in Texas as well as the overwhelming nature of slavery even during the Civil War, it is essential to look at demographics. Slavery in Texas increased rapidly from approximately 5,000 slaves in late 1836 to 27,555 in 1845 and to 38,753 in 1847. Three years later, in 1850, the number of black slaves totaled 58,161 and by 1860, as secession discussion neared, the total Texas slave population increased dramatically to 182,566.[6] Historians Mike Campbell and Richard Lowe determined that in 1850 black women comprised 50.6 percent of the slave population, and in 1860, 50.1 percent of the slave population. Using 50 percent as a basis, one can conclude that the number of black women slaves in Texas in 1850 was about 29,080 and in 1860 approximately 91,283. Furthermore, by looking at the census numbers and tax records, Campbell points out that "it is likely that Texas's slave population was approaching 200,000 at the outbreak of the Civil War."[7] This would mean that the number of black slave women when the Civil War started may have been at least 100,000. The latter is a fairly substantial number of individuals who remained subject to the confinement of slavery during the Civil War. What did they do during the war? How were they treated? What did they think of the war? What did they know about the war? And what was their reaction to freedom when that arrived on June 19, 1865? The answers to these and other questions are vital to understanding the lives of "black Texas women and the Freedom War." As former slave Lizzie Farmer phrased it, that war was "the one what set the cullud folks free."[8]

To learn what black women thought of the war and of their status as black women in white- and male-dominated Texas, one must turn to the ex-slave narratives. Those interviews, conducted by WPA. field workers during the 1930s of former slaves throughout the South, provide a substantial amount of information from the women themselves relating to black Texas women during the Civil War. Texas historians have republished many of the ex-slaves testimonies. One book, edited by Ron Tyler and Lawrence R. Murphy, contains two chapters of relevance and the other study, edited by T. Lindsay Baker and Julie P. Baker, includes sixteen slave narratives by women from Oklahoma, who as slaves resided in Texas.[9]

Randolph B. Campbell noted that by the end of the Civil War in Texas, on June 19, 1865, even a conservative estimate would place the Texas slave population at 250,000. In other words a quarter of a million black men and women were slaves waiting to be freed (slightly more than 125,000 were black women). From where did this growth emerge? Part of the answer involved a steady birth rate and a limited number of runaways, but a significant part of the growth derived from those slaves who arrived in Texas during the war with their owners and families from other Southern states and who are referred to as "refugees." As historian Dale Baum tells us, the black refugees were "slaves taken to Texas for safekeeping during the Civil War."[10]

Beginning with General U. S. Grant's successes along the Mississippi River in the spring of 1862, thousands of slaveholders from the Deep South brought their slaves to Texas to escape the advancing Federal armies. Refugees arrived principally from the states of Louisiana, Arkansas, and Mississippi, but other owners and their slaves left Missouri and Tennessee for Texas in order to retain the institution of slavery. Most of the refugees were located in the eastern third of the Lone Star State. The migration of refugees during these years represented a serious upheaval for the slaves who marched such long distances. To make matters worse, many slave families were divided by their owners' decisions to move. Sometimes only the wife was brought along, sometimes the children, and sometimes the father. Baum reviewed the census and tax returns, and determined that at least 51,000 slaves were brought into Texas during the last years of the war.[11]

During this migration, likely (using the previously mentioned 50 percent calculation) at least 25,000 black women slaves arrived in the Lone Star State. We can learn about this migratory movement from the black women's recollections as recorded in the slave narratives. Van Moore's mother told him that owners moved to Texas since the Yankees would not get this far and "they wouldn't have to free the slaves if they came way over here." Mary Lindsay, a slave in Fannin County noticed that "they was whole families of them (refugees) with they children and they slaves along, and they was coming in from every place because the Yankees was getting in their part of the country." Phyllis Petite was taken to a large plantation in Rusk County and recalled that they "went in a covered wagon with oxen and camped out along the way." As she observed, they were taken to Texas "to get away from the War," but she did not "see any war and any soldiers." Lisa Smith, who started out in Virginia, remembered that they moved often, "dat's the way it was all de time for us during de War—running away to some place or de next place." From Virginia they trekked to Arkansas, with Yankees all around. Eventually the fighting "got so hot they all had to leave," and then they migrated to McLennan County, Texas. Mattie Gilmore arrived in Texas from Mobile, Alabama; on the trip they traveled at night and rested in the daytime.[12] Many of the refugees who had not lived in Texas long enough to develop close ties immediately moved at war's end; in his study Baum estimated that undoubtedly 40 percent of the black refugees left Texas upon being freed.[13]

As Boswell noted, "While the Civil War created some disturbances of the slave system in Texas when men left for war, Texas was spared the wholesale desertion of slaves and destruction of property that other Southern states experienced." Overall, however, the Civil War created a bleak and difficult life for black Texas women. Former Texas slave Lou Smith summarized it best when she said, "Times was awful hard during the war." Black women slaves worked even harder and longer hours than before the war started. As Mollie Watson remarked, "We spun blankets durin' the war" in addition to normal duties. Black slaves received harsher punishments, especially from overseers and often from their white mistresses. Mary Reynolds remembered an overseer who beat slaves severely and "cut the flesh 'most to the bone."[14] They also had less time for relaxation.

The additional war-related pressures placed on black female slaves came about because male owners frequently entered the military service on behalf of the Confederacy. That meant more work for the remaining Texans, including black Texas women. Many Texas slave owners took along a male slave for their military service, thereby further depleting the work force, a loss filled by black women. Those losses also meant that white plantation mistresses, sometimes harsher on their slaves than the males might have been, were in charge. There are a number of reasons for this statement: first, some white women now had a chance to take out their anger and frustration on black women with whom their husbands previously had sexual relations, even if those relations were forced. As author Ruthe Winegarten put it, "these devastating forced relationships sometimes also bred hatred in the planters' wives toward their female slaves." Former slave Betty Flowers noted that "the overseer and white men took advantage of the women like they wanted to," and the women "had better not make a fuss." In a telling comment, Harriet Bartlett remarked that "they [her master and mistress] never had white children." White women also worried about maintaining discipline, and that led also to harsher punishments. Drew Gilpin Faust reports on the efforts of a white plantation mistress, Lizzie Neblett, to earn the respect of the slaves, especially the black males. Her overseers, with her direction, punished the slaves harshly. On the other hand, a female slave, Sarah, worked as a broker between male slaves and her mistress. As Faust discovered, it was the male slaves whom Lizzie Neblett feared.[15]

Whippings and violence increased; during those cruel and bitter years Harriet Robinson's mistress was the "meanest woman I ever seen in my whole life." As she asserted, "them was . . . dog days." Other female slaves reported additional incidents of cruel punishment. Molly Harrell noted that "they used to have the little whip they used on the women." The overseer where Sarah Ford labored was black; he also "was so mean I suspect the devil made him overseer down below." For a young black woman, whippings were perhaps not the worst punishment. As Rose Williams mentioned, there was one thing that her master "did to me that I can't shut from my mind." He forced her to live with a black male "against my wants." Ida Henry noted that one overseer was especially vicious. As a result "one day de slaves caught him and one held him whilst another knocked him in de head and killed him."[16]

Plantation life for female slaves meant never-ending labor beginning in childhood. During the war there was hard work with men gone—in the field, housework, cooking, sewing, dying, washing, and gardening. Almost everyone, male and female, worked in the fields. Acemy Wofford's task was to carry water. As she noted, "I didn't get around during the slave days. Just worked in the fields like a man and toted water to the master's house." Women with children, Mary Kincheon Edwards pointed out, "brought oil cloths to the field, so they could make a shady place for the children to sleep" while the mothers worked. Phoebe Henderson arrived in Texas in 1859, where she plowed and hoed, but she "worked in the house too." Most slaves received two sets of clothes and a pair of shoes per year. The homemade shoes often were red, but Eda Rains did not like the color and painted hers black. Slave diets were usually adequate, but as the war progressed less food was available. Slaves generally ate out of a tray or trough with wooden spoons; they "ate hominy, mush, grits, and pone bread for the most part," according to Harrit Robinson. Even after a long day of fieldwork, black women returned to their cabins to do their own cooking, laundry, and gardening.[17]

Black slave women during the Civil War, in spite of the increased stress, managed to survive and retain their dignity. Fortunately they did not live and work alone. They received encouragement and support from their religion, music, strong family ties, female networks, and non-work activities. Many of the slave narrative interviewees viewed religion as a special source of strength. However, not all masters approved of slave religion; Rose Williams noted that if slaves were caught praying "they'd get a whipping." But, as Mary Gaffney put it, the promise of an eternity without slavery was appealing. Charlotte Beverly "used to go to the white folks' church." Julia Francis Daniels "liked meetings just as good as [she] liked to party."[18] The type of church meetings varied; some plantation owners controlled the service where slaves were warned, as Ida Henry noted, if they would not behave "dat old Satan would git us." Favorite songs sometimes indicated a spiritual nature. Amanda Oliver, a Baptist, liked "Bound for the Promised Land." Mollie Watson revealed one slave's religious thought: after life she would be "in de nex' world whar we will be de same color an' on equal grounds."[19]

Music was also important for the strength of slave survival. Slaves sang in the fields while working. They sat around in the evening to listen and play music and sometimes dance. Mollie Watson would "ruther dance den eat"; she would "dance all night." Often their instruments were hand-made, or passed down from one generation to the next. Their music told of their spirit and interests. Amanda Oliver mentioned that during the war one refrain went:

> Lincoln rides a fine horse,
> Jeff Davis rides a mule,
> Lincoln is de President,
> Jeff Davis is de fool.[20]

However, it was the slave families that provided the most sustaining influence. Virtually every slave narrative, whether from a male or a female, mentioned family connections or ties. As Campbell wrote, "Slave families, regardless of how they were created or their size, played a vital role in providing the mental and emotional strength necessary to endure bondage." However, as he remarked, "Slave families had no legal existence in Texas."[21] Nonetheless close family ties provided slaves with love, individual identity, and a sense of personal worth. In late December, 1862, Fanny Perry sent a letter to her husband, Norfleet, who went with his owner when he left for the battlefront. Starting her letter with "my dear husband," she avowed that her "love is just as great as the first night I married you and I hope it will be so with you. . . . If I never see you again, I hope to meet you in heaven." She reflected that she had not received a letter from him, and hoped that she would soon hear from him. She continued, "I hope it will not be long before you can come home." Her husband likely received the letter, and soon thereafter left his master and the front lines. Perhaps Fanny and Norfleet were among the few fortunate Texas black slaves who learned to read and write. However, as Randolph Campbell and Don Pickens noted in their published version, possibly Fanny's letter was written by one of the owner's daughters. [22]

The importance of family to the women is apparent by the frequency with which ex-slaves mentioned members of their family. Some talked about brothers, sisters, their parents, and uncles. Sylvia King referred to her husband. Lizzie Jones remembered that she slept and worked in the "big house," while her mother stayed in the slave cabins across the field. Betty Powers came from a large family; her parents and twelve children lived in the same cabin. It was Patsy Moses' grandfather who told her about conjures and voodoo. Julia Francis Daniels remembered riding on a mule with her father to protect her near a group of soldiers when some tried to grab her and he fainted. Perhaps Mandy Morrow phrased best the importance and role of black slaves and the family when she reported that "we all lived in one big family."[23] They helped, survived, loved, supported, lived, and worked with each other.

Not all black women were slaves in antebellum and Civil War Texas; a few were free. According to the United States Census, the number of free blacks (male and female) in the Lone Star State in 1850 was 397, and in 1860 the total was 355. However, as Campbell and others have pointed out, the census certainly undercounted, and overlooked some who existed in a state of flux between slavery and freedom. Without much doubt the numbers should be doubled, and perhaps even more. Free blacks, as the Texas laws indicated, were not wanted in the state. As noticed in the discussion of Rachel Hornsby, free black women lived in a precarious situation. However, most managed to survive and even prosper. By 1860 the 174 listed free black women resided in forty of the Texas counties.[24]

Image 10. Mandy.

[Photo# PICB 19453], Austin History Center, Austin Public Library.
A woman known only as Mandy, Mrs. Eula Amelia (Caldwell) Nagle's mammy.

In spite of the severe restrictions placed on free blacks in antebellum Texas, some black women achieved a measure of success. Harriet Reynolds owned and operated a successful ranch in Jackson County; she had fourteen horses worth $500 and 250 head of cattle worth $1,500. Betsey Webster became an heiress in 1856, but it was during the Civil War that the Texas court awarded the property to her. Mary Madison arrived in Galveston in the 1840s; in 1850 she petitioned the legislature to remain in the state with a document signed by eighty-two citizens. The legislature approved her request the following year—one of only three approved. Likely Madison received strong support since she served as a nurse in Galveston. In order to remain, women needed to be assets, such as Madison, to their communities. Others worked as seamstresses, washerwomen, housekeepers, cooks, and servants.[25] In an intriguing twist to Texas race relations, Rozella, the white Jefferson County widow of a free black man of the large Ashworth family, Abner Ashworth, owned land in 1860 valued at $11,444. Rozella Ashworth also had three legally free black children, and she, as well, owned four black slaves. During the war, her son was legally cared for by a guardian.[26]

Fanny McFarland, a free black woman, whose four children were slaves, lived in Houston for years, even though she had no legal right to reside in Texas after McFarland's petition to remain in the state was denied by the legislature. She worked as a laundress and engaged in real estate speculation even through the Freedom War. George Woolfolk referred to "the remarkable land dealings of Fanny McFarland." She lived in Houston from 1834 to her death in 1866.[27] McFarland was fortunate that she was able to witness the tremendous growth of the free black population on June 19, 1865, when at least 125,000 more black women were freed. And then McFarland legally could remain in Houston, Texas.

What did black Texas slaves know about the Freedom War? There were few military engagements in Texas and those few limited to the coast. Naturally they saw soldiers, they heard gossip and rumors about the fighting, perhaps someone in their locality or plantation went to fight in the war, and they felt and witnessed the more severe punishments for slaves that frequently attended the war years. For black women, a son or husband may have attended an owner in the war. They also likely learned when a member of the household was wounded or killed in battle. On the other hand, their specific knowledge was often limited. They recalled Lincoln: he was a good man and similar to Jesus Christ and "he was nex' to God." He was the president. Easter Wells phrased it thusly, "God worked through Abraham Lincoln." Jefferson Davis did not fare as well. Frequently who he was or what position he held was not clear. He obviously was not the president, since Abraham Lincoln held that post. Maybe Davis was a senator. One of the Union soldiers marching songs, and likely sung by black workers in the fields, ended "We'll hang Jeff Davis on a sour apple tree/As we go marching on!"[28]

Annie Hawkins saw lots of soldiers. When Ida Henry's master returned from the war "he seemed a much different man. . . . He was kind and good." Amanda Oliver did not remember when the war started, but she recalled soldiers with blue uniforms. Her owners must have warned her about the Yankees, because she "was afraid of 'em." Isabella Boyd was not certain which soldiers "were the Yankees and which were the Confederates." Nancy King's master "didn't think war was right." He deserted, and soldiers came to take him back. He was ultimately killed. When Northern soldiers arrived at their house, Katie Darling recalls her mistress telling her that slaves would not be freed since they were meant to work for white people. After noticing the soldiers as they entered, she said to Katie that she did not say anything. Katie replied to the soldiers, "I'm not telling a lie; you said niggers aren't going to get free." Susan Ross's master wanted one of her brothers to go along to the war, and he refused. The master beat him so bad "you couldn't tell what he looked like."[29] Certainly from the perspective of black Texas women, the Freedom War was worth it. But when, and how, would freedom arrive. And what would it mean? They hoped and assumed that it meant getting families together, learning to read and write, and definitely land ownership for them.

Freedom arrived in Texas on June 19, 1865, when Texas black slaves were officially freed. Reactions to the freedom of the black slaves varied for white and for black. When Susan Ross's brother learned they were free "he gave a whoop, ran, and jumped a high fence," hugged his sister, and left. Molly Harrell remembered that "We all walked down the road singing and shouting to beat the band." Annie Hawkins asserted that "We was the happiest folks in the world when we knowed we was free." As she continued, "We couldn't realize it at first but how we did shout and cry for joy when we did realize it." Lou Smith reported, "When the war was over you'd see men, women, and chillun walk out of their cabins with a bundle under their arm. All going by in droves, just going nowhere in particular." However, her mother and father did not join those who left immediately. They remained on the plantation. Family members did meet after the war; Acemy Wofford's husband left Mississippi and went to Texas for her.[30]

What could impoverished and usually uneducated ex-slaves do? Elsie Reece reported that her owner "said they could stay for wages or work on halves." That pleased his freed slaves. Julia Francis Daniels's owner asked his ex-slaves to stay until the crop was laid by; they decided to stay since they "had no money and no place to go." Some owners took a more recalcitrant approach. Eli Davison's master "turned us loose with nothing to eat and almost no clothes." Isabella Boyd remarked that "when we all got free, they were a long time letting us know." Susan Merritt did not hear about freedom until September. Tempie Cummins's mother overheard that they were free, "then she ran to the field, against master's will, and told all the other slaves, and they quit work." Even though many owners just let their freed slaves go without any help, Mattie Gilmore's master "gave each of his slaves something when they were freed." Easter Wells's master told her that if she left him, "he would cut my ears off and I'd starve and I don't know what all he did tell me he'd do." On the other hand, Annie Row's master slit his throat because the slaves were freed.[31] Almost immediately after Juneteenth, the violence that would later plague Texas blacks during Reconstruction began; blacks seeking freedom were shot, some hanged, and others beaten badly.

Black Texas women did it; they endured slavery as well as the increased trauma of the Freedom War. Even though the future seemed uncertain, they could look forward to it as free women. In summarizing, perhaps former slave Acemy Wofford said it best when she ended her WPA interview, "that's all I know about slave times and when I tries to think more it brings a hurting to my head." But Betty Powers, too, spoke for the many when she quite accurately reflected that during slavery and the Civil War "they thought nothing on the plantation about the feelings of women." Yet black Texas women nurtured families, created space for the lives of the black slaves, worked, retained their spirits, and above all, set the stage for the next journey of their lives—freedom. Likely Grimes County ex-slave Eliza Elsey's reflection at the conclusion of her 1930s interview, "that all I can tell about the slave days, but I is proud we all get out of slavery and I is glad that Lincoln is the one that freed us," accurately suggests the stamina and pride of black Texas women during the Freedom War.[32]

Notes

1. Randolph B. Campbell, "Rachel Hamilton Hornsby," *Handbook of Texas Online,* accessed May 28, 2015, https://tshaonline.org/handbook/online/articles/fhobh; George P. Rawick, ed., *The American Slave: A Composite Autobiography,* Supplement, Series 2 (Westport, CT: Greenwood Press, 1979); Ruthe Winegarten, "Rachel Grumbles Enslaves Herself," in *Black Texas Women: A Sourcebook* (Austin: University of Texas Press, 1996), 12-13; James Grumbles, "Slave Narratives of Travis County," Austin History Center, Austin Public Library. On the laws affecting slavery and free blacks in Texas, see the excellent compendium edited by Randolph B. Campbell with William S. Pugsley and Marilyn P. Duncan, *The Laws of Slavery in Texas: Historical Documents and Essays* (Austin: University of Texas Press, 2010).
2. Alwyn Barr, "Black Texans during the Civil War," in *Invisible Texans: Women and Minorities in Texas History,* edited by Donald Willett and Stephen Curry (Boston: McGraw-Hill, 2005), 86-93; Randolph B. Campbell, "The Civil War and 'Juneteenth,' 1861-1865," in *An Empire for Slavery: The Peculiar Institution in Texas, 1821-1865* (Baton Rouge: Louisiana State University Press, 1989), 231-251; Bruce A. Glasrud and Ronald E. Goodwin, "On the Edge of First Freedoms: Black Texans and the Civil War," in *The Seventh Star of the Confederacy: Texas during the Civil War,* edited by Kenneth W. Howell (Denton: University of North Texas Press, 2009), 268-286; James Marten, "Slaves and Rebels: The Peculiar Institution in Texas, 1861-1865," *East Texas Historical Journal* 28 (Spring 1990): 29-36.
3. Angela Boswell, "Black Women During Slavery to 1865," in *Black Women in Texas History,* edited by Bruce A. Glasrud and Merline Pitre (College Station: Texas A&M University Press, 2008), 13-37; Winegarten, *Black Texas Women: A Sourcebook*; Ruthe Winegarten, "Slavery," *Black Texas Women: 150 Years of Trial and Triumph* (Austin: University of Texas Press, 1995), 15-37. See also Angela Boswell, "The Civil War and the Lives of Texas Women," in *The Fate of Texas: The Civil War and the Lone Star State,* edited by Charles D. Grear (Fayetteville: University of Arkansas Press, 2008), 69-81, 217-221.

4. Carl Moneyhon, "Texas in 1865," *Texas after the Civil War: The Struggle of Reconstruction* (College Station: Texas A&M University Press, 1989), 6-20, 207-8; Elizabeth Silverthorne, "The End," *Plantation Life in Texas* (College Station: Texas A&M University Press, 1986), 191-212; James M. Smallwood, "First Freedom," *Time of Hope, Time of Despair: Black Texans during Reconstruction* (Port Washington, NY: Kennikat Press, 1981), 25-42; Cecil Earl Harper, Jr., "Slavery without Cotton: Hunt County Texas, 1846-1864," *Southwestern Historical Quarterly* 88 (April 1985): 386-404; Nancy Cohen-Lack, "A Struggle for Sovereignty: National Consolidation, Emancipation, and Free Labor in Texas, 1865," *Journal of Southern History* 58 (February 1992): 57-98; Drew Gilpin Faust, "Trying to Do a Man's Business: Gender Violence and Slave Management in Civil War Texas," in *Southern Stories in Peace and War*, edited by Drew Gilpin Faust (Columbia: University of Missouri Press, 1992), 174-192.
5. See Table of Contents.
6. US, Bureau of the Census. *Negro Population, 1790-1915* (Washington: Government Printing Office, 1918), 51, 57, 218; Randolph B. Campbell, *An Empire for Slavery: The Peculiar Institution in Texas, 1821-1865* (Baton Rouge: Louisiana State University Press, 1989), 54-55.
7. Randolph B. Campbell and Richard G. Lowe, "The Slave-Breeding Hypothesis: A Demographic Comment on the 'Buying' and 'Selling' States," *Journal of Southern History* 42 (1976): 401-412; Campbell, *An Empire for Slavery*, 54-55, 231, 250-51. Quotation in note 1, p. 231.
8. T. Lindsay Baker and Julie P. Baker, eds. *Till Freedom Cried Out: Memories of Texas Slave Life* (College Station: Texas A&M University Press, 1997), "Lizzie Farmer," 21.
9. Baker and Baker, eds. *Till Freedom Cried Out*; Ron Tyler and Lawrence R. Murphy, eds., *The Slave Narratives of Texas* (Austin: State House Press, 1974), 96-112, 113-127. On the use of the Texas slave narratives see the brief and poignant essay, Randolph B. Campbell, "The Federal Writers' Project Slave Narratives as a Historical Survey," in Campbell, *An Empire for Slavery*, 261-263.
10. Campbell, *An Empire for Slavery*, 251; Dale Baum, "Slaves Taken to Texas for Safekeeping during the Civil War," in *The Fate of Texas: The Civil War and the Lone Star State*, edited by Charles D. Grear (Fayet-

teville: University of Arkansas Press, 2008), 83-103, 222-228. Quotation is title of chapter.

11. Campbell, *An Empire for Slavery*, 243-46; Baum, "Slaves Taken to Texas," 83-103; Mary Elizabeth Massey, *Refugee Life in the Confederacy* (Baton Rouge: Louisiana State University Press, 1964), 90-93.

12. "Van Moore," Tyler and Murphy, *Slave Narratives*, 13; "Mary Lindsay," Baker and Baker, *Till Freedom Cried Out*, 43-49; "Phyllis Petite," Baker and Baker, *Till Freedom Cried Out*, 73-77; "Lisa Smith," Baker and Baker, *Till Freedom Cried Out*, 90-91; "Mattie Gilmore," Tyler and Murphy, *Slave Narratives*, 12.

13. Baum, "Slaves Taken to Texas," 102.

14. Boswell, "Black Women during Slavery," 30; "Lou Smith," Baker and Baker, *Till Freedom Cried Out*, 92-98; "Mollie Watson," Baker and Baker, *Till Freedom Cried Out*, 108-111, "Mary Reynolds," *Slave Narratives* (Center for American History, University of Texas at Austin).

15. Winegarten, *Black Texas Women: 150 Years of Trial and Triumph*, quotation on 28; "Betty Flowers," Tyler and Murphy, *Slave Narratives*, 36; "Harriet Bartlett," Tyler and Murphy, *Slave Narratives*, 36; Gilpin Faust, "'Trying to Do a Man's Business'," 174-192, 241-243.

16. "Harriet Robinson," Baker and Baker, *Till Freedom Cried Out*, 83-87; "Molly Harrell," Tyler and Murphy, *Slave Narratives*, 27; "Sarah Ford," Tyler and Murphy, *Slave Narratives*, 53-54; "Rose Williams," Tyler and Murphy, *Slave Narratives*, 20-22; "Ida Henry," Baker and Baker, *Till Freedom Cried Out*, 34-35.

17. "Acemy Wofford," Baker and Baker, *Till Freedom Cried Out*, 28; "Mary Kincheon Edwards," Tyler and Murphy, *Slave Narratives*, 51; "Phoebe Henderson," Tyler and Murphy, *Slave Narratives*, 53; "Eda Rains," Tyler and Murphy, *Slave Narratives*, 73-74; "Harriet Robinson," Baker and Baker, *Till Freedom Cried Out*, 83-87.

18. "Rose Williams," Tyler and Murphy, *Slave Narratives*, 20-22; "Mary Gaffney," *American Slave*, Supplement, Series 2, V, 1447; "Charlotte Beverly," Tyler and Murphy, *Slave Narratives*, 83; "Julia Francis Daniels," Tyler and Murphy, *Slave Narratives*, 82.

19. "Ida Henry," Baker and Baker, *Till Freedom Cried Out*, 34-35; "Amanda Oliver," Baker and Baker, *Till Freedom Cried Out*, 64-65; "Mollie Watson," Baker and Baker, *Till Freedom Cried Out*, 108-114.

20. "Mollie Watson," Baker and Baker, *Till Freedom Cried Out*, 113; "Amanda Oliver," Baker and Baker, *Till Freedom Cried Out*, 65.

21. Campbell, *An Empire for Slavery*, quotations on 159, 154.

22. Randolph B. Campbell and Donald K. Pickens, eds., "My Dearest Husband: A Texas Slave's Love Letter, 1862," *Journal of Negro History* 65 (Fall 1980): 361–364; Winegarten, *Black Texas Women: 150 Years of Trial and Triumph*, 35.

23. "Sylvia King," Tyler and Murphy, *Slave Narratives*, 36-38; "Lizzie Jones," Tyler and Murphy, *Slave Narratives*, 41; "Betty Powers," Tyler and Murphy, *Slave Narratives*, 36; "Patsy Moses," Tyler and Murphy, *Slave Narratives*, 87-88; "Julia Francis Daniels," Tyler and Murphy, *Slave Narratives*, 82; "Mandy Morrow," Tyler and Murphy, *Slave Narratives*, 42.

24. Campbell, "The Law of Slavery in Texas," in Campbell, Pugsley, and Duncan, eds., *The Laws of Slavery in Texas*, 56-69; Winegarten, "Free Women of Color," in *Black Texas Women: 150 Years of Trial and Triumph*, 1-13.

25. Andrew Forest Muir, "The Free Negro in Harris County, Texas," *Southwestern Historical Quarterly* 46, no. 3 (1943): 214-238; Jackson County tax rolls, 1837-1910 (microfilm, Willis Library, University of North Texas); Winegarten, *Black Texas Women: A Sourcebook*, 257, 258, 277; Winegarten, *Black Texas Women: 150 Years of Trial and Triumph*, 7; Campbell, *An Empire for Slavery*, 205-206; Woolfolk, *The Free Negro in Texas*, 183.

26. Andrew Forest Muir, "The Free Negro in Jefferson and Orange Counties, Texas," *Journal of Negro History* 33 (1950): 183-206. Rozella Ashworth has been mentioned as a free black woman, but in fact she is listed in the 1860 US Census as white; she married a free black man, Abner Ashworth. I wish to thank Deborah Liles for her help in sorting this out.

27. Winegarten, *Black Texas Women: A Sourcebook*, 10, 258; George Ruble Woolfolk, *The Free Negro in Texas, 1800-1860: A Study in Cultural Compromise* (Ann Arbor: University Microfilms International, 1976), quotation in note 50, p. 104.

28. "Amanda Oliver," in Baker and Baker, *Till Freedom Cried Out*, 108; "Easter Wells," in Baker and Baker, *Till Freedom Cried Out*, 119; Baker and Baker, *Till Freedom Cried Out*, 125.

29. "Annie Hawkins," in Baker and Baker, *Till Freedom Cried Out*, 32; "Ida Henry," in Baker and Baker, *Till Freedom Cried Out*, 34-37; "Amanda Oliver," in Baker and Baker, *Till Freedom Cried Out*, 64; "Isabella Boyd," in Tyler and Murphy, *Slave Narratives*, 96; "Nancy King," in Tyler and Murphy, *Slave Narratives*, 99-100; "Katie Darling," in Tyler and Murphy, *Slave Narratives*, 105-106; "Susan Ross," in Tyler and Murphy, *Slave Narratives*, 110.

30. "Susan Ross," in Tyler and Murphy, *Slave Narratives*, 114; "Molly Harrell," in Tyler and Murphy, *Slave Narratives*, 115; "Annie Hawkins," in Baker and Baker, *Till Freedom Cried Out*, 32; "Lou Smith," in Baker and Baker, *Till Freedom Cried Out*, 97; "Acemy Wofford," in Baker and Baker, *Till Freedom Cried Out*, 128.

31. "Elcie Reece," in Tyler and Murphy, *Slave Narratives*, 116; "Eli Davison," in Tyler and Murphy, *Slave Narratives*, 123; "Susan Merritt," Tyler and Murphy, *Slave Narratives*, 121; "Tempie Cummins," Tyler and Murphy, *Slave Narratives*, 125; "Mattie Gilmore," Tyler and Murphy, *Slave Narratives*, 125; "Easter Wells," Baker and Baker, *Till Freedom Cried Out*, 117; "Annie Row," Tyler and Murphy, 114.

32. "Acey Wofford," in Baker and Baker, *Till Freedom Cried Out*, 128; "Betty Powers," in Tyler and Murphy, *Slave Narratives*, 36; "Eliza Elsey," in Baker and Baker, *Till Freedom Cried Out*, 16. Black Texas women faced and endured this violent, war-like period of Reconstruction; for a thorough, well-researched, and insightful study read Rebecca Kosary, "'To Punish and Humiliate the Entire Community': White Violence Perpetrated Against African American Women in Texas, 1865-1868," in Kenneth W. Howell, ed., *Still the Arena of the Civil War: Violence and Turmoil in Reconstruction Texas, 1865-1874* (Denton: University of North Texas Press, 2012), 327-351.

Image 11. Della Lowe.

DeGolyer Library, Southern Methodist University, Lawrence T. Jones III Texas photograph collection, Ag2008.0005.1.03.11

Della Lowe was only noted as someone who "sold apples in Marshall, Texas." She was listed as neither a free woman nor as someone's slave. Date on photograph is ca. 1857.

Chapter 6

Black Women and Supreme Court Decisions during the Civil War Era

Linda S. Hudson

In recent years, historians have given black women in Texas a great deal of attention, but one neglected area of study has been black women in cases reviewed by the Texas Supreme Court. The black women's names are scattered throughout appeals found in *Texas Reports*—the decisions of precedent ordered printed by the Texas Supreme Court.[1] From the days of the Republic to the Jim Crow Era, the Texas high court decided the fate of hundreds of free black and enslaved Texans named in 481 known civil and criminal appeals. At least 297 of these court decisions involved black women from eighty-one different Texas counties.[2] An examination of these decisions in the years before, during, and after the Civil War, reveals how black women came to be named in the appeals and show how legal outcomes for black women changed during the Civil War Era.[3]

West's *Texas Digest* categorizes Texas Supreme Court decisions by topic and type of case. Under the topic "Slavery," the Texas court reviewed appeals from twenty-three of the twenty-five types of slave cases such as "slaves as property," "transfer of slaves" (warranty), "hire," "crimes by slaves," "manumission," etc. Jenny B. Wahl's study of slavery in Deep South courts found that 5 to 10 percent of local slave suits were appealed, and Joseph W. McKnight in the *Handbook of Texas* states that the court ordered printed only about 20 percent of Texas appellate decisions. Thus, the Texas high court probably reviewed more than 2,400 appeals regarding thousands of black Texans in local courts. The printed decisions in *Texas Reports* do not identify all blacks named in the case files. Some court reporters only wrote "negro woman," "female slave," or did not identify slaves by gender.[4]

The Republic of Texas Congress and later the Texas State Legislature regulated working and living conditions of black Texans. The appeals show that local judges, juries, and Texas Supreme Court justices decided the fate of black persons bought, sold, mortgaged, taken for debt, divided in divorce and inheritance disputes, traded for land and general merchandise, given as gifts, hired out, neglected, abused, committed crimes, or had crimes committed against them. The courts also decided warranty cases about titles, health, and character of slaves. Legally, the enslaved workers had "double character." They were property in civil suits and persons in criminal cases.[5] State law classified the enslaved persons as chattel or movable property and counties assessed owners for the total value of slave property on county tax rolls. If owners failed to pay the taxes, others paid the tax and obtained possession of the slave. After paying taxes for two years, the taxpayer obtained a tax lien title on the person and could sell, trade, or hire them out.[6]

One change that came for black Texans with statehood in 1845 was that out-of-state creditors could sue owners for sale of or possession of slaves to pay an owner's debts. Black women stood the greatest chance of separation from family when officials auctioned them, their children, or their mates for their owner's unpaid debts, as happened in almost a third of the 481 appeals in the database of appeals. The second greatest threat to black families came with an owner's death, when heirs sued for possession of slaves, as they did in almost 20 percent of the appeals. Some suits continued after a slave's death and emancipation. In addition, seven divorce appeals before the Civil War were for division of slaves as community property.[7]

When a black woman or child over the age of six changed owners by purchase, trade, inheritance, or debt, a bill of sale provided the seller and purchaser names, the slave's name, description, value, and the value of children under age six that remained by law with the mother. The county clerk recorded the transfer, and the bill of sale became a deed or legal title to that slave then placed on the county tax roll. A warranty stated the health, character, and skills of the slave. Thirty-three appeals were warranty suits for various reasons. The enslaved persons passed from one owner to the next and from one generation to another as a more valuable type of property than real estate or livestock.[8]

The printed court decisions show how Texas slavery changed for black women over the years. Before the Texas Revolution, James Gunn, a Chickasaw Indian, freed the mixed-race Native American and black Laney, her children, and grandchildren. After Gunn's death in Lamar County in 1842, his widow sold Laney and her family into slavery. With the help of a white friend, James Colbert, Laney sued for her freedom, and in 1847, the Texas Supreme Court set Laney and her three-generation family free. Justice Abner Lipscomb explained the court decision, "Laney's freedom was granted by Chickasaw Law," and overlooking her black heritage, added, "Only [N]egroes could be slaves in Texas."[9]

Mixed-race marriage was legal in Mexican Texas. Consequently, many mixed-race couples migrated to Texas from the United States. The Republic of Texas Congress banned mixed-race marriages in 1837 and the ban continued into statehood, but with little consequence. The first mixed-marriage appeal in the Texas high court was that of Margaret Gess of New York, who lived with Adam Smith in Mexican Texas. After independence, she ran a Houston boarding house for ten years on ten acres of property that Smith held in trust for her. Smith died in 1846 and Francis Lubbock claimed kin to Smith, then claimed the land, boardinghouse, Margaret, and her daughter as assets of Smith's estate. Margaret took Lubbock to court. In the 1851 appeal, Justice Lipscomb reversed the jury decision favoring Lubbock and explained that Smith living with Margaret made her free under Spanish law. Lipscomb remanded the suit back to the lower court to decide ownership of the land. Lubbock requested District Judge C. W. Buckley decide the land ownership and was surprised when Buckley declared Margaret owner of the property. Margaret then sold the land and disappeared from Texas public records.[10]

In the first five years of statehood, appeals to the Texas Supreme Court involved eighteen black women. An 1846 appeal from Colorado County shows that Mehala was at hire for two months, but not returned to her owner. The overseer claimed she ran away, but later admitted he "chastised her." The usual amount of punishment was the Biblical forty lashes less one. The local judge dismissed the suit, but Mehala's owner, Henry Mims, appealed. Justice Royall T. Wheeler reversed and remanded the suit for retrial with eight pages of instructions for the local judge to follow. An 1849 appeal from Fort Bend County shows that Jenney and Nicey lived in Mississippi, but instead of the attorney delivering them to a new owner in that state, brought them to Texas where he sold them. The court remanded the case for retrial because the jury did not price Nicey and her infant separately as required by law. Several appeals in early statehood were about debts that followed owners to Texas. In 1849, John S. Rhea appealed a Galveston suit over an 1845 debt for Dorcas and Frances that began in Mobile, Alabama. When a creditor revised a judgment for debt in 1857, the couple was a family of five with everyone except Frances auctioned to pay their master's debts on the Galveston County Courthouse steps.[11]

The ten years from 1850 to 1860 saw black Texans increase from 27 to 32 percent of the total population. Slave-related decisions also increased, and the Texas Supreme Court printed 267 decisions concerning black Texans with 123 black women identified by name during the decade. The appeals show that some women had kind masters, but other women led difficult lives. In Bexar County, an overseer quit and sued for his wages in 1853 because the owner "would not allow him to flog the [N]egroes." Although it was illegal for slaves to be married in Texas, in an 1854 appeal from Harris County, the debtor listed three couples he asked be sold as husband and wife. In Travis County in 1855, Elijah Rawles appealed a fine imposed on him for allowing his unnamed female slave to hire herself out for more than a day at a time.[12]

Nine appeals in the decade concerned manumission of slaves by owners. Under the 1850 Texas Constitution, an owner could free their slaves after all debts were paid and expense for travel outside the state provided for in the will. In Harrison County, Charlotte's owner freed her, provided her funds, and gave her a choice of moving to a free-labor state or Liberia. Former Alabama Governor and United States Senator Gabriel Moore freed his natural black daughter Mary Minerva before he migrated to the Republic of Texas. In his will probated in Harrison County in late 1844, Moore also freed Francis, Barbara, Caroline, Matilda, their children, and several men. With statehood, the Harrison County Probate Court had an administrator hire out the Moore women and men, including Moore's daughter, to pay Moore's debts. Five appeals to the Texas Supreme Court by the Moore women and their administrators ended in 1855 when Louis T. Wigfall, the pro-slavery advocate recently arrived from South Carolina, won the women their freedom and past wages. Wigfall was not in sympathy with the women, but probably received a portion of their back wages as his fee. Two years later as a state senator, Wigfall unsuccessfully introduced a bill in the legislature to prohibit manumission by will in Texas.[13]

With a friend of the court in 1858, Betsy Webster, the slave-wife of David Webster of Galveston, won her freedom and property in the Texas courts. Betsy and Webster lived openly for thirty-plus years in Florida and Texas. Webster manumitted Betsy and willed her 5,000 acres of Texas real estate, twenty-one Galveston city blocks, and the home where she lived for more than a decade after the Civil War. Perhaps the court decisions favoring black companions called attention to the forty or more mixed-race couples then living in Texas. In 1858 the legislature made mixed-race cohabitation and fornication felonies punishable by a $1,000 fine and five years' hard labor in the penitentiary. Another state law enacted that year declared that free blacks must leave Texas or select a master. The change in state law made little difference to the mixed-race couples, the Moore women, Betsy Webster, or the 174 other free black women listed on the 1860 US census who remained in Texas undisturbed by neighbors or local authorities.[14]

The Texas court appeals show the dark side of life for enslaved women in three different appeals. In 1851 fourteen-year-old Catherine and her eight-month-old child worked and camped out with other enslaved workers in a Harrison County creek bottom where they collected bark for the local tannery. When the March rain turned to snow, the workers returned to Marshall. Catherine, who was again pregnant, was ill as she had walked barefoot in the snow the three miles back to Marshall. Catherine never recovered and she and her infant daughter both died. Mr. Crain then sued her previous owner, Mr. Murphy, claiming she was ill when he bought her the year before. While the local jury thought she was weakened by her pregnancies at a young age, Crain failed to get back the $800 he paid for Catherine. The justices thought her death was the result of Crain's neglect and remanded the case for retrial. In Cass County, Lucy's owner sold her because she was barren, the result of a recent abortion (whether spontaneous or self-inflicted the court documents do not reveal). Lucy bled continuously long after menses should have ceased, and according to her physician's testimony she died from the profuse bleeding which triggered a warranty suit against her former owner who warranted her in good health. Perhaps Lucy refused to bring a child into her world of pain. A Tyler County appeal illustrates only one example of the heartbreak that enslaved mothers faced. Winnie's mistress sold her son Champion when he turned six years old so she would not have to feed him. Later when he was older, the mistress unsuccessfully sued for his return.[15]

Local and state courts also reveal crimes committed against black women. In Harris County, J. D. Nix "committed assault and battery" upon Lucy McRea; he "cut, bruised, wounded, and beat her." The jury assessed Nix a fine of twenty-five dollars and ten days in jail. Nix appealed and claimed his behavior was legal. In 1855 Justice Wheeler warned, "Slaves are persons within the meaning of the statute concerning crimes," and added this was "a case of wanton, unprovoked, lawless violent drunkenness against the law of nature and the laws of society." In Washington County, John Stephenson beat Malissa excessively, causing her death. The district attorney prosecuted Stephenson, but the jury found Stephenson not guilty. The state appealed the decision. While owners or hirers in other states could discipline slaves as they pleased, Justice Oran Roberts quoted Texas law in 1857, "Slaves are to be regarded as persons in respect to the criminal law," and added, "It is somewhat like an assault and battery upon a child, a ward, or an apprentice." In her study of slave children, Elizabeth Rabe found the sharpest memories in the *Slave Narratives* were when children witnessed the public beatings of their parents.[16]

Living conditions for slave women were never certain and they were always at the mercy of their owners. This can be seen in the case of John Amis, former owner of "Sir Archy," a famous racehorse of the time, when he left North Carolina after the stud's death. To flee creditors, Amis took his slaves, including Betsy and her family, to Mississippi in the late 1830s, Louisiana in 1840, and then, finally, to the Republic of Texas where he accumulated more debts. In Galveston Amis's creditor-agent, John Bennett, hired out Betsy and her family to help pay Amis's local debts.

Amis died in 1846, but Betsy, her family, and other Amis slaves were the focus of suits between creditors and Amis's heirs until 1858 with local hearings, numerous trials, three state appeals, and two federal suits taken to the US Supreme Court. Family feuds for possession of slaves made up 20 percent of the Texas court appeals involving black Texans.[17]

The four years before the Civil War were the most litigious of the era with 125 slave decisions printed. While most appeals were typical of earlier ones, others were far from mundane. In Montgomery County Jane, Mary, Tamer, Harriet, Sarah, and Clarissa were objects in a bitter 1857 divorce. Jane and her children did not go to the Cartwright wife as her separate property as they normally would have. The husband claimed the children born to his wife's slave Jane and her daughter Mary were his "seed," and therefore his offspring were his property. In forming the opinion Justice Hemphill, the court's authority on family law and rumored to have two mulatto daughters, cited English Common Law, the Spanish *Las Partides*, the French Napoleonic code, and Roman Justinian *Corpus Juris Civilis* regarding offspring before he reversed and remanded the case for a local jury to decide the fate of Jane and her family.[18]

There were only nineteen appeals involving black Texans in 1860 because owners, justices, and attorneys had other priorities that fall. Local county militia companies formed, and Chief Justice Roberts called for and organized the Texas Secession Convention by the thirty-three judicial districts. Meanwhile, in Rusk County, there was justice for one enslaved woman named Vina who was murdered by the slave Calvin in 1857. Her killer lost the appeal of a mandated death sentence imposed when slaves committed murder, and he was hanged. In another Rusk County case, Sarah Devereaux's slaves farmed her plantation as sharecroppers. When their ginned and sold, but not yet paid for, cotton burned in the fire that almost destroyed the City of Henderson, Devereaux sued for their payment in the local court but the cotton buyer won on appeal because slaves could not make contracts. In Jackson County William Bracken freed his slave children on his deathbed with neighbors taking dictation and witnessing his will. Relatives challenged the will at probate and because the dying Bracken or his neighbors did not think to include specific funds in the will for his children's removal from the state. Harriet, Amanda, and Eliza became the property of Bracken's white relatives.[19]

During the four years of the Civil War, the Texas Supreme Court decided only thirty-eight appeals about black Texans compared to 125 decisions the previous four years. Slave cases declined in part because of "stay laws" not lifted until 1868 that prevented collection of debt in Texas. Also courts postponed cases with litigants away at war. Within weeks of secession in 1861, the Confederate Texas Legislature altered the Constitution to conform to other Confederate states. "No Citizen, or other person residing in this state, shall have power by deed, or will, to take effect in this State, or out of it, in any manner whatsoever, directly, or indirectly, to emancipate his slave or slaves." Previously, an enslaved person's body, time, and children belonged to their owner. Under the new law, the state dictated the use of slave property and that was anyone whose maternal lineage included a slave woman. Texas, once the liberal frontier of slavery, had become like the other Confederate states.[20]

In 1861 the court reviewed six slave cases—all criminal cases. By state law, slaves could not marry, but the Guadalupe County appeal begins ironically, "The appellant [Jack] was indicted for the murder of his wife, a [N]egro woman named Nicey." In *Jack, a Slave, v. The State* (1861) the jury sentenced Jack to death by hanging. Justice J. H. Bell was most concerned that the jury did not decide Jack's value. Since 1852, the state treasury paid an owner one-half the slave's value as determined by the court when a slave was executed by the state for a crime.[21]

Before 1858, free people of color lived in Texas under the Ashworth Act of 1840, which granted residence to free blacks of good character, such as the wealthy Ashworth family of Jefferson County. In 1858 the Texas court upheld the legislative ban on Free Negro residents and declared, "all [N]egroes were slaves *de facto.*" Consequently, before 1860, some members of the Ashworth, Thomas, and Hayes families resettled in Galveston, Brazoria, and Calhoun Counties where they were listed "white" on the 1860 census. The 1861 appeal *Ex Parte Louisa Merry* decided freed women's fates. According to Justice Bell, Miss Merry could no longer live as a free person in Texas because she was the "fruit of . . . casual sexual intercourse of [her] parents." The logic was that Negroes were slaves and slaves could not marry.[22]

Two appeals came before the court in 1862, both from McLennan County. The first case originated in 1833, when Milly Berry took her slaves to Louisiana from Mexican Texas. Berry feared the Mexican government would free her slaves, but upon arrival in Louisiana, authorities seized her slaves as contraband and sold them at auction. After 1808 the United States Constitution banned the importation of foreign slaves. This helps explain why Texans fleeing Santa Anna with their slaves stopped short of the border during the "runaway scrape." In 1862, almost thirty years later, Berry's son John regained his share of the slaves by judgment when the owner brought the Berrys' slaves into Texas. The second appeal of 1862 illustrates the conflict in opinion of local people and state justices. The case began in Limestone County before 1856, when George S. Gaines sued several men, Thomas, Colton, and others, to recover Ann, whom he claimed was his slave property. Gaines had papers that showed that Ann was born a slave for life, but Judge Henry Jewitt made Ann's freedom a separate issue because she looked white and only Negroes could be slaves in Texas. On change of venue to Tyler County, the jury gave a verdict in favor of Ann's freedom, despite evidence that Ann's mother and grandmother were slaves. After a physical examination of Ann, two physicians testified in court that they "could not detect . . . the presence of African blood in her." In the 1856 decision, Justice Lipscomb, who freed the Indian and black woman Laney in 1847, demonstrated how interpretation of race had changed. In 1856 the justice declared, "Lawful slavery is confined to the African race" and it "would so descend, *ad infinitum* so long as the descent from the slave mother could be traced though the blood be of the smallest possible amount." The evidence, he wrote, did not support the jury decision that Ann was white. Lipscomb remanded the case for retrial leaving any change in the law, he explained, "to the wisdom of the legislature."[23]

In the retrial to decide Ann's status, a special judge presided on change of venue from Limestone County to McLennan County. The jury in Waco heard evidence of Ann's African blood and enslaved mother and grandmother, and as in Tyler County, the jury voted to set Ann free. In 1862 the justices again ruled the jury decision was contrary to evidence and returned the case for retrial for a third time. The fate of Ann is unknown, but this appeal and others involving local blacks show clearly that local liberal attitudes were in conflict with the conservative statute law upheld by the conservative Texas Supreme Court.[24]

Several appeals in 1863 were about possession of slaves. In Galveston Joseph Silver sued and lost three times for the return of Frances and Dorcas to satisfy a debt paid him a decade earlier. In Jasper County Eliza Carroll's estate administrator successfully had two slave girls returned ten years after they were taken from her by mistake in 1853. In another case a Galveston County's appeal overturned a decision made nine years earlier for possession of the slave woman Ann and her five children. In Fannin County the Jamison family sued Ransom White for possession of the slave Jane given to Elizabeth Nicholson when she married and moved to Texas. In 1858 Elizabeth sold Jane and her child to pay her husband's debts. When Elizabeth died, her family wanted Jane returned. Because the deed to White did not include a required form stating the husband did not coerce his wife into selling her separate property, the title was defective, and Jane returned to the Jamison family.[25]

Why would people go to the time and expense of having slaves returned years later? Ann Lobdell, a Louisiana refugee who urged her family to migrate to Texas with their slaves, states one possible reason. She wrote of labor shortages and "Texans were eager to hire [N]egroes" and "would pay well." Additionally, the federal government compensated District of Columbia owners who freed their slaves in 1862 and after the fall of Vicksburg and Gettysburg in 1863, four Texans traded land for slaves, perhaps in hope of compensation. When the war ended without financial compensation for freed slaves, they attempted to regain their land by claiming slaves had warranty "for life" and emancipation rendered their land-slave trades invalid.[26]

The most dramatic slave appeal of 1863 was from Robertson County and concerned the murder of Daniel, the three-year-old son of James Threatt. Neighbors suspected his slaves, Ned and Elizabeth, had something to do with the child's disappearance, so they beat them with a rope until Ned said Elizabeth had put the child in a well. She countered, "He tells a lie; I can show you the child." Elizabeth then led the neighbors to a ravine, waded into the water, and carried the child out in her arms with wounds visible on his neck and head. In the appeal the district attorney implied Ned was lynched by irate neighbors when they saw the child. Threatt had owned Ned for only two or three weeks, but had owned Elizabeth for several years. Authorities charged Ned with committing the offense and Elizabeth, who had been trustworthy, was tried for aiding and abetting the crime. Elizabeth showed no malice, had no motive for murder, so the court granted her a new trial on a lesser charge.[27]

Seven appeal cases about slave women came before the court in 1864. In Washington County, the children of Robert Ferguson filed suit against their father for recovery of several named female slaves that he threatened to sell or remove from the state. Earlier, in 1845, possibly as a hedge against foreclosure, Ferguson deeded by gift the "Negroes" Mary and her two children, Sarah and Spencer, and also Rachel, America, Sophia, and Elizabeth with all their increase to his children, to have and to hold as their property after his death. On appeal Justice Moore reversed the jury decision, favoring the father's possession of the slaves and remanded the case for a jury to decide if Ferguson had recorded a deed, his children possessed the slaves, or if he filed a will, he had possession of them until his death.[28]

That year a Fayette County appeal reviewed Jack Castleman's suit against Charles Lewis and his wife for possession of Hannah and her son. Castleman claimed W. J. Hill gave the slaves to his daughter to prevent their being taken for non-payment of debt. Justice Moore left Hannah with Mrs. Lewis and wrote that Castleman lived nearby and should have known better than take a lien from Hill. In yet another Fayette County case, James Eans unsuccessfully appealed a judgment won by Sarah Sawyer and her younger siblings when they recovered their deceased mother's separate property, the slave Elizabeth and her son. Eans had purchased the slaves from the children's father, who paid property taxes on the slaves, and after his wife's death illegally filed a tax title for Elizabeth and her son who were the inheritance of his children.[29]

The last appeal during the war illustrates complications caused by spouses trading slaves. Before their trade, James T. Bloomfield owned Emanuel, and his wife Sarah Jane owned Ann and her child Eliza. The husband contracted a debt with the merchants Taylor & Hart, and then his wife died. To cover his debts Bloomfield mortgaged his wife's slave Emanuel. He then sold Ann and her child and used those proceeds for his personal use. He then gave a bill of sale to his children for Emanuel mortgaged to the merchants. Sarah Jane's father, F. M. Kendrick, then sued for control of his grandchildren's property. He appealed the jury decision in favor of Taylor & Hart, awarded Emanuel in payment of Bloomfield's debt. In trying to sort out the conundrum, Justice Bell cited *Bradshaw v. Mayfield* (1856), *Parks v. Williard* (1846), and *Edrington v. Mayfield* (1849), the prior decisions on slave trades by spouses. Bell concluded that Bloomfield held a one-third life estate in Emanuel, and that his bill of sale of Emanuel to the children could not deprive the creditors Taylor & Hart their due. Bell concluded that slave trades by spouses should have the same form as the sale of a wife's separate property.[30]

June 19, 1865, is celebrated as the day slavery ended in Texas, but freedom did not settle the legal issues involving a quarter of a million black Texans. Because of contracts for slave debt and hire, the exact date slavery ended was vital. Some Texans contended slavery ended in 1863 with passage of the Emancipation Proclamation; others said that it died with passage of the Thirteenth Amendment in December 1865. The debate continued until the court decision in *Hall v. Keese* (1868) established the exact end of slavery in Texas as June 19, 1865, when General Gordon Granger read the Emancipation Proclamation and declared all slaves in Texas free. Yet, 108 court decisions after June 1865 dealt with the lingering residue of slavery with 56 of the appeals involving former enslaved women.[31]

Most debt cases over slaves dissolved when the stay laws ceased in 1868, as slaves were no longer property. Other disputes continued with several cases that had been reversed and remanded in the 1850s being resolved after the war, such as suits over ownership of Bettie and her children in Lavaca County, Bina in Harrison County, and Violet, Julia, and Angeline in Cherokee County. In 1870 a previous slave owner, who inherited Sarah before the war, received 10 percent interest of her value from 1861 to June 19, 1865. Other appeals settled suits about women loaned but not returned, warranty suits over women with terminal illness, and past due hire of enslaved women such as the 1867 suit by Eliza's owner in Cherokee County, and by Betsy's owner in Austin County in 1870. In Leon County, Norrey's contract for hire was not paid to her owner before slavery ended. The 1868 appeal included a list of items the hirer wanted deducted from his debt as expenses required by law, including two sets of clothes, one summer and one winter dress, an underskirt, a sack, two pairs of shoes, a blanket, plus taxes and medical bills.[32]

The postwar era was one of confusion for blacks and their former owners with the Texas constitutions of 1866, 1869, 1876, and the appeals court transitioning from ex-rebels immediately after the war, to military justices during Reconstruction, and then back to ex-Confederate justices in 1874. Each political regime and court decided the issues of former slaves differently. In one appeal in 1867, Mary Lacy and Harry Pope both apprenticed their ten-year-old son Elkins in exchange for 100 acres of land from Mary Timmons. Although Pope proved that he sired Elkins ten years before, when their owner paired them at another plantation, the ex-rebel court awarded Mary custody of her son and the land because fathers of bastards had no parental authority. Reconstruction justices appointed by military authorities, however, upheld Article 12, section 27, of the 1869 Constitution that "made legitimate the marriage of all persons formerly precluded from the rights of matrimony because of the law of bondage." By doing so they recognized slave relationships as common law marriages if the couples continued their relationship after freedom. In 1870 the court recognized children of such marriages as legitimate and able to inherit property.[33]

During the military occupation of Texas, the Reconstruction justices awarded property to white men's black widows and their mixed-race children, but these awards would later be overturned. White relatives maintained that former slave-wives and children of white men had no rights of inheritance. Reconstruction justices interpreted the aforementioned Article 12, section 27 to include mixed-race couples. For example, Sam Hearne died in 1866 and left a 900-acre Brazos River plantation to his mulatto son for the care of Sam's twenty-year companion, Azeline. Hearne's white relatives filed claim to the land, valued at the time as worth $20,000, two days after Hearne died. After the death of her son from yellow fever, Azeline fought to retain her land in court. The white Hearne family persisted, and in 1884 Azeline lost the last of her land after thirteen local trials and two state appeals. The fact that Azeline Hearne was not identified in court documents as black or a former slave suggests that other black wives of white husbands may be hidden in the court appeals.[34]

With the return of former Confederates to political power in 1874, the liberal policy toward black wives of white men ended. Justice Gould, who once defended the white slave girl Ann in her quest for freedom before the war, demonstrated the change in interpretation in *Clements v. Crawford,* a landmark case in 1874. He stated that Article 12 in the 1869 Constitution was to "legitimatize children of slave couples, not those of a white man living with a [N]egro." For the first time, mixed-race couples in Texas faced legal consequences.[35]

Mixed-race couples did what they could to adapt to the changing times and attitudes. In the 1870s a white man, George Clements, lived with his wife Mary, who was a former slave, and their children." Later in the decade, when their Galveston house was in foreclosure, Mary sued unsuccessfully for homestead rights. When questioned in court, Clements testified he was not married to anyone. He had reason to lie. Between 1870 and 1885, twelve black and twelve white men served time at hard labor in the state penitentiary for cohabitation with a race not their own. In 1874 Justice Gould denied Mary a homestead, and in the same decision overruled *Honey v. Clark* (1872) that awarded the Wharton County mixed-race children of John and Sobrina Clark property valued at the time as $236,800 or $5.5 million in 2010 dollars. Previous decisions awarding inheritance to black wives and mixed-race children were also overturned, and ex-Confederate justices gave notice they would deny any future claims of mixed-race children of white fathers. Other appeals to the Texas Supreme Court show that rather than living as spouses, black women masqueraded as cooks, housekeepers, or laundresses. To show that the Clementses did what they deemed necessary to outwit the system, the 1900 census shows George and Mary living together as "white" and "married," with their two grown "white" children in a Galveston boarding house that Mary ran for "white" boarders. Sometime before 1900, Mary and her children crossed the color line in Galveston, Texas.[36]

Legal disputes over inheritance of property by black women in mixed relationships continued beyond the turn of the century. Phillis Oldham of Burleson County and Leah Foster of Fort Bend County, who were once awarded thousands of acres of land during Reconstruction, also had probate settlements overturned, and after years of litigation and intimidation, accepted 160 acres as their homesteads in the 1880s.[37] In 1907 the last appeal related to mixed-race couples was the Hardin County relationship of Maria, a woman of color, and Isaac Hamilton, a hero of the Texas Revolution who received a league of land in 1836 for wounds he received during the war. In the 1850s Isaac deeded Maria 160 acres of land held in trust for her by a trusted acquaintance until 1876 when she held title in her own name. Maria later sold the land, and the buyer subsequently sold the land to a timber company. In 1907 two court appeals by her descendants found the timberland was legally purchased by Nona Lumber Mills.[38]

The court cases about black women during the Civil War Era add yet another facet to the history of black women in Texas. The appeals reveal the lack of certainty enslaved women had in having a permanent home, a continuous mate, or if they could be separated from their children. Beatings and shortages during the war made a difficult life even worse. Any legal protections black women once had as their masters' property ended with the end of slavery. During Reconstruction and afterward, black men and women were the focus of white anger and blamed for the deaths and financial hardships of the war. Black women were shot, disemboweled, raped, and subjected to a barrage of violence and terror that swept the state. The Freedmen's Bureau recorded more than 1,500 acts of violence against black Texans with at least 350 former slaves killed between 1865 and 1868. After Federal occupation troops left Texas and the Freedmen's Bureau closed in 1870, black women across Texas were on their own.[39]

The Texas State Supreme Court decisions reflect the spectrum of conditions that free and enslaved black women experienced before, during, and after the Civil War. Their treatment ranged from leniency to cruelty, depending on the attitude of their masters.[40] The court cases also show the change in attitudes of local and state courts toward Texas black women. The liberal decisions of the late 1840s and the 1850s, when the part-black Laney was set free and Margaret Gess and Betsy Webster retained their property, contrast sharply with the seemingly white Ann kept in slavery and the loss of property by Phillis Oldham, Azeline Hearne, Leah Foster, and others after the war.

The Texas Supreme Court decisions show that the lives of Texas black women during the Civil War Era consisted of hard work, heartache, and uncertainty. They lived under the absolute control of their masters who owned their bodies, their labor, their children, and chose their mates. Although freedom brought new uncertainties, out of the crucible of slavery and its difficult aftermath emerged women of great character, enormous strength of will, and an unceasing resolve to pass on to their daughters and granddaughters great courage, an abiding hope, and a boundless determination for a better life.

NOTES

1. Angela Boswell, "Black Women during Slavery to 1865," James M. Smallwood and Barry A. Crouch, "Texas Freedwomen during Reconstruction, 1865-1874," Rebecca Sharpless, "'Us Has Ever Lived De Useful Life:' African American Women in Texas, 1874-1900," in Bruce A. Glasrud and Merline Pitre, eds., *Black Women in Texas History* (College Station: Texas A&M University Press, 2008), 13-37; Jo Ella Exley, *Texas Tears and Texas Sunshine: Voices of Frontier Women* (College Station: Texas A&M University Press, 1984), Amelia Barr relates when slavery ended for Harriet. Court cases examined in: Mark M. Carroll, *Homesteads Ungovernable: Families, Sex, Race, and the Law in Frontier Texas, 1823-1860* (Austin: University of Texas Press, 2001); Dale R. Baum, *Counterfeit Justice; The Judicial Odyssey of Texas Freedwoman Azelene Hearne* (Baton Rouge: Louisiana State University Press, 2009); Randolph B. Campbell, ed., *The Laws of Slavery in Texas* (Austin: University of Texas Press, 2010); James W. Dallam, *Opinions of the Supreme Court of Texas [Republic]* (St. Paul: West Publishing, 1883); *Texas Reports,* available online at the Portal of Texas History; Texas, Supreme Court of Texas, *Texas Reports, cases argued and decided in the Supreme Court of the State of Texas,* 1-101 (St. Paul: West Publishing Co., 1883); Linda S. Hudson, "Database: Slave Cases in the Texas Supreme Court," 481 cases listed by row with columns (1) case name, citation, justice; (2) year; (3) type of case; (4) slave gender, or name, owners, others (5) county, presiding judge (6) decision and case facts. The database will be available for research on the Portal of Texas History Online at University of North Texas Libraries.
2. Hudson, "Black Texans Database, County": Anderson, Austin, Bastrop, Bell, Bexar, Bosque, Bowie, Brazoria, Brazos, Burleson, Burnet, Caldwell, Calhoun, Cameron, Cass, Cherokee, Collin, Colorado, Coryell, Dallas, DeWitt, Denton, Ellis, Falls, Fannin, Fayette, Fort Bend, Freestone, Galveston, Goliad, Gonzales, Grayson, Gregg, Grimes, Guadalupe, Hardin, Harris, Harrison, Henderson, Hill, Hopkins, Houston, Hunt, Jackson, Jasper, Jefferson, Karnes, Kaufman, Lamar, Lavaca, Leon, Liberty, Limestone, Matagorda, McLennan, Milam, Montgomery, Nacogdoches, Navarro, Panola, Polk, Red River, Refugio, Robertson, Rockwall, Rusk, Sabine, San Augustine, Shelby,

Smith, Tarrant, Titus, Travis, Tyler, Upshur, Victoria, Walker, Washington, Wharton, Williamson, and Wood.

3. Many, but not all, Texas slave cases listed in Helen Catterall, ed., *Judicial Cases Concerning American Slavery and the Negro,* 5 vols. (Washington, DC: Carnegie Institute, 1937), and Paul Finkelman, ed., *Slavery, Race, and the American Legal System, 1708-1872,* 16 vols. (New York: Garland Publishing, 1988); C. W. Raines, *Analytical Index to the Laws of Texas 1823-1905,* 3 vols. (Austin: Von Boeckman-Jones Co., 1906); H. P. N. Gammel, Comp., *The Laws of Texas, 1822-1897,* I, "Law of May 15, 1838," mortgages, II; "Law of 11th April 1846", The Portal to Texas History, accessed May 25, 2013, http://texashistory.unt.edu/ark:67531/metaph5872; Randolph B. Campbell, *An Empire for Slavery; The Peculiar Institution in Texas, 1821-1865* (Baton Rouge: Louisiana University Press, 1989) Chapter 5 on slave law discusses some cases.; Campbell, ed., *The Laws of Slavery in Texas.*

4. William G. Myers, *Texas: A Digest of the Texas Reports,* 3 vols. (St. Louis: W. J. Gilbert, 1881), II; Myers, *Texas Digest, 1840 to date, covering Texas Reports and Southwest Reporter,* 34 (St. Paul: West Publishing Co., 1835-1879), 192-206. "Slaves" with 25 key types listed: "Nature, origin, & legality of slavery; Slave Trade; Who were slaves; Property in slaves; Rights and powers of owners; Duties and liabilities of owners; Transfers of slaves (warranty); Hiring of slaves; Fugitive slaves; Regulation of slaves, freedmen, & free negroes; Status in general; Personal rights and disabilities; Rights of property of slaves; Inheritance by, from, or through slaves; Contracts by slaves; Torts by slaves; Actions by or against slaves; Crimes by slaves; Offenses against slaves; Right to freedom; Proceedings for freedom; Manumission; Emancipation; Abolition of slavery, peonage; Legalizing cohabitation and legitimizing issue of former slaves"; Jenny B. Wahl, *The Bondsman's Burden: An Economic Analysis of the Common Law of Southern Slavery* (Cambridge: Cambridge University Press, 1998), 190. Wahl does not include Texas; Joseph W. McKnight, "Law," *Handbook of Texas Online,* accessed May 25, 2013, http://www.tshaonline.org/handbook/ online/articles/jzlph. Case files are in county clerk records and Texas Supreme Court Record Group Archives Division of the Texas State Library. Case files, if available, have names and details not in the appeals and decisions. See cases related to Gabriel Moore in Harrison County Probate Records and Texas Supreme Court Files.

5. Ariela J. Gross, *Double Character; Slavery and Mastery in the Antebellum Southern Courtroom* (Princeton: Princeton University Press, 2000), 3-9. Gross credits the term "Double Character" to Thomas R. R. Cobb, *An Inquiry into the Law of Negro Slavery in the United States of America* (n.p.: J. W. Johnson & Co., 1858); Elizabeth York Enstram, "How Dallas Grew . . . And Why," *Legacies: A History Journal for Dallas and North Central Texas,* 3, no. 2 (Fall 1991); Ruthe Winegarten, *Dallas Black Women* (Austin: Eakin Press, 2002), 50, 410. The first legal hanging of a woman in Texas was of the black Jane Elkins for killing Mr. Wisdom who hired her to keep house and care for his three children. Her conviction was not appealed; *McGee v. Currie,* 4 Tex 219 (1849) on hirer responsibility.
6. Hudson, "Database," Type 4 Property debt; *Easley v. McClinton,* 33 Tex 289 (1870) on slave mortgages usually for a maximum of 12 months.
7. *Cook v. Thornhill,* 13 Tex 293 (1855); Myers, *Digest of the Texas Reports,* "*Slaves; Auctioned in Harris County for Union Bank of Louisiana, et al. v. Stafford et al,*" 12 Howard 327 (1851), 102 slaves mortgage debt $45,000; *Randon v. Toby,* 52 US 493 (1850), 23 Africans auctioned in Harris County; *Wood v. Wheeler* 11 Tex 122 (1853), slaves sold on credit for 12 months; Hudson, "Database," Type 4.
8. Gross, *Double Character,* 16-19, bill of sale and warranty photos; Campbell, *Empire for Slavery,* 96-114; Warranty quotation in Walcott v. Hendrick, 6 Tex 406 (1851); Gammel, *Laws of Texas,* I, "Law of May 15, 1838"; Hudson, "Database" Type 7, Transfer Warranty.
9. *Mary Harvey v. Jno. Patterson, Dallam's Digest,* 370, (1840); Loren Schwensinger, ed., *The Southern Debate on Slavery* (Urbana: University of Illinois Press, 2001), vol. 1, "Petitions of Free Blacks in the Texas Legislature"; *W. G. Hill v. E. S. McDermott, Dallam's Digest,* 419, (1841); *R. M. Jones v. Laney, and Friend James Colbert,* 2 Tex 342 (1847); "Laney Colbert," Affidavit, 27 Aug 1896, 3rd Judicial Div, Indian Territory, Chickasaw Nation. Laney Colbert was 100 years old.
10. Carroll, *Homesteads Ungovernable,* 55-57, 61-66, 71-2, 145-148, 151, 224; Robert B. Shaw, *A Legal History of Slavery* (Potsdam, NY: Northern Press, 1991), 108; Jean A. Stuntz, *Hers, His, and Theirs; Community Property Law in Spain and Early Texas* (Lubbock: Texas Tech University Press, 2005), 36-37; Linda Erickson Devereaux, "William Goyens: Black Leader in Early Texas," *East Texas Historical Journal* 45 (Spring

2007): 52-57, white wife Mary Pate Sibley; Charles F. Robinson II, "Legislated Love in the Lone Star State: Texas and Miscegenation," *Southwestern Historical Quarterly* 108 (July 2004): 65-86.; *Guess v. Lubbock*, 5 Tex 535 (1851); Mark Davidson, "One Woman's Fight for Freedom; *Gess v. Lubbock*, 1851," in Campbell, ed., *Laws of Slavery in Texas*, 87-93.

11. Hudson, "Database"; *Mims v. Mitchell*, 1 Tex 433 (1846); *Mitchell v. Mims*, 8 Tex 6 (1852); Deuteronomy 25: 2-3. 40 lashes less one; *Blakley's Admin. v. Duncan*, 4 Tex 184 (1849); *Beers & Smith v. Rhea*, 5 Tex 350 (1849); *Robertson v. Smith*, 220 AL (1850); *C. O'Connor v. Silver*, 26 Tex 606 (1863).

12. Hudson, "Database"; *Meade v. Rutledge*, 11 Tex 45 (1853); *Fowler & Clepper v. Stoneum*, 11 Tex 479 (1854); *Rawles v. The State*, 15 Tex 581 (1855); *Kingston v. State*, 26 Tex S-116 (1860); Gammel, *Laws of Texas*, II, "An Act to prevent slaves from hiring own time, 9 May 1846."

13. Texas, *Constitution* (1850) Art VIII, "Slaves" Sec 1. In Virginia, Mississippi, Alabama, and Arkansas emancipated slaves could be taken to satisfy a master's debts; *Purvis v. Sherrod*, 12 Tex 140 (1854), Charlotte; Eric Foner, *Who Owns History: Rethinking the Past in a Changing World* (New York: Hill & Wang, 2002), 176, five northern states prohibited residence of blacks; *Armstrong v. Jowell*, 24 Tex 58 (1859), natural children; *Hillard v. Franz, Admin.*, 21 Tex 192 (1858), natural daughter; Hunt, *Admin. v. White*, 24 Tex 643 (1860), slave natural children; *Philleo v. Holliday*, 24 Tex 38 (1859), wife did not free; "Emancipation Petition for Henry Moore," December 8, 1853, Harrison County Historical Society Archives, Marshall, TX. Moore not willing to marry Frances as named by Moore as a condition of freedom, purchased his freedom for $800, married Amy Van Zandt in 1847, served in the Reconstruction Legislature; J. M. (Jerry) Moore, son of Henry born 1848; Federal Writer's Project, *Slave Narratives*, "J. M. (Jerry) Moore"; Randolph B. Campbell, *A Southern Community in Crisis: Harrison County, Texas 1850-1880* (Austin: Texas State Historical Association, 1983), 98, 292, 306-08, 360-1, 364; Campbell, *An Empire For Slavery*, 207; *Moore's Admin. v. Mary Minerva & her children*, 17 Tex 20 (1856); *Moore's Admin. v. Frances, her children, Barbara and others*, 17 Tex 28 (1856).

14. *Webster v. Heard*, 32 Tex 685 (1870); *Webster v. Corbett*, 34 Tex 263 (1871); "Petition to the Legislature of the State of Texas, July 21, 1856, Galveston County, Texas. Twenty-nine Galveston County resi-

dents respectfully pray 'for the passage of a law allowing Betsy, a free negro woman to remain in this state...'," Texas State Library-Archives Division, Austin, Texas. Records of the Legislature, Memorials and Petitions. Record Group 100; Jason Gillmer, "Lawyers and Slaves: A Remarkable Case of Representation from the Antebellum South," *University of Miami Race & Social Justice Law Review,* 1: 37-65. Betsy paid attorneys 1/3 of 5000 acres in 1858 as their retainer and sold city blocks to Heard and Corbett, which she regained during the war and lost in 1870 and 1871; Betsy still lived in Galveston in 1876. See "Bettsy Webster, Col, res NW corner Ave I & 15th," p. 136 in John H. Heller, *Heller's Galveston Directory, 1876-1877,* Book, 1876: (http://texashistory.unt.edu/ark:/67531/metapth636850/: accessed December 31, 2015), University of North Texas Libraries, The Portal to Texas History, http://texashistory.unt.edu; crediting Galveston & Texas History Center, Rosenberg Library, Galveston, Texas; Gammel, *Laws of Texas,* IV, Title, 12, Chap 1, Art 386, "Unlawful Marriage," 2-5 years hard labor, Chap 2, Art 388, "Incest, Adultery and Fornication," 2-10 years hard labor, Art 395a, "Every white person who shall live in adultery or fornication with a negro," Fine: $100-$1,000; Eighth Census of the United States, Population Census, Texas; Dolly Farrow Nichol, *My Thomas, Hayes, Ashworth Families* (Published by author, 2002), 16-17. In 1847 Henderson Ashworth was arrested for fornication with Letitia Stewert, a white woman, to whom he claimed marriage. Family and census records show the couple married in 1847. Lipscomb affirmed the jail sentence in *Ashworth v. State* (1853). Ashworth's father William and two uncles were born in South Carolina in the 1790s, migrated to Louisiana in 1820s, married white wives, moved to Mexican Texas in 1831 to Jefferson County, received a league and labor of land from the Republic of Texas. Henderson Ashworth was part of the Regulator-Moderator feud, which may account for his arrest.

15. *Murphy's Admin. v. Crain,* 12 Tex 297 (1854); *McFall v. Walker,* 25 Tex 328 (1860); *Gregory Admin. v. Van Vleck,* 21 Tex 41 (1858).

16. *Nix v. State,* 13 Tex 575 (1855); *State v. Stephenson and Cabler,* 20 Tex 151 (1857); George M. Stroud, *A Sketch of the Laws Relating to Slavery in the Southern States of America* (NP: NP, 1856, Rpt, New York: Negro Universities Press, 1968), 12-108. "Masters may afflict any punishment upon the person of his slave"; Andrew Fede, "Legit-

imized Violent Slave Abuse in the American South, 1619-1865: A Case Study of Law and Social Change in Six Southern States," in *The American Journal of Legal History* 29: 93-150; Thomas D. Morris, *Southern Slavery and the Law, 1619-1860* (Chapel Hill and London: University of North Carolina Press, 1996), 161, 186; Robert B. Shaw, *A Legal History of Slavery* (Potsdam, NY: Northern Press, 1991), 102-108; Mark V Tushnet, *The American Law of Slavery 1810-1860* (Princeton: Princeton University Press, 1981), 9; William E. Whiethoff, *A Peculiar Humanism in the Higher Courts of the Old South, 1820-1850* (Athens: University of Georgia Press, 1996); "An Act Concerning Slaves, February 5, 1840," in Gammel, *Laws of the Republic*; Art. VIII, "Slaves," The Constitution of the State of Texas (1846) (1850) (1861). In Texas fifty lashes was the maximum without conviction of a crime. The "usual" was thirty-nine lashes based on Deuteronomy 25: 2-3. "Forty stripes may he give him, and not exceed; lest, if he should exceed, and beat him above these with many stripes, then thy brother should seem vile to thee"; State of Texas, *The Penal Code of the State of Texas, Adopted by the Sixth Legislature* (Galveston: Galveston News Office, 1857); Mark W. Lambert, *Footnotes Newsletter Online* (Houston: Fred Parks Law Library) 16: 1, www.stcl.edu/library/FN16-1 Jones Room.html. Texas code based on Edward Livingstone's Criminal Code of Louisiana, and Jeremy Bentham's ideals, Amendments, Feb 12, 1858, took effect July 1, 1858 (accessed Feb 3, 2005); Elizabeth R. Rabe, "Slave Children of Texas: A Qualitative and Quantitative Analysis," *East Texas Historical Journal* 42 (Spring 2004): 19-22.

17. Luke Decock, "Sir Archy of North Hampton, N.C.," *Newsobserver online*, accessed March 28, 2014, http://visitnorthamptonnc.com/sir-archie-of-northampton-county-nc.html. Sir Archy stood at stud at Mowfield Plantation from 1818 until his death at age twenty-eight in 1833. Of the last twenty winning horses at the Kentucky Derby, each has Sir Archy in its pedigree. He was a charter inductee of the Thoroughbred Racing Hall of Fame. Nearly every American racehorse is related to him: Seattle Slew, Secretariat, Seabiscult, Man O'War. Of the eleven Triple Crown winners, only Citation, in 1948, did not have Archy's genes. Quarterhorses are part of Archy's legacy through his son Copperbottom owned by Sam Houston. The death of the horse at stud for a $100 fee marked Amis's financial decline; *Bennett v. Butterworth*, US 124 (1850); *Bennett v. Butterworth*, 52 US 669 (1850); *Bennett*

and Hunt, Admin. v. Butterworth & wife, 53 US 367 (1851); *Hunt, Admin. v. Butterworth & others*, 21 Tex 133 (1858).

18. Hudson, "Database," Texas State Supreme Court saw thirty slave appeals in 1856, forty-one appeals in 1857, thirty-five in 1858, and thirty in 1859. In Lamar County Mariah was auctioned for debt as were Ann, Mariah, Jenny, Lucy, Amanda, Mary, and Linda in Bastrop County and Eliza in Houston County. Inheritance battles involved Fanny and her children and Mary Ann in Houston County; Emeline, Caroline, Angeline, Lize, Phillis, and Gracy in Red River County; Primera and Hannah and her children in Rusk County; Henrietta in Bexar County; and Clara, Jane, Martha, Eliza, Nancy in Colorado County; and Charlotte in Gonzales County. Black women named in: *Allen v. Russell*, 19 Tex 88 (1857); *Gamble v. Dabney*, 20 Tex 69 (1857); *Cummins v, Rice*, et al, 19 Tex 225 (1857); *Berthlett, Jones & Co. v. Folsom*, 21 Tex 430 (1858); *Harrington v. Moore*, 21 Tex 546 (1858); *Little v. Birdwell*, 21 Tex 597 (1858); *Manly v. Culver's heirs*, 20 Tex 143 (1857); *Montgomery & wife v. Nash*, et. al, 12 Tex 158 (1859), same case, 23 Tex 156 (1859), same case, 18 Tex 747 (1857); *Trammell v. Trammell*, 20 Tex 407 (1857); *Cartwright v. Cartwright*, 18 Tex 626 (1857); James L. Haley, *Texas Supreme Court; A Narrative History, 1836-1986* (Austin: University of Texas Press, 2013), 59. Justice Hemphill lived with his slave Sabina and had two daughters, Theodora and Henrietta, whom he enrolled in Wilberforce College in Xenia, Ohio, in 1859 when he replaced Sam Houston as US senator.

19. Hudson, "Database," 1860 cases; Linda S. Hudson, "Knights of the Golden Circle in Texas, 1858-1861," in Kenneth W. Howell, ed. *The Seventh Star of the Confederacy; Texas during the Civil War* (Denton: University of North Texas Press, 2009), 52-67; Texas, *Journal of the Secession Convention*, The Portal to Texas History, accessed June 9, 2013, http://texashistory.unt.edu/ark:67531/ hetapth28537/; Ralph A. Wooster, "An Analysis of the Membership of the Texas Secession Convention," *Southwestern Historical Quarterly* 62 (Jan 1959): 328-335; *Sanders v. Devereaux*, 25 Tex Sup 1 (1860); Joleene Maddox Snider, "Sarah Devereaux: A Study in Southern Femininity," *Southwestern Historical Quarterly* 97 (Jan 1994): 479-510; Devereaux Family Papers (1805-1856), Box 2N214, "Family and Slave Records," Briscoe Center for American History, University of Texas at Austin; Hunt, *Admin. v. White*, 24 Tex 643 (1860).

20. Hudson, "Database"; "Stay Laws," *Galveston Weekly News,* Nov. 19, 1861, Dec 7, 1861; *Edmonson v. Garnett* 33 Tex 250 (1870) explains "stay laws" or postponement; *Williams v. Murphy,* 36 Tex 174 (1871); Art VIII, "Slaves," *Constitution* (1861); Art VIII, "Slaves," *Constitution* (1850); Stroud, *Sketch of Slave Law,* 96; *Geo. S. Gaines v. Ann,* 17 Tex 211 (1856); Judy Gentry, "Confederates and Cotton in East Texas," *East Texas Historical Journal* 48 (Winter 2010): 20-39.

21. Hudson, "Database"; *Jack, a Slave v. The State,* 26 Tex 1(1861); Campbell, *Empire for Slavery,* 100; *Ingram v. Linn,* 4 Tex 266 (1849) opinion explains owner's liability for slave's behavior; *Ingram v. Atkinson,* 4 Tex 270 (1849); Campbell, ed., *Laws of Slavery,* 64.

22. Douglas Hale, "Free Blacks," *The Handbook of Texas Online,* accessed December 28, 2001, http://www.tsha.utexas.edu/handbook/online/articles/view/FF/pkfbs.html; "Ashworth Act," *The Handbook of Texas Online*; *Ashworth v. The State* (1853); Dolly Farrow Nichol, *My Thomas, Hayes, Ashworth Families* (Published by author, 2002), 16-17. The Ashworths were mulatto on the 1850 Jefferson County census, stock farmers; US Eighth Census (1860) in Jackson, Brazoria, Calhoun Counties, families, listed as "white"; Ex Parte Louisa Merry (1861) no county given, but US Eighth Census (1860) Travis County lists Thomas Merry, "Mulatto,"; Angela Boswell, "Black Women during Slavery," in Glasrud and Pitre, eds., *Black Women in Texas,* 13-37.

23. *Thompson v. Berry,* 26 Tex 263 (1862); Gammel, *Laws of Texas,* "The Laws of Coahuila y Tejas" Decree 18, 15 September 1827, Art 1. All slaves registered, Art 2. Report all children born every 3 months, Art 4. Registry of slave deaths, Art 5. Owners with no heirs, slaves set free, unless owner was poisoned, Art 7. At inheritance 1/10 of slaves be freed, Art 9; all children of slaves free born and shall be educated, Decree No. 35, 24 November 1827, Art 1. A slave may choose a new master provided the new master pay the old one; *The Constitution of the State of Coahuila and Texas,* Art 13, "no one shall be born a slave in the state"; *George S. Gaines v. Ann,* 17 Tex 211 (1856); *Gaines's Admin. v. Ann,* 26 Tex 340 (1862); "Valuable land for sale" Geo. S. Gaines in *Texas State Times,* November 24, 1855.

24. *Gaines v. Ann,* 17 Tex 211 (1856); *Gaines' Admin. v. Ann,* 26 Tex 340 (1862); Thomas, Colton, or Gaines were not located in any Texas public or census records or the Portal of Texas History search. Ancestry.com, however, showed that David Thomas, acting US Secretary of War,

and J. H. Colton, a cartographer, was the maker of "Colton Map of Mexico and Texas 1856" (1865) and "Map of Texas 1864 (1866)" were in Texas at the time as was George S. Gaines, past agent to the Choctaw in Mississippi who had Texas land for sale; "Causes decided at the present session of the Supreme Court," Battesh, *Admin. of Gaines v. Ann, McLennan*, reversed and remanded, *The Texas Almanac*, Dec 27, 1862; The Ninth US Census (1870) showed Ann Gaines, black, born 1839 in Mississippi, living in Brazoria County.

25. *Munson v. Hallowell and Frankland* and *Terry v. Hallowell*, 26 Tex 474 (1863), two cases combined; "R. P. Jones, From New Orleans," *Galveston Weekly News*, Nov. 12, 1845; "Richard P. Jones (1792-1853)" partner of Charles Frankland, *Geni*, accessed January 20, 2013, http://www.geni.com/people/Richard-Payne-Jones; Ephriam Douglas Adams, ed., "British Correspondence Concerning Texas," Kennedy to Aberdeen, British Consulate, Galveston, Sept. 6th, 1843, *Southwestern Historical Quarterly* 17 (July 1913): 204, 305, 323; *Beers & Smith v. Rhea*, 5 Tex 350 (1849); *Hunt, Admin. v. Butterworth & others*, 21 Tex 133 (1858); *O'Connor v. Silver*, 26 Tex 606 (1863). Hunt, a notary, gave a complete history of the debts of Rhea, Bennett, Silver, in appeals of 1849, 1858, and 1863; *F. Holliman v. Eliza Carroll's Admin.*, 27 Tex 23 (1863); *Ransom White v. R. A. Burney, Trustee*, 27 Tex 50 (1863); Gammel, *Laws of the Republic*, "An Act Prescribing the mode in which Married Persons may dispose of their separate Property," Sec. 1, form for wife's signature.

26. Sterling (Lewis and family) papers, Louisiana State University Archives, Series I, correspondence, 1805-, B: 76-81, folder 2:18, "Natchitoches, Dec 25th, 1863, Dear Mother, . . . your affectionate daughter, A. M. Lobdell"; The District of Columbia Emancipation Act of April 16, 1862. President Abraham Lincoln signed a bill ending slavery in the District of Columbia and provided compensation to owners who were loyal to the Union of up to $300 for each freed slave. The Board of Commissioners approved 930 petitions from former owners for the freedom of 2,989 former slaves. For more see http://www.archives.gov/exhibits/featured_documents/dc_emancipation_act/; *Algier v. Black*, 32 Tex 166 (1869); *Geiselman v. Brown* 33, Tex 323 (1870); *Williams v. Wethered*, 37 Tex 130 (1872); *Fitzgerald v. Turner*, 43 Tex 79 (1875).

27. *Elizabeth, a Slave v. The State*, 27 Tex 329 (1863); Campbell, ed., *Laws of Slavery*, 64.

28. *Napoleon B. Ferguson and others v. Robert A. Ferguson*, 27 Tex 340 (1864).

29. *C. D. Lewis and wife v. Jacob Castleman*, 27 Tex 40 (1864); *James M. Eans v. S. A. Sawyer and others*, 27 Tex 448 (1864); *Sawyer v. Boyle*, 21 Tex 28 (1858); *Pridgen v. Buchannan*, 27 Tex 589 (1864); *Pridgen, Guardian v. Buchannan*, 24 Tex 655 (1860).

30. *F. M. Kendrick, Guardian, etc. v. Taylor & Hart*, 27 Tex 690 (1864); *Bradshaw v. Mayfield*, 18 Tex 21 (1856); *Parks v. Willard*, 1 Tex 350 (1846); *Edrington v. Mayfield*, 5 Tex 364 (1849).

31. Stay Laws explained in *Edmonson v. Garnett* 33 Tex 250 (1870) and *Williams v. Murphy* 36 Tex 174 (1871); *McCulloch v. Renn*, 28 Tex 793 (1866); *McLeod v. Board*, 30 Tex 239 (1867); Randolph B. Campbell, "Notes and Documents: The End of Slavery in Texas, a Research Note," *Southwestern Historical Quarterly* 88: 1 (July 1984): 71-72; Hudson, "Database," year, 1865-1907.

32. Ronald E. Goodwin and Bruce A. Glasrud, "On the Edge of First Freedoms," in Howell, ed., *Seventh Star*, 273-279, 50,000 slaves into Texas as refugees; Ralph A Wooster, *Civil War Texas* (Austin: Texas State Historical Assn., 1999), 33; *Trammell, et al. v. McDade*, 30 Tex 360 (1867); *Bingham, Admin. v. Waterhouse*, 32 Tex 468 (1870); *Holliday et al. v. White & wife*, 33 Tex 448 (1870); *Linn v. Busby*, 47 Tex 600 (1877); *Parish v. Alston*, 65 Tex 194 (1885). Other inheritance cases did not give names, only stated "slaves"; Hudson, "Database"; *Rogers v. Crain*, 30 Tex 284 (1867); *Walton v. Cottingham*, 30 Tex 772 (1868); *Williams v. Arnis*, 30 Tex 37 (1867); *Loggins v. Buck's Admin.*, 33 Tex 114 (1870); *Reavis v. Blackshear*, 30 Tex 753 (1868).

33. Hudson, "Database"; Texas Constitution (1866); Texas Constitution (1869); Paul Womack, "Judiciary," *Handbook of Texas Online*, accessed June 21, 2013, http://tshaonline.org/handbook/online/articles/jzj01, accessed June 21, 2013; *Timmons v. Lacy*, 30 Tex 115(1867); *Parker v. State*, 31 Tex 133 (1868); Barry A. Crouch, "All the Vile Passions"; The Black Codes of 1866," *Southwestern Historical Quarterly* 97, no. 1 (July 1993): 13-36.

34. Baum, *Counterfeit Justice*; Charles F. Robinson II, "Legislated Love in the Lone Star State: Texas and Miscegenation," *Southwestern Histor-*

ical Quarterly 108 (July 2004): 85-86. The names of those twenty-four men convicted of cohabitation are not given; David Work, "US Colored Troops in Texas during Reconstruction, 1865-1867," *Southwestern Historical Quarterly* 109 (Jan 2006): 337-358.

35. Hudson, "Database." Texas mixed race couples by year from sources cited previously: 1849, William and Mary Goyens; 1851, Margaret Gess and Adam Smith; 1853, Letitia Stewart and Henderson Ashworth; 1870, 1871, Betsy and David Webster; 1868, Mary Ann Franks and John Smelzer; 1871, Leah Foster and A. H. Foster; 1872, Sobrina and John C. Clark; 1873, Anna Hill and Solomon Fairfax; 1874, Sally and Augustus Catchings; 1875, Mary and George Clements; 1877, Lettuce Howell and Charles Frasher; 1878, 1883, Phillis and Otho Oldham; 1880, 1884, Sam and Azeline Hearne; Mary and Henry Moore; 1891, Katie and Calvin Bell; 1907, (2) Maria and Isaac Hamilton. See Carroll, *Homesteads Ungovernable,* for additional mixed race couples in Texas.

36. Hudson, "Database"; *Clements v. Crawford,* 42 Tex 601 (1875); Carroll, *Homesteads Ungovernable*, 55-58, 65-72, 224; *Honey v. Clark,* 37 Tex 686 (1872). Clark came to Mexican Texas and lived with Sobrina until his death in 1862. Sobrina sued for a homestead under the Fourteenth Amendment and the local jury agreed. She died in 1868; Clark's children sued as heirs under the Constitution of 1869, Article 12, Sec. 27, were awarded inheritance by jury, but it was overturned by *Clements v. Crawford,* 42 Tex 601 (1875). Ninth Census of the United States (1870) Galveston County, Texas; Eleventh Census of the United States (1900) Galveston County, Texas.

37. *Oldham v. McIver, Admin.,* 49 Tex 556 (1878). Phillis Oldham, wife of twenty-nine years, awarded husband's estate by county court in 1868, district court later claimed jurisdiction, took land away based on *Clements v. Clark* (1875); *Oldham v. McIver, Admin.,* 49 Tex S-36 (1883). Phillis sued and received homestead of 160 acres; *Bonds v. Foster,* 36 Tex 68 (1871), Foster married Leah in Louisiana, took her and children to Ohio, manumitted them, came to Texas, willed thousands of acres to wife and children. Bonds's executor claimed estate insolvent and sold the property. Leah sued for homestead of 160 acres; In 1891 Katie Bell, a white woman, was sent to prison for two years from Galveston for her attempt to marry Calvin Bell with whom she had lived for twenty or more years. Robinson, "Legislated Love," 65-86. In *Loving v.*

Virginia, the US Supreme Court (1967) made state miscegenation laws unconstitutional.

38. *Wright v. Nona Mills* 101 Tex 12 (1907) and *Nona Mills v. Wright*, 102 SW 1118 (1907) descendants of Isaac and Maria Hamilton.

39. Vicki Betts, "A Sacred Charge Upon the Land," in Howell, ed., *Seventh Star*, 257-261; Goodwin and Glasrud, "On the Edge of First Freedoms," 269-279; Brad R. Clampitt, "The Breakup: The Collapse of the Confederate Army," *Southwestern Historical Quarterly* 108 (April 2005): 498-534; Work, "United States Colored Troops," 349-351; Crouch, "'All the Vile Passions,'" 14-18, 23-26, 28-32; Texas Constitutional Convention, (1868-1869), *Journal of the Reconstruction Convention, June 1, 1868*, "The Committee on Lawlessness and Violence Report," June 30, 1868.

40. Campbell, ed., *Laws of Slavery*, 70.

Image 12. Agustina Villarreal de Benavides.

Photograph courtesy of Hector Farias.

From a prominent Laredo family, Agustina Villarreal de Benavides married Santos Benavides in 1842 when she was twenty-one. Unable to bear children, Agustina and her well-known husband adopted several children, including her husband's illegitimate son, Eraclio. She outlived her husband by seventeen years, dying February 2, 1908.

Chapter 7

Mexican-Texan Women in the Civil War

Jerry Thompson and Elizabeth Mata

The Civil War was one of the most cataclysmic and disruptive events in the frequently violent nineteenth-century history of Texas. Every man, woman, and child in the Lone Star State was somehow affected by the tumultuous events that swept over the nation. Before the bloody conflict had run its course in 1865, thousands of young Texans lay dead on a hundred distant battlefields all the way from the gentle farms and fruit orchards of Pennsylvania to the snow-crowned mountains and vast deserts of New Mexico Territory. Often overlooked were the thousands of widows and fatherless children the veterans left behind. In the southern part of Texas and along the Rio Grande, where the war had its greatest impact, many Mexican-Texan women were caught up in the conflict. As was the case elsewhere in the state, the war radically transformed the lives of these women. The effects of the struggle, both political and psychological, could be felt in South Texas well into the next century.

By the late spring of 1861, companies of men swearing allegiance to Texas and the Confederacy, frequently raised by local political leaders who often equipped the men at their own expense, were already drilling in South Texas. Leaving their wives and children, the men came in the hundreds from the farms, ranches, and small villages, "rarin' for a fight." The young recruits were told to expect a ninety-day war and so assumed that they would be home for the fall harvest. Many of the men realized that they were fighting against tremendous odds, but intoxicated by Southern pride and vigor they were anxious to achieve fame in the "glorious" struggle that lay ahead. War in 1861 was still a grand adventure.[1]

Most recruits owned no slaves and were fighting, they said, for states' rights. But underlying such rights that Southerners had argued for decades was the right to own slaves. In the tradition of the knights of Sir Walter Scott's *Ivanhoe*, one young Texan wrote of mounting his "noble steed" and "rejoicing" on his way "for the wars and the jaws of death." By 1863 the same soldier was disillusioned, weary, exhausted, and writing of the "detestable army" and praying for an end to the "bloody struggle."[2] Many *Tejanos* did not necessarily see the war as a contest between North and South, and they entered the conflict for a variety of reasons. Some had strong economic and political ties to powerful political patrons who in turn were closely associated with secessionists in Austin. A few of the older recruits were veterans of the wars in the borderlands in the era of the Texas Republic, and they knew the horrors of real combat. Few officers had any knowledge of military tactics or even how to drill their men. Training camps were established in places such as Laredo, Brownsville, Victoria, and Corpus Christi, where the young recruits, many of them *Tejanos*, were drilled. When not drilling, the men listened to fiery orators or overindulged in intoxicating spirits.

Most of the *Tejanos* who joined the military were in their late teens and early twenties, although men as old as sixty and boys as young as fourteen were not uncommon. Weapons and equipment varied greatly and were often antiquated. One young Texan recorded that his company was "armed with squirrel guns, bear guns, sportsman's guns, shotguns, both single and double barrel, in fact guns of all sorts."[3] A few men had Colt revolvers while others had only Bowie knives or butcher knives. Three companies of Texans rode off to war armed only with nine-foot-long lances that had been seized from the Mexican army more than a decade earlier. As the men and boys went off to war, women, some of them *Tejanas* (as was the case in San Antonio), frequently presented them with colorful, carefully sewn battle flags.

By the end of 1861, approximately twenty-five thousand Texans had enlisted in the Confederate Army. Of the almost ninety regiments recruited from Texas, two-thirds were cavalry, which was a very different pattern than in other states of the Confederacy. Going off to war on foot was less than honorable for Texans who spent much of their life on horseback. Of the 92,145 white males between the ages of eighteen and forty-five who were listed on the 1860 census, approximately 70,000 would serve in the Confederacy's army or the state militia. Of this number, approximately 5,000 had deserted by 1865.[4] Studies indicate that approximately 3,700 Mexican Texans served in either the Confederate Army or the State Militia. Following Lincoln's decision to occupy the Lower Rio Grande Valley in late 1863 and early 1864, almost a thousand *Tejanos* and Mexicanos joined the Union Army.[5] Two-thirds of the Texans who enlisted in either army never left the Southwest. Approximately 97 percent of the *Tejanos* who enlisted never left Texas.

For the Mexican-Texans, one of the most pressing problems before, during, and after the war was the biting and deeply rooted racism in Texas. Reeling from the racial aftermath of the Anglo-Texan victory at San Jacinto in 1836 and the creation of the Republic of Texas that followed, *Tejanos* at places such as San Antonio, Nacogdoches, Goliad and in the borderlands along the Rio Grande, were suddenly forced to adapt to American legislation that altered the region's class and gender relations.[6] Racism prevailed, despite the fact that many *Tejanos* had loyally and gallantly fought and died with William B. Travis at the Alamo and with Sam Houston at San Jacinto. The 1857 Cart War and the 1859-1860 Cortina War in the Lower Rio Grande Valley only exacerbated racial relations in Texas. In 1859 Juan Nepomuceno Cortina, at the head of 1,500 sombrero-crowned and brown-skinned angry Mexicans, was thought at one time to be marching north from the Rio Grande to murder Anglo Texans in their beds.

In many ways the new laws after 1848 loosened oligarchical control over the local population, although in a few towns such as Laredo the landed and mercantile elite continued to dominate politics and the local economy. The Civil War would also help to lure and liberate peons, whose families had been mired in poverty for generations, especially individuals who had crossed the river from Mexico. *Tejanos* of lesser means, especially those who joined the Union Army, often enlisted not to defend the Constitution and save the union but to improve their way of life, to receive a sizeable enlistment bounty, and to escape a dreary and demeaning future of indentured servitude. Many of those who came across the border to enlist brought their families with them. Once *Tejanos* put on the uniform of either the Confederacy or the Union Army, they would never be the same.

With so many men serving in the army, *Tejanas* on the South Texas border and in the south-central part of the state assumed new and expanded roles. In the absence of their husbands, some *Tejanas* had to manage family farms and ranches where they oversaw the planting, plowing, harvesting, and herding of animals, while other women successfully shifted farms from cotton to food production. On small farms Mexican-Texan women, much as their Anglo counterparts did in other parts of the state, planted gardens and worked the crops, or raised chickens, sheep, pigs, and cattle for subsistence, sale, or barter.

Image 13. Poor *Tejana* and child.

From *Le Monde Illustré*.

The contrast between rich and poor along the Rio Grande can be seen by comparing this image with that of the Benavides couple (see Image 12.) With the exception of those caught in slavery, few individuals suffered as much in Texas during the Civil War as *Tejanas*, many of whom were desperately poor as shown here.

As was the case in Laredo, a few *Tejanas* operated small businesses and shops, served as clerks, rented property, and assumed civic roles that would have been unheard of before the war.[7] In the San Antonio area, a few *Tejanas* such as Theodora Navarro, Gertrude Seguin, Susan Carbajal, Mary Garcia, and Susana Montes oversaw slaves much as their husbands and fathers had done before the war.[8] For some Mexican-Texan women on the border, the Civil War was a period of economic boom that developed as a result of the tightening Union naval blockade of the Texas coast and the ever expanding exportation of cotton into Mexico. In fact, for many *Tejanas* in South Texas, the period from 1861 to 1865 became known simply as the "cotton times."

During the war some *Tejana* mothers and their daughters raised money, sewed uniforms, and collected blankets and clothing for the rebel army. In many homes women devoted themselves to spinning, knitting, weaving, and sewing. Unable to afford coffee, women often searched for herbs as a substitute. Very poor women often lived on the verge of starvation in small adobe or board dwellings that were cold in the winter and unbearably hot in the summer. All of the women worked long hours. On the frontier, *Tejanas* also struggled with food shortages and loneliness. They worried incessantly about Lipan Apache and Comanche Indian raids. Yet for many Mexican-Texan women, the war was a welcome reprieve from the constant stress of pregnancy and childbearing.

Some of the best-known Hispanic women during the Civil War were Cubans. Lola Sánchez came from a large Cuban family that settled near St. Augustine, Florida. Angered that her father was accused of being a Confederate spy, Sánchez assumed that role herself. When Union troops occupied her Florida home, she overheard their plans and informed nearby Confederates of a pending raid. Perhaps even more famous was a Cuban immigrant, a teenager from New Orleans named Loreta Janeta Velázquez, who enlisted in the Confederate Army against her soldier-husband's wishes. As the cross-dressing Lt. Harry Buford, Velázquez fought in several battles, including the First Battle of Bull Run and Shiloh, where she was wounded, before later serving as a Confederate spy. Losing faith in the Confederate cause, by 1863 Velázquez was spying for the Union. In 1876 she scandalized America by revealing her role-breaking sexuality in the memoir, *The Woman in Battle.* Velázquez also had the temerity to criticize the war.[9]

Undoubtedly the most famous *Tejana* during the Civil War was the unfortunate sixty-three-year-old Josefa "Chipita" Rodriguez. Reportedly born in Mexico in 1799, Chipita is thought to have moved with her father to the Nueces River community of San Patricio de Hibernia when she was very young. Her father Pedro was thought to have deserted from Gen. Antonio López de Santa Anna's army in the waning months of the Texas Revolution. By the time of the Civil War, not far from San Patricio on the banks of the Aransas River, Chipita was furnishing travelers on the Cotton Road leading to the border with hot meals and a bed on the porch of her cabin. When a horse trader named John Savage was murdered with an axe near her residence, presumably for the $600 in gold he was carrying, Chipita and Juan Silvera, who may have been her illegitimate son, were accused of robbery and murder.[10]

Although John Savage's gold-filled saddlebags were found untouched near Savage's horse, which raised substantial doubt as to the motive for the crime, it was widely rumored that Savage's bloody corpse, which was found stuffed in a burlap bag, was the work of Chipita's bloody axe. Both Rodriguez and Silvera were indicted and convicted in the Fourteenth District Court of Judge Benjamin F. Neal. Although Chipita maintained her innocence throughout the trial, she refused to testify in her own defense and remained silent, perhaps, it has been speculated, to protect her guilty son. Despite a recommendation of mercy by the all-Anglo jury, Judge Neal ordered Chipita to be executed. While she was being held in the home of Patricio County Sheriff William Means at Meansville, two unsuccessful attempts to lynch the sixty-three-year-old *Tejana* were thwarted. According to legend, Chipita was also kept in leg irons and chained to a wall at the county courthouse for a time.

Local legend has it that children brought her candy and corn shucks to make cigarettes. During a rainstorm on Friday, November 13, 1863, Chipita was taken from the county courthouse and hanged from a large oak tree. Her last words were said to have been, "No soy culpable" (I am not guilty). One witness to the hanging claimed to have heard a moan from Chipita's makeshift coffin as she was being buried in an unmarked grave. Many believe that her ghost continues to haunt San Patricio to this day, especially when a woman is to be executed.[11]

Through the years Chipita has become a folk legend. Her enduring legacy has been the subject of two operas, numerous monographs and endless newspaper accounts. Rachel Bluntzer Hervert's lengthy poem, "Shadows on the Nueces," and Teresa Palomo Acosta's poem, "Chipita," both portray the unfortunate *Tejana* as a heroine.[12] In 1985 state senator Carlos Truan of Corpus Christi asked the Texas legislature to absolve Chipita Rodriguez of murder, and the Sixty-ninth Legislature passed a resolution to that effect, which was signed by Governor Mark White. Chipita's hanging remains a significant and eerie episode of the *Tejana* experience during the tumultuous era of the Civil War.[13]

Chipita provides an excellent example of the marginality that many *Tejanas*, especially those who were poor, experienced within the United States legal system. *Tejana* washerwomen, ranch or farm workers and servants, as well as some homeowners, had little recourse against violent sexual assault. Such women struggled to punish their assailants, and officials were slow to arrest perpetrators of sexual assaults.[14] Frequently, the heaviest burden of prosecution fell on the female victims. The Rio Grande Frontier presented a special problem for prosecutors in that criminals could easily slip across the international boundary. Religion was undoubtedly another reason for prejudice.[15]

Largely because of the racism that existed in Texas, a number of *Tejanos*, many taking their families with them, fled to Mexico during the war. One such individual was Capt. José Ángel Navarro, Harvard University's only *Tejano* in the Confederacy and the son of José Navarro of Texas

Revolution fame, who fled to Mexico in 1863. Writing from San Fernando de Rosas, Coahuila, south of Eagle Pass, on December 1, 1863, Captain Navarro told Santiago Vidaurri, governor of Nuevo Leon and Coahuila, that he had arrived in Mexico "for the purpose of settling permanently." It "is enough to tell you," Navarro went on to say, "that I left because the military authorities in San Antonio treated me unjustly."[16] Writing from Brazos Santiago on the coast near Brownsville only weeks before the end of the war, Antonio Abad Dias, a fifty-year-old second lieutenant in the Union Army, could only recall with horror the crimes inflicted on *Tejanos* by Confederate authorities, especially after the controversial 1862 draft. The "horrible and animalistic acts," he wrote, were "not unlike a swarm of bees and boils the blood in your veins."[17]

Serious problems broke out in the predominantly *Tejano* Second Texas Cavalry (Union) when less than a year after the regiment was recruited in the Lower Rio Grande Valley, it was decided to transfer the men to Louisiana. Many of the officers who resigned argued that they had enlisted only for the war in Texas, and they could not be separated from their wives and children. For instance Second Lt. Santos Cadena submitted his resignation in May 1864, saying that he knew little English and was concerned about the welfare of his family in Rio Grande City. "I have a large family from whom I have been long separated and who now require my immediate presence and support," the thirty-year-old Cadena wrote.[18] The large number of desertions in the regiment was thought to be the result of many of the men leaving the army to "visit their homes and fear to come back."[19] Desperate for food to support their families, many of the men who deserted were selling their arms and equipment in Mexico.

Retaining some of the Spanish law relating to family relationships, *Tejanas*, depending on age and marital status, had the right to establish contracts, had control over their own property (as was the case with some of the Benavides women in Laredo), and they could sue and be sued in court. Women from the landed and mercantile elite, because of the family's literacy, wealth and political clout, could pursue litigation of any nature, while the poor and dispossessed women rarely shared that recourse.[20] Although there are few judicial records from the Civil War era involving *Tejanas*, there is at least one case in 1863 of a *Tejana* who, while gambling, stabbed a man over a disagreement at a ranch near Brownsville.[21] Shortly after the war, a woman in San Antonio named Mariana killed another woman at a *Diez y Seis de Septiembre* fandango.[22]

The mob violence against *Tejanos* that peaked in the decade before the war seems to have subsided somewhat during the war, although the violence rose again in the 1870s. The mistreatment of Mexican-Texans, regardless of gender, reflected the "deep-seated racial prejudice on the part of Anglo-Texans." When four *Tejano* deserters were apprehended a few miles from San Antonio, they were disarmed, but then released. It was feared that if they were taken to San Antonio, vigilantes whom one observer characterized as a "blood-thirsty mob" would "hang them in the plaza."[23] In fact mob violence against Mexican-Texans in the Lone Star State was "greater in scope and longer in duration than anywhere in the United States."[24]

Another aspect of the war on the Texas-Mexico border that influenced *Tejanas* was the flight of runaway slaves into Mexico. At the same time, debt peons from Northern Mexico fled into Texas. All of them sought refuge and freedom on the other side of the river.[25] While there were few slaves along the Rio Grande, slavery remained relevant in the area, because runaway slaves frequently passed through the region on their flight into Mexico. Before the war, Guadalupe County passed a resolution prohibiting "Mexican peons" from entering the county "because of their alleged sympathy with bonds-people."[26] Although there is evidence that some of the population, especially in the areas of San Antonio, Gonzales, and Goliad, assisted runaway slaves, there is also evidence that some *Tejanos* were involved as slave catchers. For example, in November 1860, Santos Benavides, who was a leading economic and political force in Laredo, was praised by the *Corpus Christi Ranchero* for apprehending runaway slaves. Evidently Benavides had even crossed into Mexico in search of runaway slaves, hoping to collect reward money.[27] So extensive had been the flight of slaves from Texas that armed expeditions frequently crossed the Rio Grande in search of runaway slaves.[28] Another prominent border resident of the Lower Rio Grande Valley, Rodrigo Hinojosa, was also praised for capturing two runaway slaves and returning them to their owners in Texas.[29]

There is also evidence that African Americans and Mexicans, in defiance of the miscegenation laws in Texas, intermarried on both sides of the river. Even before the war, mixed marriages, especially between *Tejanas* and Anglo or European males, had become common in Texas, especially in places such as Brownsville, Laredo, and San Antonio. *Tejanas* were considered legally white and could marry Anglos or European immigrants, but not someone of African descent. As early as 1837, Texas had enacted an anti-miscegenation law that barred marriage between whites and anyone of African descent.[30] From the time of the Spanish conquest, the Catholic Church had maintained the sole authority to sanction marriage and was the only recognized church. However, when South Texas and much of the borderlands (including the area south of the Nueces River) fell under American control following the Treaty of Guadalupe-Hidalgo in 1848, marriage options and religion choices expanded greatly. There seems little doubt that the pattern that developed after the arrival of Anglo-American colonists in Texas was due to the decreasing influence of the Catholic Church over marital issues, and interracial marriage accelerated in the chaos of the war in 1861.[31]

Several mixed marriages between *Tejanas* and Anglo and European males were essential to the cause of the Civil War in south Texas. Such marriages gave Anglo and European men access to land and power. In Laredo interracial unions among the landed and mercantile elite resulted in racial lines becoming excessively blurred. Within a generation it became difficult to judge an individual's ethnicity by their first or last name. One such Laredo union occurred on June 1, 1857, with the marriage of John Zirvas Leyendecker, an immigrant from the German state of Nassau who became a captain in the Confederate Army, to Maria Andrea Benavides, the younger sister of Santos Benavides.[32] Andrea later suffered a miscarriage in August 1857 after five days of excruciating pain, but she went on to give birth to four children over the next five years. The couple also adopted a young Anglo-Texan orphan in Fredericksburg on December 24, 1861.[33] Tragedy struck the family when Andrea became critically ill of consumption and died in the midst of the war on September 11, 1863. During the several months of her illness, Andrea was nursed by a sister, Juliana, whom Leyendecker married at the St. Augustine Church in Laredo during August 1865, with Santos Benavides and his wife Agustina acting as sponsors. Besides caring for her sister's five children, Juliana gave birth over the next fourteen years to ten children. She lived until June of 1926, outlasting her soldier-husband by twenty-four years.[34]

Perhaps the most significant mixed marriage in South Texas was that of Petra Vela to a Quaker-educated rancher and steamboat entrepreneur named Mifflin Kenedy, who had become one of the most influential men in the Lower Rio Grande Valley. Another successful and significant marriage was that of Salomé Ballí, whose first husband, John Young, had died in 1859. Her second marriage to John McAllen produced a son, John B. McAllen, who along with a son by her first marriage, John B. Young, inherited a vast ranching empire in Hidalgo County.[35] In the Lower Rio Grande Valley, Edward Doughtery, an Irish immigrant who served as one of Brownsville's first alderman and Cameron County district attorney, married María Marcela Garcia in 1847. The couple raised seven children. A leading and influential political figure in the Lower Rio Grande Valley, Doughtery had fought at Palo Alto and Resaca de la Palma during the Mexican-American War. He established the small trading community of Rudyville near Relampago in Hidalgo County. As state representative on the eve of the Civil War, Doughtery introduced a bill in the legislature in 1859 that called for the creation of a peonage system in Texas similar to that of Mexico. In a heated debate on the floor of the House of Representatives, Ángel Navarro, one of the few *Tejanos* in the legislature at the time, vociferously opposed the bill, saying that it was "an insult to the Mexican population of the State of Texas," and that it would drag "the poor and degraded natives" into bondage and "deprive them of their liberty [and] their earnings." The measure went down in defeat by a vote of forty-two to thirty-two.[36]

In San Antonio one of the more significant mixed marriages was that of Carolina Angela de la Garza, who was wed to Bartholomew Joseph DeWitt, a prominent frontier merchant, sutler, and one of the founders of San Angelo. In fact the settlement of gambling houses, saloons, and trading posts on the North Concho River was named in honor of his wife. Over the years "Santa Angela" was corrupted to "San Angela," and eventually the name was changed to San Angelo in 1883. The mother of five children, Carolina died unexpectedly in San Antonio in 1866, perhaps a victim of the cholera epidemic that swept the city at that time.[37] A sister, Margarita de la Garza, was married to James L. Truehart, a well-to-do Virginia-born city alderman. Vicenta Yturri, from one of San Antonio's leading families, was married to Ernest B. Edmunds, a respected Louisiana merchant.[38]

In the lingering legacy of the long Spanish colonial era, men remained the principal patriarchs in a "hierarchical society sanctioned by both the Catholic Church and the state for the purpose of maintaining social and political stability."[39] Although they could not vote, *Tejana* women exercised leadership roles, especially landholding women, including *Tejanas* such as the De la Garzas and Yturris. Not only did they retain their traditional female roles in society, which included childbearing and childrearing, cleaning, preparing food, spinning, weaving, and making clothing, but the war also thrust them into roles and additional labors that were normally those of men. Moreover, unlike Spanish law, which had granted them a larger degree of equality, English common law saw *Tejanas* as inherently unequal. For example, Agustina Villarreal de Benavides, the wife of Col. Santos Benavides, the highest ranking Mexican Texan in the Confederate Army who commanded a Civil War regiment that bore his name, exercised considerable economic independence. A family crisis occured in the midst of the war when her colonel-husband fathered a child with Josefa Gonzalez in Guerrero, Tamaulipas, in 1863. In time, however, the child, Santos Eraclio Villarreal de Benavides, was accepted by the family, and Agustina saw to his rearing and education. Two decades later, Benavides would remember how his "dear wife" received Eraclio at "two years of age" and how "she raised him and took care of him as a mother until [his] death" in Monterrey, Nuevo León, at the age of nineteen in June of 1883.[40]

In some rare instances the position and rank of *Tejanas* seems to have increased within the social, political, and economic spheres during the war. Although in most cases women's rank in society did not come close to the status or prestige of men, their standing at home and in their community enabled them to gain a degree of power, confidence, and influence. Of course, the range of confidence and influence varied greatly between the lower and upper classes of *Tejanas. Tejana* elite in San Antonio helped to supply their husbands with clothing, often learning how to card, spin, and knit wool. Everyone, rich and poor alike, planted gardens and learned to do without the basic staples they had enjoyed in the antebellum years.[41]

A large majority of the women of Mexican ancestry living in Texas during the Civil War were classified as non-elite. Many of these women were washerwomen, ranch workers, and domestic servants. The workload of their personal household duties was piled on top of their other responsibilities. Some *Tejanas* were able to earn a small wage that went directly to household and family expenses, which were mostly under the authority of the male head of the family. Seldom were women allowed to list "homeowner" below their name on legal documents. Studies indicate that many Mexican-Texan women married very young, and many took on heavy workloads at the age of fifteen or sixteen and in some cases as young as thirteen. For example, Senovia Cervantes, who applied for a pension at the age of seventy in 1899, shortly after the death of her husband, recalled how she was only thirteen when she married her soldier-husband, Manuel Cervantes, in San Antonio in 1859.[42] Like other young women, she would have barely begun puberty.

Some *Tejanas* in San Antonio and along the Texas-Mexico border and the Gulf Coast were attracted to the army to wash, cook, or serve as prostitutes. Prostitutes provided their services in their own huts or tents, or in the soldiers' tents. Undoubtedly, as was the case elsewhere, prostitutes did double duty by cleaning, cooking, washing, and performing other traditional domestic female tasks. Many men saw prostitutes (many of them company laundresses) as having been forced into prostitution as a result of the exigencies of war, and viewed them sympathetically.[43]

Brothels thrived in Texas border communities such as Brownsville, across the Rio Grande in Matamoros, and downriver at Bagdad. Venereal diseases, especially syphilis and gonorrhea, were rampant, plaguing one out of every twelve soldiers. The *Brownsville Ranchero* described Bagdad at the mouth of the Rio Grande as a place where "fandangos were held every night and women as beautiful as houris exhibit their charms, without the least reserve."[44] Bagdad, another observer said, consisted of "dirty looking buildings" where "blockade runners, desperadoes, the vile of both sexes, adventurers, the Mexican and the rebel" gathered, and "numberless groggeries and houses of worst fame [where] vice in its lowest form held high carnival."[45] Women were arrested in San Antonio for allegedly keeping "a disorderly house for the purpose of public prostitution, and as a resort for prostitutes, vagabonds, free negroes, and slaves."[46]

The traditional assumption has been that Mexican-Texan women in the mid-nineteenth century were largely enslaved by their dominant husbands, that their lives were spent largely at home, and that they had little to no public voice or forms of independence. However, historian Omar S. Valerio-Jiménez, in his in-depth study on the Mexican-American search for personal identity, ably argues that *Tejanas* had gained a large degree of political and social independence and influence in the years leading to the Civil War. This may be true, but as Valerio-Jiménez goes on to conclude, *Tejanas* were still faced with severe and often debilitating ethnic and gender discrimination.[47] Moreover, no one in Texas during the Civil War, with the exception of slaves and especially Unionists (who were brutalized and sometimes hanged), were as badly discriminated against as *Tejanas.* This was especially true of anyone who was of dark complexion and who had recently arrived in the state and knew no English.

While scholars have noted that Anglo women's growing independence was significantly greater than that of their minority counterparts at this time, Valerio-Jimenez believes the gap was not significant, largely as a result of the decreasing influence of the Catholic Church in Texas over marital issues and the drastic increase in interethnic marriages (normally an Anglo male marrying a Mexican-Texan female, as previously noted).[48]

The years leading to the Civil War brought a flood of families into Texas from Mexico. Most were escaping the cruel and ruthless Mexican justice system, as well as the political turmoil and instability south of the border. They were hoping for a better way of life north of the Rio Grande. Many of the "non-elitist women" who crossed the border settled in areas such as Laredo, Brownsville, San Antonio, and along the lower Nueces and San Antonio rivers. They were, much as those who illegally crossed the Rio Grande 150 years later, aware of their unfortunate circumstances and the fact that they were vulnerable to rape, kidnapping, assault, abandonment, and even incest. Valerio-Jimenez writes that lower-class *Tejanas* quickly became aware that such offenses would not be ignored under the American judicial system, and they felt better prepared in taking jobs as washerwomen, maids, or servants.[49] Unfortunately, it was in such work places that the women were susceptible to acts of violence and cruel behavior. Even though the women felt safer in Texas, they were subject to economic privation if their husbands, brothers, or fathers were arrested and incarcerated. There is some evidence, Valerio-Jiménez believes, that during the war it was probable that a large number of impoverished *Tejanas* claimed that their husbands were off fighting, when in reality they were imprisoned. This excuse allowed for them to receive aid from neighbors and local charity forces.[50]

In contrast to the lives of *Tejanas* in counties such as Cameron, Hidalgo, and even Bexar, where there were large numbers of Mexican Texans, the situation in Webb (Laredo) was somewhat different. Here the Mexican Texan elite (such as the García, Sanchez, Farias, Martinez, and Benavides families) had always dominated the county, both economically and politically. Although the *Tejano* elite in the Lower Rio Grande Valley had largely been pushed aside and excluded from political office and the poor in counties such as Cameron were seen as little more than illiterate peons, the elite in Laredo traditionally dominated the political scene.[51] Yet all along the border and elsewhere, Mexican-Texan women continued to live much as they had before the war, mired in a life of poverty, fear, and uncertainty. It is true that some lower-class men did fight on the Union side "to seek revenge against the largely pro-Confederate American minority by siding with the Union."[52] Consequently, this meant an even harsher life for the *Tejanas* left behind at home, for once rumor spread that their husbands were fighting for "the enemy," prejudice and racism only increased.

An analysis of Texas Confederate Pension applications by *Tejana* widows in the period from 1899 to 1917 provides a revealing glimpse into the lives of these poor—often desperately poor—aging widows who were dependent upon the generosity of the state for postwar pension benefits. In awarding pensions for Confederate service, Texas, like most other Southern states, confined its relief to veterans or their widows who were residents of Texas and who were disabled or indigent. Those who did list an occupation frequently indicated they were continuing to work into their late sixties and seventies as laundresses or domestic servants.

Receiving a pension required a written and certified application that consisted of a series of questions relating to age, health, income (if any), date and place of marriage, residence, as well as the military service of the deceased husband and the unit he had served. The application had to be signed by the county judge and approved by the county commissioners. For most *Tejanas*, the pension was their only source of income. Most of the widows were illiterate and dependent on the county judge for assistance in completion of their applications. Beginning in 1899 when pensions became available, at least seventy *Tejana* widows (mostly in Bexar and Webb Counties) successfully completed applications. In some instances they included mortuary warrants in hopes of recovering expenses for the burial of a deceased husband, usually forty-five dollars: forty dollars for the casket and five dollars for the hearse.[53]

In Bexar County, for example, Juanita Castillo, signing with an "x," did not get around to applying for a pension until 1917 (at the age of seventy-three), when she was living at Elmandorf, southeast of San Antonio. Her husband, Sevariano Castillo, who had died in 1893, had been with Capt. Joseph M. Penaloza in the Eighth Texas Infantry and had ridden with Col. Santos Benavides later in the war. Castillo indicated that she was only sixteen when she was wed at the beginning of the war in 1861.[54] Legend holds that many couples married at the start of the war for the sake of "living in the moment." Marriage at a young age was common for Mexican-Texan women, however, especially in the mid-nineteenth century.

Many of the widows owned no property. An exception was Lucia de Treviño, who at age sixty-eight applied for a pension in Laredo in 1899. The literate Treviño proudly owned a house valued at $700. In fact the 1900 census shows that Treviño was the head of a household and was financially responsible for three children.[55] Since her husband died in 1876, it is probable that Trevino achieved a slightly higher socio-economic status than other pensioners, and she may have exaggerated the degree of her indigence. Her ability to read and write, not to mention her property status, made her somewhat unique among the *Tejanas* who sought a pension after 1899.[56] Rosa F. de Ceballos, who had married Pedro Ceballos in San Antonio in 1853, indicated in her pension application that she was striving to make a living by her sewing. Her husband, a silversmith born in Mexico, had helped to raise a company for the Third Texas Infantry. The captain had been forced to resign in November 1863, largely because he was "a Mexican and of limited English education." The resignation was said to have been "an act of charity to his family" because senior officers in the regiment did "not want to disgrace him." In 1864, however, Ceballos became an ordnance officer in Col. Santos Benavides' regiment in the more relaxed ethnic environment at Laredo. After the war Ceballos became a deputy sheriff in Bexar County, but following his death in 1894, Lucia had slipped into poverty.[57]

Almost all of the Mexican-Texan women pensioners in Webb County had married men who had ridden with Col. Benavides during the war. One such individual was Andrea F. DeLeza, a poor "washer woman" who lived in a small "lumber" house valued at forty dollars on a lot owned by the city of Laredo for which she paid no rent. She had married her husband, Clemente, at the end of the war at St. Augustine Church in Laredo.[58] Francisca J. de Jiménez, sixty-two and a "domestic," applied for a pension in 1899, saying that her husband, Angel Jiménez, who passed away in 1894, had also served in Benavides' Regiment.[59] A sixty-seven-year-old "washer woman" named Carlota Guerrero de Escobar, who lived in a house valued at fifty dollars on the outskirts of Laredo, said that her husband Felix Escobar had fought on the border with Benavides. The two had wed in the small village of San Ignacio eight years before the war.[60]

Unfortunately for historians, few personal letters or other documents relating to the lives of low income *Tejanas* who lived in the tumultuous years from 1861 to 1865 are known to exist. Although the pension records indicated that a number of widows became impoverished in the late nineteenth and early twentieth centuries, a few women did live comfortably before, during, and after the war.[61]

Partly as a result of the widespread illiteracy among *Tejana*s, who had never had the opportunity for an education, there are few existing letters or other documents dating from the war of historical significance. A set of valuable letters by two very well-educated and literate brothers-in-law, Capt. Joseph Rafael de la Garza and Capt. Manuel Yturri y Castillo, provide the historian with a window into the war. Capts. Yturri y Castillo and de la Garza were two of the few elite *Tejanos* from South Texas. Both men were fluent in English and Spanish, and were part of the ranching and landholding Bexareño elite. Their correspondence reflects each man's deep affection for their families in San Antonio, as well as the loneliness and desperate conditions among many soldiers at the time. Most of de la Garza's letters were written to his mother, María Josefa Menchaca de la Garza, while Yturri's letters were mostly to his wife, Elena.[62] Although Captain de la Garza was killed at the bloody Battle of Mansfield in 1864, the letters of the two men reveal their relationships with their wives, mothers, and sisters. Through their many letters written from the fields of Arkansas and the swamps of Louisiana, Yturri's and de la Garza's correspondence offers a window into the daily lives of *Tejana* women during the war and their everyday struggles.[63] Their letters illuminate the strong relationships that existed in the two very influential and extended families, especially between the men and the important women in their lives. For instance in most of Captain de la Garza's letters, it is evident that the bond between mother and son, as might be expected in Hispanic families, was much stronger than what existed between him and his sisters.[64] He continuously asked for prayer and a quick response to his correspondence. "I am tired of writing home," he wrote, "but it seems all of you have forgotten me completely. How much work can it be for you to sit down and write a few lines?"[65] De la Garza could be very demanding in his letters to his mother, sometimes asking for money, on one occasion to pay for a chair he had purchased.[66] Such correspondence indicates the subservient role that women played in the war, and the assumption that women were expected to cater to the men in their life.[67]

Throughout the war the twenty-four-year-old Capt. Manuel Yturri carried the heavy burden of a husband in the form of constant worry about the welfare of his family. In 1862 when Yturri left for the war, he not only said goodbye to his twenty-one-year-old wife, Elena, but also left his one-year-old son, Manuel Jr. Yturri's letters are filled with worry for his family, especially the various illnesses they endured and their economic stress. Yturri frequently reminded his "beloved Elenita" to write him constantly and to keep him informed about events in San Antonio.[68]

Although her letters are sadly missing from the historical record, it is obvious that Elena Yturri took control over the financial responsibilities of the family and as well as the social obligations of a young *Tejana.* In a letter fragment that dates from 1864, Yturri writes: "My darling, you can't imagine what I would give to be by your side. I would gladly be a private in Texas only to see you and our children again and be at home a month at your side . . . Instead here we have a miserable life eating corn bread, coffee made from corn without sugar . . . I have no money, not even one cent and if I had it it wouldn't help because here you can't find anything."[69]

The war had been a painful and trying time for Elena Yturri and hundreds of other Latinas. It was a time of hunger, weariness, and despair that would not soon be forgotten. *Tejanas* experienced racism, gender discrimination, endless hardships, hunger, fear, and in many instances, the loss of loved ones. But they had lent hearts and hands on the home front in the nation's greatest struggle: the Civil War. With time, the war would fade into memory, and the contributions the *Tejanas* made would largely be forgotten.

Image 14. Mexican-Texan Confederate Widows.

Bexar

Russell, Saluda	Turner, Julia	Varga, John (Mrs.)
Tijerina, Juliana Vargas de	Uriega, Justa Villagran de (Mrs.)	
Townsend, Flora	Valdez, Apolonia	

Karnes

Flores, Reter

Matagorda

Flores, Isabel

Victoria

Espitia, Fernandes

Wilson

Aguilar, Estefana M. de	Gortari, Maria T.	San Miguel, Florencio C.
Arredondo, Guadalupe	Griego, Clara M. de	Trevino, Pilar F. de
Balades, Sicilia	Lang, Julia	Ximenes, Antonia C.
Botello, Carlota	Orasco, Vicentia Mindiola	Ximenes, Josefa C.
Cardenas, Amelia	Reed, Lucinda	Ybarbo, Vital (Mrs.)
Garza, Ester V.	Roxo, Maria Engracia	Zerda, Mariade Jesus

Zapata

Navarro, Gunersinda R. de

Webb

Alafila, Francisca Baco de	Gamboa, Jacinta R. de	Mendiola, Andrea G.	DeZapata, Amada G. de
Alegria, Jesusa Gonzalez de	Garcia, Crescencia R. de	Mendiola, R. B. De (Mrs)	Zuniga, Felilpa Flores de
Botello, Antonia Gonzales de	Garcia, Helena G. de	Molina, Juana Z. de	
Botello, Ignacia S. de	Garza, Adelaida M. de	Molina, Juanita de	
Ceballos, Rosa F. de	Gil, Cecelia H. de	Moreno, Natividad R. de (Mrs)	
Chevalier, Margarita C. de	Gonzalez, Celedonia G. de	Ochoa, Antonio Trevino de	
Ciprian, R.S. de (Mrs)	Guer[r]ero, Romana R. de	Olbera, F.M. de (Mrs)	
De Mendiola, Paula Gonzales	Guzman Veronica G. de	Olvera, Refugia B. de	
Deleza, Andrea F.	Herrera, Francisca Torres	Paredes, Nasaria R. de	
Escamilla, Anestacia F. de	Herrera, Romana Luna de	Ramirez, Jesusa L. Vda. de	
Escobar, Carlota Guerrero de	Jimenez, Francisca J. de	Riojas, Nestora G. de	
Gamboa, Gertrudes C. de	Juarez, Susana Telles de	Trevino, Lucia R. de	

Table 1: Confederate Mexican-Texan Civil War Widows

Image 15. Texas Union Widows.

Bexar	Presidio, Jeff Davis
Fisk, Simona (50)	Ash, Margarita (45)
Gonzalez, Jose[fa] (41)	
Duval	**Nueces**
Morales, Macima V.; Morales, Jesus	Villa, Juana (26)
El Paso	
Acosta, Valentina; Acosta Nicolas	
Escabante, Josefa A.; Escabante, Ramon	

Table 2: Widows of Texas Union Veterans as Determined by the Census

NOTES

1. Ralph A. Wooster, "Texas in the Civil War," *Handbook of Texas Online,* accessed December 24, 2013, http://www.tshaonline.org/handbook/online/article/qds02. Perhaps the best overall study of Texas in the war is Ralph A. Wooster, *Texas and Texans in the Civil War* (Austin: Eakin Press, 1995).
2. Jerry D. Thompson, ed., *Westward the Texans: The Civil War Journal of Private William Randolph Howell* (El Paso: Texas Western Press, 1990), 55; and William Randolph Howell to Sallie Patrick May 4, 1863, William Randolph Howell Papers, Center for American History, University of Texas at Austin.
3. Martin H. Hall, *Sibley's New Mexico Campaign* (Austin: University of Texas Press, 1960), 37.
4. Wooster, "Texas in the Civil War," 2.
5. Jerry Thompson, *Vaqueros in Blue and Gray* (Austin: Presidial Press, 1976); Jerry Thompson, *Mexican Texans in the Union Army* (El Paso: Texas Western Press, 1986).
6. Omar S. Valerio-Jiménez, *River of Hope: Forging Identity and Nation in the Rio Grande Borderlands* (Durham: Duke University Press, 2013), 176.
7. See for example, Invoice signed by Josefa Treviño, October 1-November 30, 1862 (twenty dollars rent for quarters for Capt. Santos Benavides at Laredo); Teresa Benavides, April 1-30, 1863 (fifteen dollars rent for office of commanding officer at Laredo), and Agustina Benavides, May 1-31, 1863 (fifteen dollars rent for room for quartermaster at Laredo); All in Confederate Papers Relating to Citizens or Business Firms, 1861-65, Record Group 109, Roll 58, National Archives, Washington, DC. Agustina Villarreal de Benavides was the wife of Col. Santos Benavides, the highest ranking Mexican-Texan in the Confederate Army. To some extent the war was very much a business affair for the Benavides family.
8. Eighth Census, Slave Schedules (1860), Bexar County, Tex., NA

9. "Rebel: Loreta Velázquez, Secret Soldier of the American Civil War." A WPBT, PBS documentary; Loreta Velázquez, *The Woman in Battle: The Civil War Narrative of Loreta Velázquez, Cuban Woman and Confederate Soldier.* Ebook (2013).

10. The scholarship on Josefa "Chipita" Rodriguez is abundant. Rachel Bluntzer Hebert, *Shadows on the Nueces* (Atlanta: Banner, 1942); Vernon Smylie, *A Noose for Chipita* (Corpus Christi: Texas News Syndicate Press, 1960); Ruel McDaniel, "The Day they Hanged Chipita," *Texas Parade* (September, 1962); Ruthe Winegarten, *Finder's Guide to the Texas Women: A Celebration of History Exhibit Archives* (Denton: Texas Woman's University Library, 1984); and Marylyn Underwood, "Rodriguez, Josefa [Chipita], *Handbook of Texas Online,* accessed December 24, 2013, http://www.tshaonline.org/handbook/online/articles/fro50.

11. Silvera was given five years in the state penitentiary, *The Ranchero,* October 29, 1863.

12. "The Hanging of Chepita [*sic*] Rodriguez," accessed December 23, 2013, http://www.tamu.edu/faculty/ccbn/dewitt/irishchipita.htm. In *From San Patricio de Hiberia: The Forgotten Colony.* This website also has the "Minutes of the District Court of San Patricio County," along with the indictment and sentence: "The State of Texas vs. Juan Silvera and Chepita [*sic*] Rodriguez." Another fascinating case of hanging was that of a *nuevomexicano* woman, Paula Angel, who was hanged in Las Vegas, New Mexico, in April 1861. Angel would go down in history as the first and last woman to be executed in New Mexico. Robert J. Tórrez, *Myth of the Hanging Tree: Stories of Crime and Punishment in Territorial New Mexico* (Albuquerque: University of New Mexico Press, 2008).

13. Rodriguez was the second woman to be legally hanged in the Lone Star State.

14. Valerio-Jiménez, *River of Hope,* 188.

15. See Jean A. Stuntz, "Tejanas: Hispanic Women on the Losing Side of the Texas Revolution," in Mary L. Scheer, ed. *Women and the Texas Revolution* (Denton: University of North Texas Press, 2012), 56.

16. Ángel Navarro to Santiago Vidaurri, December 1, 1863, Correspondencia de Santiago Vicaurri, Archivo General del Estado de Nuevo León, Monterrey, Mexico.
17. Pronunciamiento, Antonio Abad Dias, April 17, 1865, Cecilio Vela Papers, private collection.
18. Santos Cadena to G. W. Paschal, May 19, 1864, Cadena Compiled Service Record, Group 94, Adjutant General's Records, National Archives.
19. John L. Haynes to F. J. Herron, May 2, 1864, Regimental papers of the Second Texas Cavalry, RG 94, NA.
20. Ibid. Also, Manuel G. Gonzales, *Hispanic Elite of the Southwest* (El Paso: Texas Western Press, 1989).
21. Brownsville *Daily Cosmopolitan*, November 5, 1863.
22. San Antonio *Herald*, September 21, 23, 1865.
23. R. H. Williams, *With the Border Ruffians: Memories of the Far West, 1852-1868* (Lincoln: University of Nebraska Press, 1982), 75.
24. William D. Carrigan and Clive Webb, *Mob Violence against Mexicans in the United States, 1848-1928* (New York: Oxford University Press, 2013), 56. Nine *Tejanos* and *Mexicanos* whom Confederate authorities labeled "Black Republicans" were massacred at the Clareño Ranch in Zapata County on the Rio Grande in April 1861. In March 1863 the murder of teamsters along the Cotton Road in the vicinity of the King Ranch, similar to the violent racial intolerance that characterized the infamous Cart War in 1857, forced Confederate authorities to issue orders for the apprehension of the individuals responsible for the murders. See Jerry Thompson and Lawrence T. Jones III, *Civil War and Revolution on the Rio Grande Frontier: A Narrative and Photographic History* (Austin: Texas State Historical Association, 2004), 36, 43.
25. James David Nichols, "The Line of Liberty: Runaway Slaves and Fugitive Peons in the Texas-Mexico Borderlands," *Western Historical Quarterly* 44 (Winter 2013): 413-33. The degree to which there was an organized underground railroad in Texas and to what extent *Tejanos* and *Tejanas* played a role in the escape of slaves into Mexico has yet to be fully explored.
26. Arnoldo De León, *They Called Them Greasers: Anglo Attitudes toward Mexicans in Texas, 1821-1990* (Austin: University of Texas Press, 1983),

49-50; for reaction to interracial marriages in San Antonio, see San Antonio *Herald*, June 15, 1858.

27. Corpus Christi *Ranchero*, November 17, 1860; Thompson, *Vaqueros in Blue and Gray*, 12.
28. For an excellent study of escaped slaves and fugitive peons, see James David Nichols, "The Line of Liberty: Runaway Slaves and Fugitive Peons in the Texas-Mexico Borderlands," *Western Historical Quarterly* 44, no. 4 (Winter, 2013): 413-33.
29. Ibid., March 17, 1860. Also, San Antonio *Herald*, February 6, 1858, May 19, 1858 and Corpus Christi *Ranchero*, July 6, 1861.
30. Valerio-Jiménez, *River of Hope*, 196.
31. Ibid., 188. Although the Republic of Texas claimed the Rio Grande as its southern and western border, it was unable to exert political or military control over communities such as Laredo, Santa Fe, or Albuquerque.
32. Felix Garcia, *The Children of John Z. Leyendecker: A Brief Genealogical Sketch* (Laredo, 1984), 9-11, 20-24; Angel Sepulveda Brown and Gloria Villa Cadena, eds., *San Agustin Parish of Laredo Marriage Book I, 1790-1857,* 238. Leyendecker was born on September 10, 1827, at Saynerholz amt Walderodt in the German Duchy of Nassau and was baptized in the parish church of Mendt.
33. Maria Isabela was born on July 2, 1858; Maria Juana on October 23, 1859; Lucia Pragedis on July 21, 1861; and John during the war on November 2, 1862, at Fredericksburg, where the couple lived part of the time. John was born "sickly," however, and died at Fredericksburg five days later. He was buried in the Catholic Cemetery in the community.
34. Baptismal Records, St. Augustine Church Archives, Laredo, Texas. Also, Garcia, *Descendants of John Z. Leyendecker*, 20-33.
35. Armando C. Alonzo, *Tejano Legacy: Rancheros and Settlers in South Texas, 1734-1900* (Albuquerque: University of New Mexico Press, 1998), 168.
36. *State Gazette Appendix Containing Debates in the House of Representatives* (Austin: John Marshall and Co., 1860), 62-63; Jerry Thompson, *Cortina: Defending the Mexican Name in Texas* (College Station: Texas A&M University Press, 2007), 36.

37. Jerry Thompson, ed., *Tejanos in Gray: The Civil War Letters of Captains Joseph Rafael de la Garza and Manuel Yturri* (College Station: Texas A&M University Press, 2011), xvii-xviii.
38. Ibid., xx.
39. Alonzo, *Tejano Legacy*, 273.
40. Santos Benavides, Affidavit, July 10, 1883. Document in private possession.
41. Lola Council Ellsworth, "San Antonio During the Civil War" (Master's thesis, University of Texas, 1938), 77-78.
42. Senovia Cervantes, Pension Application No. 8965, Bexar County, December 14, 1916, Texas State Archives, Austin, Texas.
43. Gloria Sananes Stein, *Civil War Camp Life: Sutlers, Sex and Scoundrels* (Xlibris, 2008), 61.
44. Corpus Christi *Ranchero*, June 15, 1867.
45. *New York Herald*, July 29, 1865.
46. Bexar County court records as quoted in: Ellsworth, "San Antonio During the Civil War," 106.
47. Valerio-Jiménez, *River of Hope*, 190, 197.
48. Ibid.
49. Ibid.
50. Ibid.
51. Ibid., 167.
52. Ibid., 249. At the beginning of the war, the family patriarch Basilio Benavides and Ángel Navarro, who represented Bexar County, were the only *Tejanos* in the Texas Legislature.
53. See for example: Eligio Herrera, Pension Application No. 4335, Webb County, August 17, 1899, Texas State Archives.
54. Juanita Castillo, Pension Application No. 34189, May 19, 1917, Bexar County, Texas State Archives.
55. Lucia de Trevino, Pension Application No. 4355, August 17, 1899, Webb County, Texas State Archives; and Twelfth Census of the United States (1900), Webb County, Texas, NA.
56. Ibid.

57. Pedro Cevallos, Compiled Service Record, Confederate Adjutant General's Office, RG 109, National Archives; Thompson, *Vaqueros in Blue and Gray*, 141; Thompson, ed., *Tejanos in Gray*, 34, 105, 108, 114-16.

58. Andrea F. DeLeza, Pension Application No. 4320, August 17, 1899, Webb County, Texas State Archives.

59. Francisca J. de Jimenez, Pension Application No. 4336, July 12, 1899, Webb County, Texas State Archives.

60. Carlota Guerrero de Escobar, Pension Application No. 4321, July 13, 1899, Webb County, Texas State Archives.

61. Valerio-Jiménez, *River of Hope*, 167.

62. Thompson, ed., *Tejanos in Gray*, ii-xv.

63. Ibid.

64. Ibid.

65. Ibid., 9.

66. Ibid., 15.

67. Ibid.

68. Ibid., 33.

69. Ibid., 78.

Image 16. *Helena Landa Fending off Robbers*

Painting by Michael Waters [Image 075-0003]. Institute of Texan Cultures, UTSA Libraries, San Antonio, Texas.

Chapter 8

Courage on a Texas Frontier

German Texas Unionist Women on the Civil War Home Front

Judith Dykes-Hoffman

> By this time they had entered the house and taken hold of my husband. I was not too dumbfounded with terror to know what it meant, and resolved to make a desperate effort to render my husband all possible aid, or to at least enable him to defend himself.... That was the last time I ever saw him alive.
>
> Clara Feller, German Pioneers in Texas.[1]

Clara Feller's story represents only one of many told by German Texas Unionist women who lost husbands, brothers, fathers, and sons because of their anti-Confederate stance during the Civil War. Whether they openly opposed slavery or simply refused allegiance to the Confederacy, men risked being executed for their beliefs, which in turn threatened the women with grave personal loss. Unionist women dealt with the usual turmoil that war brings, but also faced and often resisted hostile forces. Some of them avoided losing loved ones and friends by helping them hide in caves, attics, cellars, and in open fields. These women kept their men's whereabouts a secret from Confederate neighbors and from the soldiers sent into the area to conscript the men into military service. In secret they took food and other necessary provisions to them during their sequester. Still other women endured the Civil War alone while their husbands, fathers, and brothers escaped Confederate conscription and persecution by moving North or to Mexico. In sum the German Unionist women of Comal, Kerr, and Gillespie Counties of central Texas experienced the war under harrowing circumstances. During these tumultuous years they not only struggled to protect their families but simply to survive.

Tens of thousands German immigrants came to Texas starting in the mid-1840s. They sought economic, political, and religious freedoms and opportunities. Most of these German pioneers carved their new homes and towns in the three central Texas Hill Country counties mentioned above. They found a sparsely settled area with mostly Comanche inhabitants, and many Texans considered this region the edge of civilization—the Texas frontier. The women who emigrated from Germany to Texas during this time left behind a world and a way of life familiar to them. According to historian Lauren Kattner, life in nineteenth-century Germany emphasized "the importance of work, social order, and religion." It was a place where young boys and girls learned a "work ethic, occupational hierarch[ies], and religious tenets" specific to their community.[2] The poem, "Wuerde de Maenner," or "Men's Position of Honor," taught in Hanoverian schools as early as 1841, best exhibits the social and occupational order of nineteenth-century German life. In it men were honored before women, then, in descending order, homage was given to other groups. At the top was the prince, followed by the orator, teacher, singer, artist, judge, doctor, warrior, forester, merchant, artisan, and finally the farmer. As to religion, Lutheranism and Catholicism were the dominant belief systems and these were passed down through the generations.

For German women, and the newly arrived German-Texan women, the transmission of cultural ideas and customs occurred through their mothers' teaching, especially during their early years of life, a period referred to by Kattner as the *Wartezeit.* As girls grew into women, formal education, religious confirmation, and outside work or domestic service all socialized them to appropriate cultural behavior. Kattner points out that families' economic standings also influenced their daughters' cultural training. Wealthy families often sent daughters abroad to learn "needlework, household management, and to receive a liberal education." Middle class families enrolled their daughters in "regionally advanced schools" for similar liberal educations, "as well as lessons in patriotism." Less-affluent families prepared their daughters for "teaching positions or engaged [them] in volunteer work among the poor." Once formal education ended, or domestic service ceased, the women returned home to receive further household and childcare training. This was largely in preparation for their future roles as wives and mothers. Kattner states that for most young women this period of cultural training and indoctrination led either to "teaching or welfare work, [entering a] nunnery . . . or most likely marriage."[3] In the midst of building new homes and communities, the German women living in central Texas Hill Country worked towards recreating this system in this new world.

They could not imagine that they would be Civil War participants within fifteen years. Yet when Texas seceded from the United States in February 1861, and when civil war erupted in April the same year, German-Texans faced war. At this point they had to decide where their loyalties lay. Those who chose to side with the Confederacy faced the cruelties of war, while those who remained loyal to the United States, the Unionists, would come to experience a different kind of agony. At first most Unionists were left alone by those who supported secession. After all, both sides included people who were neighbors and friends. The younger men who championed the Southern cause eagerly enlisted in home guards, Confederate cavalry, and infantry units, while the older men helped to mobilize community resources in preparation for war. Those loyal to the Union kept quiet, left the state, volunteered for home guard duty, or created Union Loyal Leagues.[4] Confederate women organized themselves into groups such as the Southern Ladies Aid Society of New

Braunfels, Texas. They collected such supplies as winter clothing for use by Confederate volunteers and organized farewell parties for departing soldiers.[5] Like men, Unionist women publicly voiced their disapproval without undue fear of harsh reprisal. However, by the spring of 1862, changes had come to Texas and to all the other Confederate states.

By 1862 both the US government and the Confederacy realized that the war would last longer than predicted and that they needed more soldiers. In April the Confederate government therefore enacted a conscription law that decreed "all able-bodied white male citizens between the ages of eighteen and thirty-five [were] liable to service for three years." It also required that "one-year volunteers remain in the army for two more years."[6] Conscription was not favorably received by many Americans; therefore, political leaders linked it to patriotism. They knew that winning a long war required men's military service and citizens' loyalty. Pockets of Unionism, however, existed throughout the South and increasingly concerned the Confederate government and its military leaders. In some cases Confederate citizens formed vigilante groups.[7] Texas was no different. Violence erupted in 1862 in the northern Texas counties of Cooke, Grayson, Wise, Denton, and Lamar. The "Great Hanging" of Gainesville referred to forty hangings of Unionist men in October 1862 following "several years of vigilante action against persons accused of fostering disorder on the North Texas frontier."[8] Cities such as San Antonio (Bexar County) and Austin (Travis County) also contained many Unionists who risked being "attacked on the street or along back roads," or arrested for using seditious language.[9]

German-Texan Unionists were singled out and attacked for their beliefs, as were other Unionists. Confederate officials, who remembered the strong resolutions passed against slavery by the 1854 Texas State Convention of Germans, viewed non-slaveholding Germans, particularly those who retained their German culture, with caution. Accordingly, in the spring of 1862, Texas Governor Frank R. Lubbock and Gen. H. P. Bee of Laredo decided to declare martial law in the Hill Country counties.[10]

Newspaper reports of this declaration startled the Germans. The declaration ordered all males over the age of sixteen to appear before the county marshal and furnish "such information as may be required of him." It also ordered all individuals who claimed citizenship to take an oath of allegiance to Texas and the Confederate States of America, and warned that they were to "not convey to [the] enemies any information whatever, or do any act injurious to the Confederate States or beneficial to the United States."[11] Thus, anyone who openly declared loyalty to the US government or tried to aid the Union cause would be considered in rebellion by the Confederacy, and thereby a traitor. The declaration also advised people to turn in the names of anyone they believed disloyal. Martial law and the Conscription Act placed the Texas German Unionist men and women in a difficult and dangerous situation.

These two decisions angered many German-Texans. Throughout the South, the Conscription Act proved extremely unpopular and many men refused to enter military service, or left not long after they enlisted. Women throughout the South helped to support the men by hiding and caring for those who refused to enlist, especially those who shared a kinship or anti-Confederate sentiments. German-Texan women from Comal, Kerr, and Gillespie Counties demonstrated the same support towards the German-Texan men who deserted or avoided the draft. One Gillespie County deserter, Peter Bonn, was quite crafty in his methods. According to family records, Peter swore allegiance to the United States on May 23, 1860, after he was granted citizenship. When civil war erupted he was "drafted into the Confederate [A]rmy" and stationed on the Texas coast. He left behind a young wife and two small children on the family farm. On several occasions Peter and a friend, Conrad Hahne, "would desert and come home afoot to do field work." Peter "disguised himself as a woman" to escape detection while he worked in the field. This masquerade worked, for he was never caught by officials.[12]

Confederate military leaders stationed in the area wrote of their frustration in trying to enforce conscription. Capt. Edmund P. Turner, writing to Superintendent of Conscripts J. P. Flewellen, "called attention" to German-Texas settlements. Frustrated, he wrote that "resistance to conscription is seriously contemplated" by them. Flewellen in turn wrote to A. J. Bell, an enrolling officer. He stated that the Germans were "remarkably stubborn" and "do not intend to submit to enrollment." He wanted an entire company placed under his command to bring in the dissenters. If caught, these men received harsh retribution.[13]

The Unionist women of Comal County, however, escaped the worst of the persecution and danger. Unionist sentiment in New Braunfels, Comal County's largest town, and its surrounding communities never grew to the levels that it did in Kerr and Gillespie Counties. Neither were the small number of Unionists in the county as vocal or visible as those in other counties. The majority of the diminutive group farmed in the countryside and did not actively campaign against secession. In February 1861 return on the vote to ratify or reject Texas's secession from the Union revealed that only 86 of 325 voters voted against secession. Not long after this vote Comal County organized more than 250 men, almost all entirely of German descent, into two cavalry units and one infantry unit for service in the Confederate Army.[14]

The local newspaper, the *Neu-Braunfelser Zeitung*, issued no pro-Union statements during the war years. Editor Ferdinand Lindheimer, a quite prominent and highly respected New Braunfels citizen, was a staunch supporter of states' rights and secession. Most Comal County Germans accommodated or eventually supported the Confederacy for the reason that Lindheimer outlined in his response to the 1854 German Texas Convention: "Negro slavery is an evil which threatens the continued existence of the Union. Its abolition must be left to the several states in which it exists. We German-speaking Texans are not in a position to suggest a solution but feel that the federal government should not interfere in this question."[15] Thus, the Germans of this area who accepted the actions of the Confederacy did so because they basically believed in states' rights. Their suppression in Germany by an aristocratic government perhaps caused many to be suspicious of a strong federal US government. In contrast, a small group of Unionists in Comal County strongly opposed slavery and secession.

Comal County's Unionists did not experience the level of persecution suffered by those in Kerr and Gillespie Counties. Evidence shows that only a few Comal men died for their loyalist beliefs. Of course the women still suffered hardships. They lived day-to-day during wartime not knowing if tomorrow would bring death to male kinfolk. Like women elsewhere, Comal's Unionist women experienced the war in isolation and without male protection in a patriarchal society. Their menfolk generally joined Confederate military units in hope of eventually deserting and reenlisting in Unionist companies. Others fled north to Union lines or south to Mexico. Some simply hid in surrounding caves and fields.[16]

Anna Katherine Tays's two sons, both from Comal County, were both Unionists. Johann Heinrich Tays obeyed his Confederate conscription orders but at the first opportunity abandoned his Brownsville unit and boarded a Union warship scheduled to sail to New Orleans. At New Orleans, Tays enlisted with the First Texas Cavalry Regiment, but was soon wounded while standing guard in the city of Baton Rouge, Louisiana. His injuries resulted in a military discharge, but, possibly because he feared a hostile reception in his hometown, Tays went to St. Louis, Missouri, to wait out the war. Not until Reconstruction, sometime in the late 1860s, did he feel it was safe to return to New Braunfels. Anna Tays's other son, Henrich Friedrich Tays, was not as fortunate. His Union loyalties resulted in his capture and murder at the Battle of the Nueces, sometimes referred to as the Nueces Massacre, in August 1862. Thus, Anna grieved the loss of one son and worried for many years about the safe return of the other one.[17]

While Anna Tays anguished over her sons, she still had her husband's company and protection. Other women carried on daily life without their husbands' aid. In a society where men controlled the business, financial, and political worlds, women found it difficult to function on their own, let alone in solitude with the stigma of being a Unionist, or the wife of one. Yet many German-Texas women survived the Civil War without the company of their husbands. Helena Landa, for example, wife of prominent and wealthy New Braunfels merchants Joseph Landa, found herself alone after her husband's forced exile in 1863.

Joseph Landa, one of Comal County's few German slaveholders, was forced to flee Texas after he freed his five slaves in response to President Abraham Lincoln's Emancipation Proclamation. According to his son, Harry Landa, Joseph's action provoked "The Golden Circle," a secret society whose purpose was to "ferret out and convict anyone of abolitionist tendencies." Joseph Landa was "tried" and found guilty of abolitionism by the organization, which then instructed him to settle his affairs and leave the country. Joseph fled to Matamoros, Mexico, in 1863 and left his wife, Helena, in charge of the family general store, flour mill, saw mill, and cotton gin. Harry recalled that the area soon became "over-run with bushwhackers, scalawags and out-laws, not identified with the regular Confederate Army" and that his mother had a difficult time protecting their property. For example, not long after Joseph's departure a band of "ruffians" entered their general store with robbery on their minds. He remembered that his mother, Helena, who was alone in the store with her seven children, chased off the would-be robbers at gunpoint. Harry marveled at his mother's "ability and courage in protecting property during the absence of her husband" and proclaimed her "a brave and courageous mother." She was also apparently an efficient accountant, for when Joseph Landa returned to New Braunfels after the war, he found his businesses fiscally sound.[18]

Like Comal County, Kerr County contained primarily German communities. Unionists, however, were much more numerous here than in Comal County, and they took a more vocal and visible stance against secession. For example, only 86 of 325 men, or 26 percent of those who voted, did so against secession in the Comal election, while in Kerr County 53 of 87 voters, or 61 percent, voted against secession.[19]

Image 17. Kerr, Gillespie, and Comal Counties in central Texas.

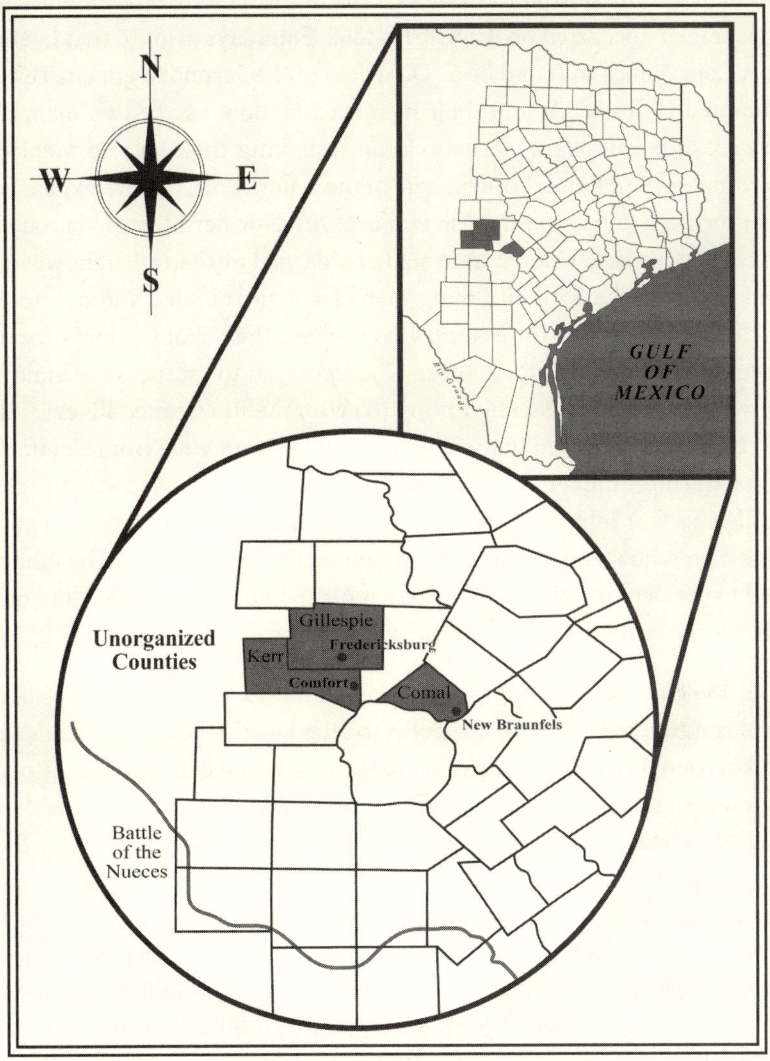

Map 3

The inhabitants of Comfort, Comal County's largest community, suffered greatly during the war as a result of the Battle of the Nueces. This tragedy occurred on August 10, 1862. Four days prior to that fateful day, Capt. James Duff and Lt. C. D. McRae of the Second Regiment Texas Mounted Rifles, CSA, and their men tracked down sixty-two men, all but six of whom were German-Texans, making their way to Mexico. Writing in 1901, Emma Altgelt, wife of the founder of Comfort, explained that the men hoped to establish contact with Northern forces via routes in nearby Mexico. Confederate soldiers learned of their plan, however, and followed the band of young men. They surrounded and overtook the Unionist band at the Nueces River where they shot the majority of them. According to Altgelt, those who managed to escape were hunted down and "killed while attempting to swim the Rio Grande River."[20] In all, thirty-six men died in the Nueces battle; fifteen were from Comfort, a staggering number considering the small size of the town. Nueces battle survivor John W. Sansom remembered in 1905 that of the twenty-plus men who escaped death, eleven joined the Union Army. The others fled to Mexico or California, or they returned home where they hid out during the remaining years of the war.[21]

In 1865, three years after the battle, relatives and friends of the slain men traveled to the battle site, collected the bleached bones of the dead, and carried them back to Comfort for proper burial beneath a limestone monument that commemorated their actions. Prior to this trip, the mother and the sister of slain sixteen-year-old Henry Steiler traveled to the tragic spot where he fell to bury Henry's remains. Wilhelmine Steiler and her mother rode unescorted on horseback through Confederate ranks who, according to family records, left them alone after learning of their daring mission. Upon reaching the site, Wilhelmine realized that she was not strong enough to both dig a grave and lift her brother's body, so she hid him under brush weighted down by rocks in order to keep the animals from dragging his remains away. The two women returned home and, later, Wilhelmine returned to the makeshift grave, recovered her brother's body, and took it back to the family farm for proper burial.

Henry Steiler's mother never fully recovered from the loss of her son or the trip to collect his remains.

To Comfort's Unionists, the men and women who endured the Battle of the Nueces were heroes. In addition, many more Unionists experienced the dangerous threats of the "haengebande." The "haengebande" was the name given to a group of men, headed by James Waldrip, who primarily terrorized Gillespie County's Union sympathizers. The Unionists in this county experienced similar experiences as those in Comal and Kerr Counties, but endured the terroristic activities by the Waldrip gang.

The population of Gillespie County, especially its largest community, Fredericksburg, was also primarily of German heritage. Gillespie citizens overwhelmingly opposed secession; 400 of its 467 eligible voters, or 85 percent, voted against it. These German-Texans did not agree with slavery or secession, and felt extreme loyalty towards the United States, the country they had pledged to support. In addition, because Fredericksburg was located on the outer edge of settled territory, people there worried about losing the protection provided by federal troops stationed at area forts against Indian raids. For some their very survival might be at stake if Texas seceded from the Union. Women in particular worried that the withdrawal of federal protection, simultaneous with men's conscription into military service, would leave them vulnerable to the Comanches who often ventured onto their farms and into their homes. Thus, with Texas's withdrawal from the Union in February of 1861, tremendous struggles began for Unionist women as well as men.

After the onset of war, some Unionists in Gillespie County joined others in escaping to Mexico. Balthasar Blum of Fredericksburg decided in 1862 to evade Confederate military service by going to Mexico. Before he left, he took his new wife Margarethe, their infant daughter, and two daughters from his previous marriage to live in San Antonio where he felt they would be safe. A year later Margarethe and the three girls joined him in Mexico where they lived until the end of the war. Louis Martin, who headed to Mexico in June 1864, did not escape physical danger.

Confederate soldiers stationed near the Nueces River stopped his wagon, captured him and another passenger, Eugene Frantzen, and hanged them both. Louis's widow Elizabeth drove their horse-drawn wagon to the Mexican border, where she recovered his body and returned with it to Fredericksburg. Like Wilhelmine Steiler, Elizabeth traveled alone from Fredericksburg to the Texas-Mexico border, despite the danger of encountering Confederate soldiers and Indians. Her personal fears came second to her desperate desire to recover her husband's body.[22]

While some women helped their men escape to the North or to a foreign country, others helped the men hide in the surrounding area. After the Battle of the Nueces, those who managed to survive and return to their homes had to be protected from pro-Confederate soldiers and citizens caught up in the anti-Union frenzy. It was no secret what would become of Unionists if captured, especially since Texas Hill Country Germans were placed under martial law in May 1862, on grounds of being in open rebellion against the Confederacy. Amalia Betz Kammlah protected her husband, Henry Kammlah II, after he was wounded at Nueces. She concealed him in some of their pastures and took food, water, and other necessities to him during his seclusion. Josephine Ransleben helped hide her brother, William Klier, and her brother-in-law, Julius Schlickum, both of whom were Nueces survivors. She took care of their needs for the rest of the war years.[23]

When Governor Lubbock declared martial law in May 1862, the government stationed Capt. James Duff, the same individual who led Confederate troops at the Battle of Nueces, in Gillespie County to oversee the implementation of the decree and catch would-be deserters. County citizens grew to despise Duff because they considered his tactics crude and harsh. R. H. Williams, a Confederate soldier assigned to Duff's company and instructed by the captain to get Unionists to swear Confederate allegiance, recalled some of the carnage in his memoirs. He described one Unionist's house, which the group passed as they traveled through the area, as "desolate . . . wasted and destroyed." The man who owned the house was in hiding to avoid conscription, and his wife had been "brought into the camp with her children." According to Williams, the destruction to their home was extensive:

> About twenty acres of land had been cultivated on the side of the valley, cleverly irrigated by the stream running through it. Now the crops were trampled and destroyed, and not a living thing was to be seen on the place; even the bee-hives in front of the comfortable log house were overturned and empty. The poor little furniture in the living room, and the loom in the kitchen, had been smashed; and all this had been done by some of our marauding parties by our Captain's orders.[24]

In August 1862 Duff ordered his men to round up and bring in the Unionist men hiding in outlying areas so they might convert them "to the true faith by means of the halter." He dispatched two other groups of approximately twenty-five men, Williams recalled, "with wagons to bring in from the scattered ranches the wives and children of those who had taken to the mountains." Days later they returned with women, children, and some men. The men were guarded by the soldiers while the women were sent on to Fredericksburg where local officials imprisoned them.[25] On August 15, 1862, the *Neu-Braunfelser Zeitung* reported the arrest and imprisonment of "the wives and children of eleven families" in Fredericksburg.[26]

Captain Duff was just one individual who tormented the German Unionist men and women. James Waldrip and his band of Confederate patriots, the "haengebande," carried out some of the more notorious deeds against them. Most people living in Gillespie County knew Waldrip prior to the war and generally liked him. By the end of the war he was the most hated man in the county. Somewhere in these years Waldrip and his group of twenty to thirty men became caught up in the anti-Unionist frenzy that resulted in the murder of many Unionists. Waldrip kept a list of known and suspected Unionists whom he and his men then targeted for death. Once a man's name made the list, his men systematically went to his home, usually at suppertime, took the Unionist away, and hanged him.

Mathilda Wagner, who lived in Fredericksburg as a young girl, remembered that the notorious gang killed a close family friend who was hiding from the vigilante thugs. Every morning the friend returned home from his secluded place to check on his family and bring water to his pregnant wife and children. Waldrip's gang learned of his routine and killed him one morning as he drew water from a stream.[27] Conrad Wehmeyer, with the help of his wife, Louise, also hid from Waldrip. When Louise learned that her husband's name was on Waldrip's list, she hid him in a friend's attic until the danger passed. During this time she continued to run the day-to-day affairs of the bakery her husband had operated. She went about business as usual to keep Waldrip unsuspicious and also to evade probing questions about Conrad's absence.[28] Louise successfully protected her husband's life.

William Feller, Justice of the Peace, and Louis Schuetze, a local schoolteacher whose names appeared on Waldrip's list, were not as lucky as Conrad Wehmeyer. Clara Feller, wife of William Feller, and Louise Schuetze, daughter of Louis Schuetze, described how the men died and how their deaths affected their lives. In an 1882 letter and, later, in a 1925 interview, Clara Feller recalled that Waldrip, along with thirty to forty horsemen, rode at "full speed up to [their] door" the evening of March 9, 1864, just as the family sat down to supper. The men told William that he was to come with them for he was under arrest. It was common knowledge, she said, that her husband was a "staunch opponent of slavery" and was "free in his denunciation of various outrages that had been committed" in the area, especially the "Nueces butchery." William asked the men what the charges were and demanded that they produce an arrest warrant. Clara stated that the men told her husband "to never mind about the warrant, and you'll find out what for when you reach the place to which we are taking you." After a small scuffle during which Clara Feller attempted to hand her husband a pistol, "one of the men, a powerful fellow, saw what [she] was doing, grabbed [her] arm and wrenched the pistol out of [her] hand." The gang put Feller on a horse and rode off away from the house. Clara, who "begged and pleaded that [she] be allowed to go with [her] husband," remembered the last words spoken to her by her husband were ones of assurance that everything would be all right. He wanted her "to stay with the children." She recalled she did as told out of love for him and concern for their children, who were in tears after witnessing the whole affair.[29]

Clara recounted other details of that "cold, stormy night." She kept vigil throughout the evening, long after the children went to sleep. She knew that she probably would never see her husband of thirteen years return alive, which was finally confirmed when friends arrived with the news she dreaded. She recalled that they told her, "Mrs. Feller, be prepared for the worst! Mr. Burg has been shot down in front of his house, and Mr. Kirchner and Mr. Blank taken away." She further recalled that on Monday, only two days before, the community had buried Mrs. Burg. With Mr. Burg's death, seven children became orphans that night. In fact Clara wrote, "in a span of three short days twenty children were made fatherless." These included her own seven children aged two through twelve years.[30]

Louis Schuetze, local schoolteacher and sometimes preacher, suffered a similar fate as William Feller. Mathilda Wagner recalled that Schuetze was a "prominent and influential" person who was an outspoken adversary of slavery and a staunch Unionist. It was also well known that his brother Julius, a music teacher for the children of former governor Sam Houston, had openly opposed Texas's secession. These facts caused Waldrip to add Schuetze's name to his murder list, especially after some of his men heard him speak of his love for the United States one night at a local bar. Schuetze had dared also to describe the proud moment when he took his oath of allegiance to the United States after his emigration from Germany.[31] Words such as these incited Waldrip's rage and catapulted him into action on the night of February 24, 1864.

Schuetze's daughter Louise recalled the details of that evening in a deposition she gave to the coroner on February 26 and 27, 1864, two days after the murder. She testified that at approximately 7:00 p.m. her father turned away an individual who knocked at their front door. Schuetze told the caller that it was too late in the evening to receive anyone, and to return in the morning. The man outside retorted that if the door was not opened "he would knock it down." At that point the Schuetzes realized there were many men outside; Louise went to the window, opened it, and called for help. Someone from outside fired a shot through the window and then the "front door was broken in and the men rushed through." In an adjoining room, Schuetze and Louise hid from the intruders. When the men tried to break down that door, Schuetze retreated to the kitchen to escape the danger. Waldrip's men, however, eventually made their way to him.[32]

Louise testified that the band of men "dragged" her father outside. He pleaded for his life, reminding them that "he had formerly always been disposed to be friendly towards them" and imploring them to "consider his large family." After Waldrip's men carried Schuetze outside to the front of the house, Louise, who remained detained inside by one of the men, heard a blow and her father cry out. After a brief conversation between Waldrip and Schuetze, she recalled her father "called out 'Louise, come here!'" She stated in the deposition that she "tore herself loose and hurried" to her father, who told her: "My Louisa, they are going to hang me!" The men mounted their horses and dragged her father away. Before they left, one gang member assured Louise that they only wanted her father's testimony in regards to other Unionists. She cried out for help when one of the men returned for Schuetze's revolver, but the man reiterated that no one would be harmed, and they only wanted his testimony against others. When he rode away "at full speed," Louise "ran to town in order to get help."[33]

Nearby neighbors tried to render aid but were also threatened by the Waldrip group. C. Krauskopf testified that he heard Schuetze cry for help and beg the men to "think of my family." He, William Wahrmund, and John Meusebach had grabbed their guns and "walked towards the house when six threatening men ran at us." Seeing a "larger armed crowd close to the [Schuetze's] house" the men realized they were overpowered and turned back towards town. They hurried to the church, rang the bell in alarm, and hoped that the ringing would "bring up all the troops which could be assembled." The next day, however, some local citizens found Schuetze's lifeless body some three miles north of town "with a rope around his neck, hanging from a bough of a live oak. His hands were bound behind his back, and on the left side of his forehead a wound was found." A coroner's jury ruled that he was "violently murdered between the 24th and 25th of February."[34]

Louise Schuetze witnessed the kidnapping of her father that left her mother a widow, and herself and siblings fatherless. Like Louise, Clara Feller watched helplessly as her husband was forced from their home to meet a similar fate. The women grieved as any woman would who faced the murder of a loved one during wartime or peacetime. In addition, these women lived with the fact that Confederates viewed these men's deaths as one less traitor to deal with and not worthy of much attention. Nevertheless, they knew they did all they could to help.

The experiences of Unionist women in Comal, Kerr, and Gillespie Counties varied according to where they lived. Comal County contained fewer loyalists than the others, which spared its citizens the harsher treatment meted out to loyalists in other counties. This area lacked vigilante groups such as the "haengebande," nor were Confederate troops stationed there as existed in Gillespie County. Those who harbored anti-Confederate views never organized into a formal group as they did in Kerr County and they tended to keep their political views to themselves. Those who felt strongly enough about their union beliefs typically left Texas or hid to avoid Confederate military service. Others joined Confederate units, but abandoned them at first opportunity to enlist in Union units. However, throughout all three areas, the German-

Texas Unionist women participated as much as they could within the confines of nineteenth-century gender roles. Upon war's end the women and men returned to the work of building communities and repairing relationships in the Texas Hill Country. Their stories and experiences add to a growing body of literature of Texas women at war. As well there are more stories waiting to be researched and written about of the Texas Hill Country German women of the Civil War era.[35] As historians continue to dig deeper and reexamine Texas women's experiences during the American Civil War, a more accurate picture will develop that will rightfully incorporate the German-Texan women into this important part of American history.

Notes

1. Don H. Biggers, *German Pioneers in Texas: A Brief History of Their Hardships, Struggles and Achievements* (Fredericksburg, TX: Fredericksburg Publishing Co., 1925), 76-77.
2. Lauren Kattner, "Growing Up and Town Development: Social and Cultural Adaptation in a German-American Town" (Master's thesis, University of Texas at Dallas, 1987), 8.
3. Ibid., 10.
4. According to Guido Ransleben, Union Loyal Leagues were not to cause dissension between Unionists and Confederates, but to "take such actions as might peaceably secure its members and their families from being disturbed and compelled to bear arms against the Union." They were also created to offer protection from Indian attacks. State officials became alarmed at the creation of these groups, which led to harsh reactions by the state in spring 1862. See Guido Ransleben, *A Hundred Years of Comfort in Texas: A Centennial History* (San Antonio: The Naylor Co., 1954), 105.
5. *New Braunfels Zeitung*, September 20, 1861, and September 27, 1861.
6. James McPherson, *Battle Cry of Freedom, The Civil War Era* (New York: Ballantine Books, 1989), 430.
7. Victoria Bynum, *Unruly Women: The Politics of Social & Sexual Control in the Old South* (Chapel Hill: University of North Carolina UP, 1992): 111-150; Wayne Durrill, "An Uncivil War," *Southern Exposure: A Journal of Politics & Culture* 18, no. 1 (April, 1947); and William T. Auman, "Neighbor against Neighbor: The Inner Civil War in the Randolph County Area of Confederate North Carolina," *North Carolina Historical Review* 56, no. 1 (January, 1981).
8. Richard B. McCaslin, *Tainted Breeze: The Great Hanging at Gainesville, Texas 1862* (Baton Route: Louisiana State University Press, 1994), 1; Claude Elliott, "Union Sentiment in Texas, 1861-1865," *Southwestern Historical Quarterly* 50 (April 1947): 455; Walter Buenger, *Secession and the Union in Texas* (Austin: University of Texas Press, 1984), 55-56.

9. James Marten, *Texas Divided: Loyalty and Dissent in the Lone Star State, 1856-1874* (Lexington: University Press of Kentucky, 1990), 62.

10. Robert Shook, "German Unionism in Texas During the Civil War and Reconstruction" (Master's thesis, Southwest Texas State University, August 1957), 46; *Neu-Braunfels Zeitung*, June 20, 1862.

11. Oscar Haas, *History of New Braunfels and Comal County, Texas: 1844-1946* (Austin: The Steck Co., 1968), 191; *Neu-Braunfels Zeitung*, June 20, 1862.

12. Gillespie County Historical Society, *Pioneers in God's Hills: A History of Fredericksburg and Gillespie County People and Events* (Austin: Von Boeckmann-Jones, 1974), 7.

13. Edmund P. Turner to J. P. Flewellen, December 4, 1862 and J. P. Flewellen to A. J. Bell, November 28, 1862, *The War of the Rebellion: A Compilation of the Official Records of the Union and Confederate Armies*, ser. 1, 15 (Washington: Government Printing Office, 1886), 886-887.

14. *Neu-Braunfelser-Zeitung*, March 1, 1861; Haas, *History of New Braunfels*, 153-171.

15. *Neu-Braunfelser-Zeitung*, May 26, 1854.

16. Hanno and Alvin Welsch, Interview by Herb Skoog, 4 Oct. 1878, "Reflections" interview 101, transcript, Sophienburg Archives, New Braunfels, Texas, 4-5.

17. Tays-Clemens Family Papers, Malmstead Family Private Collection, New Braunfels, Texas.

18. Harry Landa, *As I Remember* (San Antonio: Carleton Printing Co., 1945), 19-23.

19. Ransleben, *A Hundred Years of Comfort*, 80.

20. C. D. McRae report of battle to Maj. E. F. Gray, August 10, 1862 *Official Record*, ser.1, 9, 614-615; Emma Murck Altgelt, "Die Kolonie Comfort," trans. Guido Ransleben, *The Comfort News*, June 5, 1969.

21. Ransleben, *A Hundred Years of Comfort*, 114; John W. Sansom, *Battle of the Nueces in Kinney County, Texas, Aug. 10th 1862* (San Antonio, 1905).

22. Gillespie County Historical Association, *Pioneers in God's Hills: A History of Fredericksburg and Gillespie County People and Events*, 2 vols. (Austin: Von Boeckmann-Jones, 1947), 18-19, 128.

23. Ibid., 73, 170.

24. R. H. Williams, *With the Border Ruffians, Memories of the Far West 1852-1868*, ed. E. W. Williams (New York: E. P. Dutton and Co., 1907), 238.

25. Ibid., 236-237.

26. *Neu-Braunfelser Zeitung*, August 15, 1862.

27. Jo Ella Powell Esley, *Texas Tears and Sunshine* (College Station: Texas A&M University Press, 1985), 111.

28. Evelyn M. Carrington, *Women in Early Texas* (Austin: Jenkins Publishing Co., 1975), 282.

29. Clara Feller to unnamed group, November 25, 1882, letter in possession of Mrs. Reinhard Enderlin, Fredericksburg, Texas; Biggers, *German Pioneers in Texas*, 75-77.

30. Biggers, *German Pioneers*, 75-77; Clara Feller to unnamed group, November 25, 1882.

31. Esley, *Texas Tears and Texas Sunshine*, 111; Clarke Schuetze to Maury Maverick Jr., August 3, 1988, transcript from the collections of the Vereins Kirche Archives, Gillespie County Historical Society, Inc., Fredericksburg, Texas; Sworn Statement of Winifred Schuetze Cade to Maury Maverick Jr., August 8, 1988, transcript from the collections of the Vereins Kirche Archives, Gillespie County Historical Society, Inc., Fredericksburg, Texas.

32. Louise and her father were at the family's second home located closer to town. It was customary for Mr. Schuetze to stay at this other location while at work, then when time allowed to return to the main residence several miles away where his wife and children stayed. This particular day, Louise accompanied him to the second home. Julius Schuetze, "My Experiences in Texas," *Texas Vorwarts*, June 25, 1886, transcript from the collections of the Vereins Kirche Archives, Gillespie County Historical Society, Inc., Fredericksburg, Texas.

33. Ibid.

34. Ibid.

35. Angela Boswell, "The Civil War and the Lives of Texas Women," in *The Fate of Texas: The Civil War and the Lone Star State*, ed. Charles D. Grear (Fayetteville: University of Arkansas Press, 2008), 69-81;

Melanie Kirkland, "Texas Woman at War," in *Texans and War: New Interpretations of the State's Military History*, eds. Alexander Mendoza and Charles David Grear (College Station: Texas A & M University Press, 2012), 69-96.

Image 18. Mahuldah Clark.

Courtesy of Keith and Colleen Clark Carri.

Wife of Nathaniel Clark, victim in the Great Hanging at Gainesville.

Chapter 9

"In Favor of our Fathers' Country and Government"

Unionist Women in North Texas

Rebecca Sharpless

They came to the North Texas forests and prairies from the east, from the Ohio Valley and the Old Northwest Territory. They trekked overland, sometimes on foot and sometimes with ox carts, across miles of open countryside until they reached the hamlets that would be their new homes. Towns were few and far between, and forts staffed by the US Army protected them from attack by the Native Americans who still lived just to the west. The women and men who settled North Texas in the 1850s found fertile land and wide skies and a country that was being split apart in the prelude to a great civil war.

The population of North Texas grew dramatically during the 1850s. As the rumblings of war grew louder, some of the new arrivals surely wondered what they had gotten themselves into by moving to a slave state. As Texas called a secession convention and individual counties voted on whether to leave the Union, many North Texans wanted to remain in the United States. In Collin, Jack, Montague, Fannin, Grayson, Lamar, and Cooke Counties, a majority of voters cast their ballots in favor of staying in the Union, and in four other counties, a sizeable minority did so as well.[1] But the majority of voters across the state chose overwhelmingly to leave the United States, and those who opposed secession found themselves severely tested by the events of the next four years and beyond. The Civil War brought discord and death to the spacious prairies and thick woodlands just south of the Red River.

Because women had no public voice, their political engagement and loyalties defy easy assumptions, and indeed a number of families in North Texas had sons in both the Union and Confederate armies.[2] But through their words and actions, women clearly manifested themselves as political thinkers and actors. They followed their men's public activities with interest and knowledge. As historian Amy Murrell Taylor points out, kinship ties strongly influenced the stances of both men and women, and husbands and wives or mothers and sons often shared their beliefs.[3] Their social status as women shielded the white female supporters of the Union from the vicious punishments meted out to many of the men. The war and its related fury nonetheless changed the lives of these women forever.

As tensions grew between those who favored slavery and those who did not in the late 1850s and early 1860s, threats increased against the lives of Unionists, perceived as traitors to the Confederacy. An untold number of North Texas families simply left the area, seeking homes where their politics would not endanger them.[4] For the women in these families, only recently arrived in Texas, dissent meant disruption once again, and many must have contemplated yet one more move with heavy hearts.

Particularly dramatic was the attempted escape from Fort Worth of Northern Methodist missionary Anthony Bewley and his wife, Jane Winton Bewley, in the summer of 1860. Northern Methodists were particularly suspect as abolitionists, and they found themselves under intense scrutiny from pro-slavery partisans. The Bewleys were no strangers to controversy, having experienced condemnation for their Unionist views in Missouri as early as 1850 and creating strains between Jane Bewley and her sisters.[5] They had already fled Texas once in late 1859, after pro-slavery forces disrupted the Northern Methodist Episcopal annual conference in Collin County. Jane and Anthony Bewley and their family returned to Texas in the spring of 1860, against Jane's wishes. To the fears of Jane and their friends, Anthony replied: "Let them hang or burn me on my return, if they choose; hundreds will rise up out of my ashes."[6]

Despite Anthony's bravado, on the day that suspected Unionist William Crawford was hanged in July 1860, the Bewley family fled Fort Worth. Charles Elliot, a writer for the Northern Methodist church, noted that they left behind all their belongings and traveled by cover of darkness. Jane Bewley participated actively in the flight: "The first two or three nights of their journey Mrs. Bewley kept watch, and then they drove and watched alternately. Mrs. Bewley often drove while Mr. Bewley slept. They pursued their journey often at night, and mostly through byways, to shun exposure."[7] A posse seized Anthony Bewley in Missouri on September 5. Not realizing the gravity of the situation, Jane Bewley did not attempt to see her husband, "a circumstance she greatly regrets." The mob returned Anthony Bewley to Fort Worth and hanged him from the same tree where William Crawford died. Jane Bewley and the children, the youngest of whom was only four years old, were stranded in Missouri. Jane Bewley's concerted efforts to save her husband came to naught.

While their sisters headed north, other Unionist women stayed behind. They managed alone in a hostile environment while their husbands avoided Confederate service in several ways. The men might leave Texas, go into hiding, or even join US troops. By supporting their men's decisions, the women acted against the Confederacy and, tacitly, in favor of the Union. Northern Methodists Jane Brown Condit and her husband, William Spangler Condit, for example, had immigrated to Lamar County from Kentucky in 1851, and William prospered as a stocker raiser. Early in the war, vigilantes ordered William to leave the region, and he went to his mother's home in Kentucky. Jane and their ten children remained in Lamar County, and William died before he could return to Texas.[8] Jane coped by herself, taking care of the household as best she could, undoubtedly fearing for her husband's safety and then mourning his death.

In some rural areas, notably the forks of the Sulphur River, Unionist men "took to 'the brush'—thickets, bottomlands, or other wooded areas" rather than be drafted into the Southern army. Confederate general Henry E. McCulloch in 1863 estimated that a quarter of the population of Fannin County was aiding deserters. The men in hiding depended on their families to supply them with food and clothing.[9] Mary Ellen Terry Chamblee, a native of Greene County, Illinois, kept track of her Unionist husband, Frank, with a code of carefully placed sticks. She met him regularly, bringing food for almost three years. If the Chamblees thought that Frank was safe at war's end, they were mistaken, for in the spring of 1865, a group of assailants appeared at the Chamblee home. Mary Ellen attempted to help Frank elude them by disguising him in her clothes. The ruse failed, and Frank was murdered, rendering futile Mary Ellen's years of efforts.[10] Countless other men, however, succeeded in hiding out, and their wives and families made possible their safekeeping.

Some Texas men headed north and joined the Union army, undoubtedly creating extremely uncomfortable situations for the women whom they left behind. William Gaston, a Mexican War veteran, came from Illinois to Titus County, where he met and married Amanda Perkins in 1860. Threatened with charges of treason against the Confederacy, William fled Texas, leaving Amanda and their young son. William traveled to Springfield, Missouri, and joined the Sixth Missouri Cavalry. Through a letter published in a Fort Smith, Arkansas, newspaper in 1864, he urged Amanda to escape to his previous residence in Illinois. She remained in Titus County, however, doubtless deeply concerned about her husband's military service in hostility to her country of residence.[11] William returned safely to Texas after the war, although possibly missing a leg. William and Amanda apparently made little secret of their joy in the Union victory, in 1868 naming a newborn second son Philip Henry Sheridan Gaston in honor of the Union general who oversaw the military occupation of Texas. The Gaston family eventually left Texas, however, and resettled in Missouri.[12]

Another group of women, likely fearful and often alone, were the wives of a group of influential North Texas Unionists who fought exhaustively to keep Texas from seceding. When faced with defeat, these men placed their loyalty with their new home state rather than the United States, to the extent of even joining the Confederate Army.[13] No words have survived from the women who were married to these men, yet one can imagine their taking a keen and anxious interest in the goings-on in their home counties and in Austin. Women such as Eliza Smiley Armstrong, Harriet Shields Epperson, and Mary Gattis Latimer, whose legislator husbands all worked to keep Texas in the Union, may well have been relieved that age or disability precluded their men from serving in the Confederate Army. One could wonder about the response of Kentucky native Emily Irwin Williams. Her husband, Lemuel Hardin Williams, was a wealthy Lamar County slaveholder, yet he voted against secession in the state convention. After Texas seceded, he then proceeded to raise a company for the Confederate Army and served in the Indian Territory. Emily remained behind with seven children and seven slaves.[14] Confusion, grief, anger, and worry may well have filled Emily Williams's mind during Lemuel's tumultuous journey from Unionist leader to Confederate commander.

The foremost Unionist in North Texas was James Webb Throckmorton of Collin County. Annie Rattan Throckmorton, born and reared in Illinois, married him in 1848 and moved to the prairie outside of McKinney. Rearing ten children, Annie Throckmorton remained at home while her husband's work as a Texas state representative and US congressman took him first to Austin and then to Washington DC. Annie Throckmorton eagerly kept abreast of James's thoughts and actions. Historian Pearl Cashell Jackson wrote that Annie Throckmorton "spent every spare moment reading that she might be well informed on the topics of the day, and be able to discuss them with the husband she idolized. . . . She even read dull Congressional Records while her husband was in Congress so as to write intelligently to him on the questions that were absorbing his mind." When asked how she could bear to read the *Congressional Record*, Annie Throckmorton replied, "I began it as a duty; now I find it necessary and really enjoy it."[15] One can imagine women such as Annie Throckmorton, well informed and attentive, having strong opinions about the fate of the Union in Texas, and being pummeled by the shifting currents around them. Certainly they must have felt great anxiety as their husbands weighed their futures and ultimately threw in with the rebellious South. At times they surely feared for their husbands' lives as the men fought for a cause in which they did not believe. James Throckmorton faced Union fire in battles in Oklahoma and Arkansas before returning safely to Collin County.

Like many other parts of the Confederacy where Union sentiment was strong, North Texas was the site of bloody retribution against Unionists. Deadly outbursts occurred throughout the region for the duration of the war. Women experienced the violence firsthand, although no white women were physically harmed.[16]

Black women were a different matter. Pro-Confederacy Texans worried incessantly about slave rebellions, which they believed would be stirred up by abolitionists. While slave women were few in number in North Texas, clearly white Southerners believed that they were fully capable of political thought and political action and greatly feared them.[17] Slave women suffered dearly because of white Texans' suspicions.

Fannin County in particular was the site of retaliations against slave women who were thought to be rebellious. In February 1860 a slave named Emma and two men allegedly murdered their master and his family, and all three were hanged.[18] During the hot and fear-wracked summer of 1860, the body of outspoken Confederate sympathizer Alfred E. Pace's six-year-old son was found in a water hole. One of Pace's female slaves, whose name was never given in print, confessed to strangling the boy because he had said something to his mother that caused the slave's own son to receive a whipping. While a substantial minority of Bonham citizens wanted to burn the woman alive, she was hanged instead. Her actions, said a writer in the *Texas Advocate,* were stirred up by Northern Methodist abolitionists.[19] And when W. W. Stell's Paris home caught fire in July 1860, one of his female slaves confessed to the arson.[20] Although Confederates may not have believed that slaves were capable of coming up with plans of their own, they assumed that the slaves were certainly able to execute the suggestions of the people who sought to free them. This agency by slaves, real or imagined, was absolutely intolerable to the Confederates, and the slaves paid with their lives. Unlike white women, female slaves met the same fate as men who were suspected of violence against their owners. Their slave status, not their sex, decided their fates. Pro-slavery Texans would not tolerate insurrection by any bondsperson, male or female.

A handful of white women spoke out boldly against the Confederacy. Confederate officials tended to disregard them, not holding them responsible for actions for which their menfolk were imprisoned or executed, though their deeds and language sometimes surpassed the men's in treasonous content. Lucretia Hawley, for example, came to Texas with her husband, Elias Hawley, and her daughters from a previous marriage in the late 1850s. Shortly after war broke out, Elias Hawley abandoned his wife and fled Texas. Some of her neighbors suspected that she was a Union spy. In June 1862 Lucretia Hawley, her daughters, and two men attempted to leave Gainesville but were stopped. Although the men in their company were imprisoned, the women were not. In October Hawley and one of the men, John Cottrell, attempted to "escape" Cooke County and made it only as far as western Grayson County. Cottrell was executed in late 1862; Hawley's fate is unknown but she evidently was not killed as a traitor.[21]

The most extreme incidence of violence against northern sympathizers occurred in Cooke County, with its close-knit community of Unionists, many related by blood or marriage.[22] Forty-one men were hanged in October 1862 and several others killed, accused of treason against the Confederacy. No women were arrested or hanged in Gainesville despite their evident interest and involvement in the activities before, during, and after the hangings. When investigators, fearing a plot against the Confederacy, searched Unionist homes, they allegedly found "large quantities of powder, lead and cartridges... concealed in beds, ladies' wearing apparel & in every conceivable secret place," indicating that some of the women were tacitly involved in secreting weapons in their homes and personal possessions. While apparently no women were actual members of the so-called Peace Party, an early chronicler of events indicated that they "seemed to be well instructed concerning the organization."[23]

Although women seldom bore arms, Illinois native Salina Dukes McGuire, a mere twenty-three years old and likely pregnant with her first child, expressed her political leanings with a gun in early 1862. When vigilantes tried to impress her husband, Cornelius McGuire, into service against suspected Hopkins County Unionists, Salina McGuire threatened the terrorists with a rifle and forced them off the family property.[24] The vigilantes did not return.

Surely one of the boldest Unionist women in North Texas was Sarah Francis DeLemeron, a native of Morgan County, Illinois, who left no doubt as to her political affiliation. She and her husband, Joel, a Mexican War veteran, married in 1854, settled in Cooke County, and accrued considerable wealth. Joel DeLemeron fell under suspicion in 1862 because he had rendered aid to Nancy Ware and Elizabeth West Boyles, whose husbands were missing after a roundup of Unionists in Gainesville. Confederate operative George Bradly, posing as a Unionist, came to the DeLemeron home on October 30, 1862, trying to trick Joel DeLemeron into betraying his Unionist sympathies. Joel DeLemeron demurred, claiming to be neutral. Sarah Francis, however, wished Bradly "great success" in his fictional plot against the Confederacy and reproved her husband, saying that "he could do so, too, if he were not afraid." DeLemeron then confessed to repairing Nancy Ware's wagon and loaning Elizabeth Boyles a horse to help her escape from Cooke County to Missouri. Sarah DeLemeron then said, "If the truth must come, my husband is as good a Union man as I am a woman—and I am as good as they ever make 'em." After elaborate machinations to entrap him, Joel DeLemeron was arrested, found guilty, and sentenced to life in prison.[25]

Joel DeLemeron was imprisoned in Austin, and Sarah followed him there. She launched a legal appeal for his release but soon effected a different type of liberation by smuggling him a saw and auger. He quickly escaped from prison and headed for Mexico. Sarah was "threatened with hanging" but escaped in the night. She and her young child arrived in St. Louis in September 1863. She told her story to the media and observed that there was a "'right smart Union feeling in Texas, but they dar'nt own it.'"[26] Sarah and Joel were eventually reunited and in 1900 were living in southern Illinois.[27]

Joel DeLemeron was unusually fortunate in being sentenced to prison, for across North Texas Confederate partisans killed Union sympathizers throughout the 1860s. Most of these men were married and often had families with numerous children and infants. As their men were rounded up, sometimes tried and sometimes not, and hanged, wives, daughters, and sisters participated in the proceedings in a variety of ways. A number of men were hanged in private, out of sight and without the knowledge of their families. In Hopkins County in February 1862, members of the Howard and Hemby families were physically prevented from seeing their menfolk before their deaths. According to Benjamin Ober, who observed the hangings, some of the condemned men's wives showed up but "were driven away with threats without a sight of their loved ones."[28] These women were left widows without witnessing the executions that caused their losses.

During the trials and executions of the men in Gainesville in October 1862, their families paid close attention. Mahuldah Hicklin Clark not only monitored the trial of her husband, Nathaniel Clark, but also kept an account of events, which has not survived. Her son, Lemuel Clark, wrote in the early twentieth century, "Now it mite be asked by some how I knew so mutch a bout this matter. I will tell you why. My mother an foalks was rite there, and she was a cloast observer an kep a note of all things pertaining to the crime."[29]

As the Cooke County men were rounded up, tried, and hanged, their families crowded around, weeping and sometimes screaming.[30] Traumatized children recalled for many years seeing their fathers hanged.[31] When three-year-old America Jane Dawson (whose name perhaps reflected her family's political leanings) went with her mother to recover the body of her father, Arphax Dawson, she saw children kicking at his corpse lying in the street.[32] A number of the families were unable to retrieve the bodies of their loved ones, which were subsequently buried in shallow graves on the banks of Pecan Creek. Heavy rain washed some of the corpses from the ground, while others were uncovered by rooting hogs. Half a century later, Lettie Diston recalled seeing a hog dragging her stepfather's arm "over town."[33]

Some of the condemned men left wills to direct affairs after their deaths, indicating their concerns about their bereaved families. Henry Field, for example, left his pregnant sixteen-year-old daughter Lydia Field McCool, whose husband William would soon be killed, three cows and calves and a roan filly colt. To his wife, Mary Ann Bail Field, he left "for her and my infant childrens benefit and maintanence the improvements on their land, two mares, a filly, a colt, all the 'cattle' and 'movable effects.'" The two youngest Field children would not be old enough to remember their father.[34]

Northern Methodist missionary Anthony Bewley, hanged in Fort Worth in 1860, left a poignant letter for his wife, Jane. He proclaimed his innocence and noted the difficulty that the situation presented to her: "You, my love, will have the lasting satisfaction to know that your husband was innocent, for you have been with me for some twenty-six years, and your constitution is emaciated and gone down to feebleness." Anthony wanted to smooth the future for his family:

> You will have to spend the remaining part of your life as a bereaved widow, with your orphan children, *with one blind daughter*. . . . Tell George and baby, when they get old enough, they must seek religion and be good boys, and meet pa in heaven. I want William and John, as they are the oldest, to be good to their mother and their blind sister. Do with your scant means as you think best. I have feelings—I can not tell you *how* I feel for you. . . . I can only leave you in the hands of Him in whom I put my trust. . . . Dear Jane, I can not tell you what is the best course for you to pursue, but I want you to get somewhere that the children can have a chance at school. . . . I do hope that the good Lord will comfort and guide you to the best conclusions.[35]

Jane Bewley had the small comfort of knowing that her husband was thinking of her and their children even as he became a sacrificial victim to the Unionist cause in the South.

The killings were, of course, devastating to the survivors. Some women lost both husbands and fathers. Many of the women still had numerous children at home; several from Gainesville had infants, and at least two were pregnant when their husbands were killed. When Lydia McCool gave birth to a son in the spring of 1863, she named him William after his murdered father, commemorating the loss of her beloved.[36] The widows' problems were both psychological and practical, as Mahuldah Clark indicated in a letter to her son in February 1863, a scant four months after her husband's hanging: "Times is hard. I hird [heard] that some of the men at Gainesville was a going to administer [confiscate] on the mens property that was hung. If thay do I want you to come and tend to it for me. I dont want them gentlemen to have any thing that I have got. . . . Tell Evaline and Cynthia if they knowed how lonesome I was they would come and stay with me."[37] Clark was worried about Confederate designs on her property as well as emotionally overwhelmed in the loss of her husband of twenty-one years.

The bereaved coped with their losses in a mixture of ways. For the most part, they suffered in private—but not always. Their public protests make clear that many of the women had political leanings of their own and believed that their opinions had weight. One of the first victims of the furor against suspected Unionists was William Crawford, who had immigrated to Tarrant County with his wife Mary Crawford and their four small children from Minnesota in 1860. Possibly because of northern publications sent to Crawford by family members (and confiscated by local authorities), Fort Worth pro-slavery forces believed him to be an abolitionist and lynched him on July 17, 1860.

The widowed Mary Crawford returned to Minnesota and in September 1860 wrote for the local newspaper her account of events, which was then picked up by national outlets such as the *New York Tribune* and the abolitionist newspaper *The Liberator.*[38] In her essay Crawford depicted her husband as a hardworking family man, desirous of better land and opportunity and completely unaware that he was suspected of being an abolitionist. As she told the story, William left their house in Fort Worth on the morning of July 17 with their two small sons to bring in a load of sand. According to the boys, a local merchant, Charles Turner, his overseer, and another man overtook their father and accused him of promising to help a slave run away. By the time the little boys arrived to summon their mother, their father had been hanged from a pecan tree. Mary Crawford wrote, "My grief, my indignation, my misery, I have no words, no desire to describe." A postmortem inquest said that William Crawford was hanged by "some person or persons to the jurors unknown" and found that Crawford "richly deserved his fate." Searchers scoured the Crawford home for evidence of Unionist activity but found nothing. At that point, Mary Crawford decided to take matters into her own hands, and she sent for Turner, the alleged murderer. When he refused to go to her, she went to his store with a loaded pistol: "I wished to confront him with my boys, and if he showed signs of guilt to shoot him down." Thinking of her children, however, Crawford left without firing a shot.

A week after the murder, the family set out from Fort Worth. Funds from a local benefactor enabled the destitute family to reach their relatives in Minnesota, where Mary Crawford wrote her account of the outrage. Turner felt sufficiently stung by Crawford's accusations that he published a rebuttal of the charges in the *Dallas Herald* the following spring.[39] While Mary Crawford could not prevent the death of her husband and elected not to carry out blood vengeance, she could name his alleged killer and at least make him defend himself in a public forum.

Most of the victims of Confederate violence were buried quietly or their families were unable to retrieve their bodies. Caroline and Lizzie Boyd of Collin County, however, used their father's memorial as a means of venting their anger at his murderers. When Confederate soldiers hanged Hugh Boyd in March 1864, the sisters erected a tombstone over his grave, reading, "Murdered by a band of traitors because of his devotion to the federal government."[40] The Boyd women made clear their sentiments about both the Confederacy and their father's violent end.

Bereaved women had little choice but to move on with their lives. Most had children to think of and little means to provide financially for their families. Like the Crawfords, some families of the men hanged in Gainesville left Texas shortly after the murders, heading for Union territory. Dicy Chiles, widow of Henry Chiles, took her eight children, including "a babe of only a few weeks old" and immediately went to Lamar County, Texas, then to Knox County, Illinois, at the end of the war.[41] Adelia Knowles Kilborn, widow of Hiram Kilborn, and her three youngest children moved to Bourbon County, Kansas, sometime before 1870.[42] The women could not or would not stay in the region whose people had taken their men from them.

Even in their grief, families divided by the war could not be reunited. North Carolina native Austin Glenn was a farmer and minister, probably Northern Methodist Episcopal, and he was hanged in Hunt County in early 1863, although one of his sons and a son-in-law were in the Confederate Army. According to family stories, Austin's widow, Rhoda, three adult sons and their wives and children, as well as six unmarried children departed Texas the morning after the hanging, not slowing until their wagon broke an axle in Arkansas. They eventually made their way to southern Illinois, where they had relatives, and the adult sons joined the Union Army. But their married daughter, Missouri Ann Glenn Ball, remained in Texas because her husband, Joseph Ball, was in the Confederate Army. Two of the Glenn brothers died in the war: one in Confederate service and another in the Union Army.[43]

Some women, like Mary Crawford and Mary Ellen Alexander Goss, widow of Curd Goss, returned to the places that they had come from before moving to Texas, but always in the United States rather than the Confederacy. In Goss's case that refuge was DeKalb County, Missouri, where her youngest son had been born about 1858. In 1870 she had several hundred dollars to her name, and her oldest son, age twenty, was farming and supporting his three younger siblings.[44] Eliza Jane Dougherty Harper, widow of Manadier Harper, went back to central Illinois where she and her husband had married in 1845. In 1870 she was in Peoria, eking out an existence by taking in laundry. Her three oldest children helped support their family, which included a daughter who was only a few months old when her father was killed.[45]

Some of the refugees—perhaps most—sought sanctuary with their kin. A single woman without a male relative for protection would be vulnerable to all sorts of difficulties, not the least of which would be financial survival. Margaret Kendrick Chiles, widow of Ephraim Chiles, left Texas immediately after Ephraim's murder with her three small sons. Heading first to Iowa, she eventually arrived in St. Clair County, Missouri, near her brothers and remained there the rest of her life.[46] Lydia Field McCool took her two children and went to live with her grandparents and sister in Iowa.[47]

Because Northern Methodists considered Anthony Bewley a martyr, Jane Bewley received help from strangers as well as her family. Marooned with her children in Missouri, Bewley eventually made her way to the home of her daughter and son-in-law in Allen County, Kansas. She nearly died of pneumonia, but in March 1861 set out for Baldwin City, Kansas, and was again ill with pneumonia for almost six months. Contributions from strangers enabled Jane Bewley to buy a small home and get medical help for herself and her blind daughter, Catherine.[48] She remarried in 1863. In 1872 a Methodist writer observed that "the Northern Indiana Conferences adopted Mr. Bewley's children, and are educating them."[49]

Like Jane Bewley, a number of the widows remarried within a short period of time, sometimes within a matter of months after their husbands died. In nineteenth century America a single parent had a difficult time raising a family alone, and both males and females usually remarried after the death of a spouse. The women of North Texas married men from Union states who likely shared their political allegiances. Susan Mary Hedenberg Thomas, widow of Eli Sigler Thomas, married fellow Illinoisan William Carrel Hayes in Grayson County in May 1863, and they moved west to Jack County, Texas, an area even less sparsely populated than North Texas, which had voted not to secede from the United States. Jane Stalcup Dawson, with five children of her own, two of them toddlers, wed Kentucky native Creed T. Walthall in January 1864 in Sherman. Walthall was a widower with eight children, and the couple added two more sons to the blended family.[50] New partners could provide fresh starts and stability for women and their children.

For the women who stayed in North Texas, whether single or married, the adjustments took a long time, if they came at all. In June 1869, six years after her husband's murder, Susan West Leffel, widow of David Leffel, was living in Pilot Point, Denton County, the home of many fellow Unionists. In a letter to Texas Governor Edmund J. Davis, she complained about the ill treatment that the families continued to receive. She reminded Davis of the plight of the Unionists and observed that her family and others remained vulnerable to predations by former Confederates: “In the first place the vigilent committy hung my husband (at the time they hanged so many at Gainesville) on the account of his Union proclivities, and left me in a sad and mornful condition but still after I have had all that to endure and my family and many of our sympathizing friend (that the leader of their familys were taken off by those nocternal visitors and destroyed by the hanging) are ever since the war as the carcas to the Eagel.” She complained of unwarranted arrests, thefts, pistol-whippings, and “slanders.” She continued to grieve for her husband despite the passage of time: “It is indeed hart rendring that my husband, as kind as he was, and great sorce of my comfort & living should be hanged and his helpless family, (with many others) are as barbrsly treated as tho we were even aliving with the Indians; simply for them to take vengance uppon us because we were and are in favor of our Fathers Country and Government.”[51]

Leffel neatly summarizes the plight of Unionist women in North Texas: kept from direct political action themselves, they nonetheless viewed the United States as the land of their ancestors, and they defended it passionately with the only tools available to them as women: words and care for their loved ones. While many of their men paid for their loyalty with their lives, the women remained behind and paid throughout their lives instead.

The women most affected by the secession of Texas likely never completely recovered from the tumult surrounding the Civil War. Some were uprooted, some forced to reconcile conflicting political views, and some suffered significant losses of family members. As the years wore on, the violence in North Texas became a taboo subject, and the women must have wondered how they could bear witness to all that they had experienced. It remains for others, a century and a half later, to remember the women who loved the Union as much as their menfolk did.

Notes

1. The author gratefully acknowledges the generous help of research assistant Meredith May; Robyn Reid of the Mary Couts Burnett Library, Texas Christian University; Colleen Clark Cari, moderator of the Facebook group Gainesville Texas—The Great Hanging—October 1862 Civil War; and Cathy Magleby, creator and moderator of the blog Gainesville, Texas 1862. All citations from the blog are used with permission of Cathy Magleby. Walter L. Buenger, *Secession and the Union in Texas* (Austin: University of Texas Press, 1984), 67.
2. James Lemuel Clark, *Civil War Recollections of James Lemuel Clark*, ed. L. D. Clark (College Station: Texas A&M University Press, 1984), 113, 117.
3. Amy Murrell Taylor, *The Divided Family in Civil War America* (Chapel Hill: University of North Carolina Press, 2005), 4, 41-42; Keith S. Bohannon, "They Had Determined to Root Us Out: Dual Memoirs by a Unionist Couple in Blue Ridge Georgia," in *Enemies of the Country: New Perspectives on Unionists in the Civil War South*, ed. John C. Inscoe and Robert C. Kenzer (Athens: University of Georgia Press, 2001), 104.
4. James Marten, *Texas Divided: Loyalty and Dissent in the Lone Star State, 1856-1874* (Lexington: University Press of Kentucky, 1990), 44; Richard B. McCaslin, *Tainted Breeze: The Great Hanging at Gainesville, Texas, 1862* (Baton Rouge: Louisiana State University Press, 1994), 36.
5. Charles Elliott and Leroy Monroe Vernon, *South-Western Methodism: A History of the M.E. Church in the South-west, from 1844 to 1864* (Cincinnati, OH: Poe and Hitchcock, 1868), 29.
6. Elliott and Vernon, *South-Western Methodism*, 156.
7. Elliott and Vernon, *South-Western Methodism*, 157-58.
8. David Pickering and Judy Falls, *Brush Men and Vigilantes: Civil War Dissent in Texas* (College Station: Texas A&M University Press, 2000), 54; "William Spangler Condit," accessed December 22, 2013, http:// http://www.findagrave.com/cgi-bin/fg.cgi?page=gr&GRid=67916671; Eighth Census of the United States, 1860.
9. Pickering and Falls, *Brush Men*, 15.

10. Pickering and Falls, *Brush Men*, 16, 21, 102-3.

11. Pickering and Falls, *Brush Men*, 168.

12. Tenth Census of the United States, 1880.

13. Thomas C. Dyer, "Vermont Yankees in King Cotton's Court: Cyrena and Amherst Stone in Confederate Atlanta," in *Enemies of the Country: New Perspectives on Unionists in the Civil War South*, ed. John C. Inscoe and Robert C. Kenzer (Athens: University of Georgia Press, 2001), 127.

14. A. W. Neville, "Williams, Lemuel Hardin," *Handbook of Texas Online, accessed December 22, 2013,* http://www.tshaonline.org/handbook/online/articles/fwi29; Eighth Census of the United States (1860), Lamar County, Texas, Schedule 1 (Free Population); Eighth Census of the United States (1860), Lamar County, Texas, Schedule 2 (Slave Population).

15. Pearl Cashell Jackson, *Texas Governors' Wives* (Austin: E. L. Steck, 1915), 65, 69-70.

16. The death of a Mrs. Hillier in Clark County, Arkansas, was the only documented death of a white woman near Texas during the war. Unionist Frederick Sumner told of her death in the spring of 1862. Her husband, a Northerner, was suspected of Union sentiments and tried before a provost-court. Given a choice of hanging or joining the Confederate Army, he chose the latter. His wife erupted in the court, saying "she wished to God the Union army would advance and take possession of Texas, that her husband might return and provide for his family." After the husband reported for military duty, six men, dressed in women's clothes, came to her house and accused her of being an abolitionist. According to Sumner, "They dragged her to the nearest tree, and, regardless of her pleadings for mercy, to spare her life for the sake of her innocent children, they put a rope around her neck, swung her up, and left her in her death-struggles, in the presence of her terrified little ones, till next morning, when some of the neighbors took down the body and buried it." A depiction of the hanging appeared in *Frank Leslie's Illustrated Newspaper* in 1864, showing three small children pleading for their mother as she is hoisted up by men wearing dresses. See Thomas L. Wilson, *Sufferings Endured for a Free Government: A History of the Cruelties and Atrocities of the Rebellion* (Washington, DC: Thomas L. Wilson, 1864), 260; McCaslin, *Tainted Breeze*, 57; *Frank Leslie's Illustrated Newspaper*, February 20, 1864.) Hillier's

outburst scarcely branded her an abolitionist; rather, her desire to keep her husband at home echoed the cries of women across the Confederacy, fearful of losing their means of support. See Drew Gilpin Faust, *Mothers of Invention: Women of the Slaveholding South in the American Civil War* (Chapel Hill: University of North Carolina Press, 1996), 238-44.

17. Randolph B. Campbell, *An Empire for Slavery: The Peculiar Institution in Texas, 1821-1865* (Baton Rouge: Louisiana State University Press, 1989), 264-66, 275.

18. Donald E. Reynolds, *Texas Terror: The Slave Insurrection Panic of 1860 and the Secession of the Lower South* (Baton Rouge: Louisiana State University Press, 2007), 23.

19. Pickering and Falls, *Brush Men,* 11; *Clarksville Standard,* June 30, 1860. According to the *Texas State Gazette,* July 7, 1860, the murder was one of "several" in Fannin County "caused by Abolitionists tampering with the negroes."

20. Pickering and Falls, *Brush Men,* 12.

21. Sam Acheson and Julie Ann Hudson O'Connell, eds., "George Washington Diamond's Account of the Great Hanging at Gainesville, 1862," *Southwestern Historical Quarterly* 66 (January 1963): 402-4.

22. The known family ties among the Gainesville victims are explored in the blog *Gainesville, Texas 1862,* moderated by Cathy Magleby. Susan Emeline West Leffel, the wife of David M. Leffel, and Elizabeth West Boyles, the wife of William Boyles, were sisters. Cloe Carter Floyd, wife of Thomas B. Floyd, and Anne Carter Morris, wife of M. Wesley Morris, also were sisters. Lydia Field McCool was the daughter of Henry Field and the wife of William McCool, who was hanged in the latter part of 1862. Mary Ann Dawson Dye also lost both her father, Arphax R. Dawson, and her husband, Rama Dye. Cynthia Ann Neely Martin lost her husband, Richard N. Martin, while her brother's wife, Elizabeth Burch Neeley, lost her father, Barnabus Burch. Margaret "Peggy" Kendrick Chiles and Dicey A. Kennedy Chiles were married to brothers, Ephraim and Henry Chiles, respectively.

23. Acheson and O'Connell, "George Washington Diamond," 362.

24. Pickering and Falls, *Brush Men,* 57; "Salina Dukes (b. 26 Feb 1839, d. 25 Jul 1916)," accessed Dec. 27, 2013: familytreemaker.genealogy.com/users/g/r/i/Patricia-A-Griffith-NE/WEBSITE-001/UHP-0199.html.
25. Acheson and O'Connell, "George Washington Diamond," 409-13.
26. Milwaukee *Daily Sentinel,* September 14, 1863; San Francisco *Bulletin,* September 30, 1863.
27. Twelfth Census of the United States (1900), St. Louis, Missouri.
28. Pickering and Falls, *Brush Men,* 61.
29. Clark, *Civil War Recollections,* 104.
30. Acheson and O'Connell, "George Washington Diamond," 362, 381, 389.
31. Letter from Ruth Sheppard, Auburn, Washington, to "Jean and Leon," no date, in possession of Colleen Clark Cari.
32. Facebook posting by Cindy Spears Faulkner, February 14, 2011, to Gainesville Texas—The Great Hanging—October 1862 Civil War group, accessed December 22, 2013, https://www.facebook.com/groups/40399537273/.
33. McCaslin, *Tainted Breeze,* 90; Clark, *Civil War Recollections,* 108-9.
34. *Gainesville, Texas 1862* blog: "Henry Field," blog entry by Cathy Magleby, August 20, 2009, accessed December 22, 2013, http://gainesvilletx1862.blogspot.com/search/label/Field-Henry; Eighth Census of the United States, 1860.
35. Elliott and Vernon, *South-Western Methodism,* 164-65.
36. *Gainesville, Texas 1862* blog: "William R. Rhodes," blog entry by Cathy Magleby, September 28, 2008, accessed December 22, 2013, http://gainesvilletx1862.blogspot.com/search/label/Rhodes-William%20R.; "Eli M. Scott Family," blog entry by Cathy Magleby, November 18, 2008, accessed December 22, 2013, http://gainesvilletx1862.blogspot.com/search/label/Scott-Eli; "Bennet C. Barnes," blog entry by Cathy Magleby, October 15, 2008 , accessed December 22, 2013, http://gainesvilletx1862.blogspot.com/search/label/Barnes-Bennet; "Lydia Field McCool--Her Story Continues," blog entry by Cathy Magleby, September 17, 2009, accessed December 22, 2013, http://gainesvilletx1862.blogspot.com/search/label/McCool-William; "Who's Who? The Morris Men," blog entry by Cathy

Magleby, March 25, 2011, accessed December 22, 2013, http://gainesvilletx1862.blogspot.com/search/label/Morris.

37. Clark, *Civil War Recollections*, 115-16.

38. Mary Crawford, "A Wife's Account of Her Husband's Murder" in *The Liberator*, 31, vol. 14 (April 5, 1861); originally published in the *Waseca (Minn.) Citizen.*

39. Letter from Charles Turner to the Dallas *Herald*, April 16, 1861.

40. J. Lee Stambaugh and Lillian Stambaugh, A History of Collin County, Texas (Austin: Texas State Historical Association, 1958), 69.

41. McCaslin, *Tainted Breeze*, 188; *Gainesville, Texas 1862* blog: "A Martyr for His Country," blog entry by Cathy Magleby, February 29, 2012, accessed December 27, 2013, http://gainesvilletx1862.blogspot.com/search/label/Chiles-Henry.

42. *Gainesville, Texas 1862* blog: "Preacher . . . Not the Kind That Preached for Money," blog entry by Cathy Magleby, February 12, 2012, accessed December 27, 2013, http://gainesvilletx1862.blogspot.com/search/label/Kilborn-Hiram.

43. Pickering and Falls, *Brush Men*, 81, 99-100.

44. Ninth Census of the United States (1870), DeKalb County, Missouri.

45. *Gainesville, Texas 1862* blog: "Eliza Harper—Wash Woman," blog entry by Cathy Magleby, May 21, 2008, accessed December 27, 2013, http://gainesvilletx1862.blogspot.com/search/label/Harper-M.D.

46. *Gainesville, Texas 1862* blog: "Dicey Chiles," blog entry by Cathy Magleby, October 16, 2008, accessed December 27, 2013, http://gainesvilletx1862.blogspot.com/search/label/Chiles-Ephraim.

47. *Gainesville, Texas 1862* blog: "Lydia Field McCool: Her Story Continues," blog entry by Cathy Magleby, October 17, 2009, accessed December 27, 2013, http://gainesvilletx1862.blogspot.com/search/label/McCool-William.

48. Elliott and Vernon, *South-Western Methodism*, 179-80.

49. Homer S. Thrall, History of Methodism in Texas (Houston: E. S. Cushing, 1872), 125.

50. "Jane Caroline Stalcup Walthall," accessed December 27, 2013, http://www.findagrave.com/cgi-bin/fg.cgi?page=gr&GRid=27993297.

51. *Letter from Susan West Leffel to Edmund J. Davis, June 11, 1869,* Texas Governor's Office Records, Archives Division, Texas State Library, Austin, on *Gainesville, Texas 1862* blog: "Left me in a sad and mornful condition: Susan Leffel, widow of David Miller Leffel," blog entry by Cathy Magleby, April 20, 2011, accessed December 27, 2013, http://gainesvilletx1862.blogspot.com/search/label/Leffel-David%Miller.

Image 19. Sarah Katherine "Kate" Stone.

Courtesy John Q. Anderson Papers, Mss. 2156, 2162, Louisiana and Lower Mississippi Valley Collections, LSU Libraries, Baton Rouge, LA.

Chapter 10

"They Call Us All Renegades in Tyler"

Elite Refugee Women in Civil War Texas

Candice N. Shockley

In August 1863 the *Galveston Weekly News* published Lt. Col. Caleb Goldsmith Forshey's sardonic account of the tide of elite planter families flowing westward into Texas in an "exodus" following the surrender of Vicksburg, Mississippi. In considerable detail, Forshey described the "woe begone [*sic*]" crowds of once-regal elites huddled alongside "sullen" enslaved persons and "crippled mules" under "crazy carts and rickety wagons" in a "serio comic [*sic*] encampment" as they fruitlessly sought shelter from driving rain and sucking mud. With their "wan visages" and "dirty and patched habiliments," Forshey declared, "such droves of tatterdemalions would defy the pencil of Hogarth." Casting the Sabine River as the biblical River Jordan and Texas as the "Promised Land," Forshey wryly suggested that privileged Louisiana refugees expecting succor and protection be "placed at work upon the formidable line of fortifications… located along this western bank of Jordan." Three months later, J. W. Johnson of Boggy Depot, Choctaw Nation, took a strikingly different tone in a letter to the *Houston Tri-Weekly Telegraph* regarding a party of Confederate soldiers' wives bound for Texas from Union-occupied Missouri.[1]

Extolling the "patriotism, forbearance and long suffering" of the group, Johnson reported that while the women had no idea if their husbands still lived, they vowed "THEY would shoulder the musket and BREAST the storm of battle and fall a sacrifice upon the altar of their country's freedom" should the need arise. Johnson went on to encourage the "Ladies of Texas" to heed the example set by the Missouri women's "patriotic course" as Texans had "as yet…felt none of the hardships and privations of this war…"[2]

Nearly 250,000 white Southerners fled their homes and communities during the Civil War. While Federal troop occupations or the catastrophic physical destruction of battle forced many to seek shelter in neighboring Southern states, a large number of elite slaveholders voluntarily retreated in advance of such circumstances in order to preserve personal material property and enslaved populations. Confederates made clear distinctions between those planter-class refugees, many of whom intentionally evacuated prior to invasion in the interest of retaining personal wealth, and displaced persons—typically soldiers' families and occupants of the middle and lower rungs of the socioeconomic order. Those distinctions often caused refugees to be characterized as either "patriots" or "cowards," and in many cases determined the degree of assistance and inclusion offered. Displaced persons overwhelmingly inspired sympathy, public calls for aid, and ardent praise of their patriotic sacrifices. Elite refugees frequently encountered open censure, charges of cowardice, and a general lack of benevolence, particularly when accompanied by large groups of enslaved persons.[3]

Although wartime leaders—and postwar popular memory—promoted the image of a Confederacy wholly united in support of a "Cause" that superseded all other loyalties and interests, the experiences of elite refugees attest to a significant source of internal divisions on the Southern home front. Furthermore, the circumstances of war profoundly transformed the South's deeply rooted ideological constructions and prescriptions. Venerated in antebellum culture as the exemplar of "true" womanhood, the Southern Lady[4] occupied a privileged, protected position second only to elite white males at the apex of society. As the Civil War shattered the Southern social, political, and economic hierarchy, however, it destroyed the sources from which elite women drew understanding of their own identities and self-worth. The emergence of new wartime ideologies installed a new paragon of virtuous womanhood—the Confederate Woman—upon the pedestal formerly occupied by the revered Southern Lady. In his study of human mobility during the Civil War, Yael Sternhell argued that mass physical movements of Southerners provided the "fullest incarnation" of the war's transformation of antebellum civilization. Indeed, for many elite Ladies across the Confederacy, the refugee experience further revealed the complete and irreversible destruction of Southern culture and society. For many planter-class women who sought sanctuary in the Lone Star State, refugeeing in Texas proved no different.[5]

During his 1863 tour of the Confederacy, Arthur James Lyon Fremantle, then a lieutenant colonel in the British army, remarked that "in this country, where every white man is as good as another, by theory, and every white female is by courtesy a lady, there is only one class." While the common-born soldier of a complex, rigidly stratified British social order might indeed have perceived wartime white Southern culture as rather egalitarian, the single truth in Fremantle's observation existed in the words "by theory." In 1860 only one-third of the South's free population held enslaved persons, yet that minority controlled nearly 95 percent of the region's agricultural property in terms of land and human chattel. Of those slaveholders, only 12 percent could be considered "planters." Most historians agree that the planter class generally encompassed whites who held more than twenty enslaved persons; the most exclusive stratum, elite planters, held one hundred or more enslaved persons. Scholars continue to debate the criteria required to classify middle-ranking Southerners. Sometimes termed "plain folk" or "yeomen," smaller slaveholders and non-slave owners fell between the planter class and the landless "poor whites" in the Southern economic hierarchy. Contemporary acknowledgement of membership in the planter aristocracy that dominated the social, political, and economic realms of the antebellum South, however, demanded much more than the accumulation of material wealth.[6]

In his study of Southern race relations, Joel Williamson argued that the Southern antebellum social hierarchy reflected decades of elite slaveholders' efforts to construct a superior "organic society" in which every individual played a strictly defined role. As Catherine Clinton contended in her study of antebellum plantation mistresses, elite males developed rigid race, gender, and class ideologies to justify the enslavement of people of African descent and maintain absolute authority over Southern society, politics, and economy. In that world, fulfillment of ideological constructs defined identity, determined stature and desirability, and theoretically assured a productive and peaceful civilization. According to Williamson, the slaveholding class expected plain folks to recognize their proper places in society and reinforce cultural prescriptions in exchange for paternalistic protection and guidance.[7]

Similarly, as Drew Gilpin Faust argued in her examination of the Civil War's influence on gender constructions, planter-class men also required the support and participation of elite women to ensure the perpetuation of the Southern power structure. As Anne Firor Scott pointed out in her analysis of the patriarchal system, the elite planter family served as the model for this idealized organic society and validated the absolute authority of the planter patriarch. To preserve their influence, material empires, and way of life, elite males promoted a reciprocal relationship that promised protection, provision, and veneration in exchange for elite women's fulfillment of the "Ladyhood" ideal. According to Faust, the characteristics ascribed to "Ladies"—gentility, domesticity, willing subservience, and constitutional and emotional delicacy – purportedly demonstrated true femininity and the epitome of womanhood. Additionally, outward manifestation of those "inherent" traits illustrated the alleged necessity of a Lady's utter dependence upon the patriarch.[8]

Therefore, while the designation of "Lady" compelled elite women to abide by strict conventions, it also entitled them to deference and privilege within a culture that denied women nearly any formal political and economic voice or authority. Fulfillment of the Southern Lady ideal afforded a superior moral influence within homes, local communities, and society that women of the lesser classes could not obtain. Furthermore, these deeply ingrained ideological constructions ensured that many elite women's conceptions of personal identity and worth rested on the extent to which they embodied the Ladyhood ideal. While the Civil War stripped away every vestige of normality for Southerners, it also positioned elite women in roles and situations far beyond the bounds of traditional cultural mores and divested them of the identity that protected and privileged them above all other women.

In March 1861 newly elected Vice President Alexander Stephens unambiguously outlined the Confederate government's founding principles, declaring that the South's "social fabric" rested upon the supremacy of the white race and the subjugation of people of African descent through enslavement. Therefore, he claimed, "all of the white race, however high or low, rich or poor, are equal. ..." In order to secure the support of all white Southerners—a measure of vital importance to the Confederacy's ability to wage war—political leaders, ministers, and the press heavily promoted an allegedly democratizing national identity based upon racial unity. Although white supremacy had been a predominant factor in the antebellum social hierarchy, Southern war propaganda deliberately elevated patriotic virtue over traditional class constructions. Furthermore, as historians such as James McPherson and LeeAnn Whites contended, to create an all-encompassing Confederate nationalism, leaders exploited Southerners' deeply rooted belief in the sacred obligation to defend hearth, home, and honor.[9]

In his study of Southern concepts of honor, Bertram Wyatt-Brown argued that defense of home and family constituted a fundamental moral imperative within antebellum culture. According to Wyatt-Brown, honor served as the cornerstone of the South's ethical code and provided meaning to white Southern lives regardless of class or gender. Therefore, through various means white men and women of all ranks established and maintained the honor of family and community through manifestations of fundamental elements such as valor. While the patriarchal system emphasized traits that purportedly rendered Ladies dependent upon white males for defense of their honor, Southern notions of valor also esteemed particular expressions of courage for women, such as unflagging endurance in times of strife. In the absence of male protection, then, women were expected to assume the zealous defense of households and communities. Southern leaders' two-pronged appeal to white supremacy and homeland defense actualized a Confederate nationalism that, for many non-slaveholding men and women, justified fighting a war that protected the institution of slavery and a social, economic, and political system that had perpetuated their own subordination. Because the ascendance of Confederate identity transcended class differences, however, the wartime environment provided opportunities for plain folk to gain a social parity that had been unattainable in the antebellum hierarchy.[10]

At the onset of war, elite Ladies fervently declared their willingness to present an unyielding, united front and to sacrifice personal well-being for the greater cause of the new nation. Southerners regarded themselves as the true inheritors of American revolutionary heritage, and many women of the planter aristocracy evoked the Revolutionary generation in vehement pledges to defend the Confederate home front. Margaret Ann "Meta" Morris Grimball, member of one of South Carolina's oldest and wealthiest planter families, disparagingly recounted in her diary the panicked flight of Beaufort citizens prior to the 1861 Battle of Port Royal. Grimball, a descendant of Continental Army general and Declaration of Independence signer Lewis Morris, scornfully remarked, "the women were seized with a perfect panic and many fled into the interior; such terror stricken creatures disgrace their Revolutionary Ancestry." In April 1861 the *Georgia Southern Confederacy* published an "appropriate communication" regarding "The Duty of the Ladies." In her submission "Ziola" affirmed the equal readiness of "Southern heroines of '61" to uphold the sacrifices of their "ancestors of '76." In fact she proclaimed, "were every man shot down in our ranks, there would not be wanting women who would shed their hearts' blood rather than submit to the base invaders of our soil."[11]

As Faust contended, because the war effort necessitated women's support on the home front, the Southern press strongly encouraged the formation of this new sacred embodiment of womanly virtue and honor: the Confederate Woman. According to this emerging female archetype, the Confederate Woman not only stoically bore any personal sacrifice for the cause but also embraced the ancient, venerated obligation to fiercely protect home and community. Initially, Confederates seemed to give equal esteem to traditional traits ascribed to ideal Southern Ladies and the evolving characteristics of Confederate Women. The *Texas Republican* provided an elaborate introduction to a transcription of Sallie O. Smith's address on behalf of the "Ladies of Marshall" to the departing W. P. Lane Rangers. According to the newspaper's editors, Smith appeared "beautifully and tastefully attired" as she arrived on "an elegant milk-white steed." Upon presenting a battle flag to the company, Smith, a "model of ease, grace, and loveliness," delivered a spirited promise to the Rangers. "When your dead bodies lie piled in hecatombs," she vowed in a "musical" voice, "some Southern Pentheailea...some *Boadiceas*, burning with Southern fire...like Pallas...rush with dagger in hand and achieve victory or immolation."[12]

While elite Ladies across the South invoked Revolutionary legacies and mythological warriors, Texans emphasized their particular heritage in creating standards for true patriotic dedication to their cause. An 1862 letter from women of southern Bexar Country addressed the "Ladies of San Antonio" and recalled the "patriotism and generosity ever distinguishing" women of Texas. The women also announced their commitment to uphold their heritage of female valor, declaring "we have no fears feeling fully equal to the task of self-defense." Texas women also drew upon the hallowed inheritance of the Texas Revolution in pledges to sacrifice personal interests in the fight for "independence and liberty." During a July 1861 flag presentation to the Fayetteville Academy Guards, Mary B. Breeding reminded her male classmates of "our fathers" relentless fight for Texas's independence from Mexico, admonishing the "true Texas boys" to "maintain the blood-bought honor of your fathers or never return to us."[13]

Southern newspapers heralded women who adopted this burgeoning Confederate identity that measured value by degree of sacrifice for the cause and demonstration of patriotic courage rather than class. The *Atlanta Southern Confederacy* reprinted a Texas woman's August 1861 letter under the headline "A Lady with the Right Spirit," characterizing her sentiments as "pure and lofty patriotism." Describing the departure of her four sons for war, the woman admitted that while "my boys were... far dearer than my own life," she hoped "the last Southern man on earth—my sons among them—may fall on the field of battle" to defend the honor of home and family. As for the possibility of Confederate surrender, she continued, "I had rather, a thousand times, see their heads laid low in the grave, than live to see them submit...." Such expressions illustrate the developing wartime expectations of ideal women. The effusive approval of Southern leaders and members of the press further ensured that the Confederate Woman replaced the Southern Lady as the preeminent model of female virtue on the home front.[14]

In spite of thousands of similar vows made by women across the South, when theoretical sacrifices for a unified cause became imminent reality, some elites abandoned previous pledges in favor of conserving personal wealth and resources. Four months after Meta Grimball condemned the cowardice and selfishness of South Carolinian planters who had chosen to escape in advance of Federal troops, Grimball's husband evacuated his own large enslaved population. When eighty-four bondsmen escaped the family's Saint Paul's Parish rice plantation, the Grimballs abandoned their home and fled to Spartanburg, remaining there for the duration of the war. In her diary, Grimball confessed that although she and her peers along South Carolina's coast had been "so loud in their expressions of determination while the war was in Virginia, [we] feel very faint now that it has come upon us."[15]

Many of the elite slaveholding families of the Lower Mississippi River valley grew equally apprehensive as Federal troops captured Confederate forts along the river near Tennessee and Missouri. Fearing the likely confiscation of personal assets, including enslaved populations, as well as the escape of enslaved persons into Union-occupied areas, many planter families decided to flee rather than attempt to defend their homes and communities. In April 1863 twenty-two-year-old Louisianan Katherine "Kate" Stone and her family abandoned Brokenburn, their 1,260-acre cotton plantation near the Mississippi River. When a friend learned of the family's decision to leave, Stone admitted in her diary, she "sent me word that I was a great coward to run away." Outside the relatively isolated confines of rural plantation society, many elite refugee women experienced blatant incivility, social ostracism, and public criticism for the first time in their lives as a result of the radical social transformations that enshrined the Confederate Woman in place of the Southern Lady.[16]

In answer to the question "To be or not to be—a Refugee," a letter published in the *Georgia Southern Banner* advised civilians to resist the urge to flee, declaring that those who remained in their home communities "suffered less than the friendless refugee seeking hospitality among strangers who have not the means, if they had the inclination, to tender their hospitality." According to Faust, Southerners likely began using the term *refugee* in late 1861, in reference to the incredibly wealthy South Carolina planter families—such as the Grimballs—who abandoned immense Sea Island cotton and rice plantations and attempted to relocate enslaved populations prior to Union naval attack. Some

Texas Confederates shared Grimball's initial disdain for the "uncalled for" hysteria of slaveholders, declaring of many Gulf Coast planters' 1863 decampment for the state's interior, "We think they are scared before they are hurt." Others complained that "useless" evacuations of "women and children and household plunder" impeded troop movements, monopolized railroads, and consumed food resources vital to the army. As war intensified and increasing numbers of civilians arrived in Texas in search of "safer" environments, criticism of planter-class refugees grew considerably more overt.[17]

In October 1861 the *Clarksville Standard* reprinted a letter sent from a regiment in North Fork Town, Creek Nation (present-day Oklahoma), concerning planter refugees headed for Texas. The authors condoned the deliverance of women and children to Texas but declared that the slaveholders must "return to their native State to drive back so wicked an enemy." After all, the authors affirmed, "Sacrifices of person and property will have to be made. Our cause is common and all should share alike." By 1863 thousands of refugees streamed into Texas as Gen. Ulysses S. Grant commenced his devastating Vicksburg Campaign, followed the next year by another wave attempting to escape the path of Gen. Nathaniel P. Banks's march along the Red River to Alexandria, Louisiana. To many refugees Texas seemed unlikely to fall into Federal hands as it was geographically removed from most major combat zones. In March 1862, after guerilla warfare destroyed much of Osceola, Missouri, several individuals, recently returned from the Lone Star State, convinced 1st Lt. John Weidemeyer of the Sixth Missouri Infantry of its security. According to Weidemeyer, "All advised me to have my family go to Texas."[18]

The state's vast and sparsely populated lands also offered possible economic opportunities for refugee slaveholders, and Texas's shared border with Mexico provided access to international cotton markets for planters possessing the means to relocate enslaved persons. Sugar planters James and Eliza McHatton Ripley vacated their home near Baton Rouge in 1862 and fled west, having already transferred their enslaved population to a family member's Texas plantation earlier that year. According to Ripley, the couple sought refuge in the state because their enslaved people "were there at peaceful work," the couple believed the Union army "could never get a foothold on its boundless prairies," and "if worse came to the worst" they could escape farther south to Mexico. As early as 1862 many other elite Louisiana planter families chose to desert their home communities to protect personal holdings. Kate Stone described the exodus in her small, close-knit neighborhood near Omega in June of that year, reporting in her diary "a good many planters are leaving...and sending their Negroes to the backcountry." Two of the largest slaveholders in the parish, she continued, "are said to be already on their way to Texas with the best of their hands."[19]

Several months later, Stone's elder brother took leave from the army to relocate "the best and strongest" of the family's 150 enslaved persons to Texas. Two months after, Stone's widowed mother Amanda followed with daughter Kate, the younger Stone children, a niece, and several domestic servants. As the *Southern Banner* would warn one year later, the Stones found many Texans possessed "neither the means nor the inclination" to grant them warm welcome. In late August 1863 Stone described the "first instance of liberality" the family encountered since their arrival in Texas three months earlier, when a Smith County family provided the Stones with a night's lodging and "did not charge us a cent." One month later, Stone continued her record-keeping of Texan benevolence when the family met a "second man...in Texas...to have goodwill for refugees and sympathy for their troubles."[20]

Unlike elite refugees, many dispossessed plain folk and soldiers' families reported that Texans extended sympathetic welcomes, greeting them as compatriots and offering assistance and comfort. In 1863 a Georgia newspaper illustrated Confederates' distinctions between planter-class refugees and displaced plain folk. The newspaper's editors declared they had "uttered not a word of expostulation" when elite refugees, "the wealthier ones," complained of "cold[-]shouldered" ostracism and "extortionate charges" extended by fellow Confederates. Now however, the editors continued, Federal troop incursions deeper into the South created refugees of a different character. "Instead of coming among you as voluntary refugees they come as exiles forced from their homes by the tyrant," the "wives and little ones of those in the field standing between us and danger." Echoing this reproval in an address published by a Houston newspaper, "Ceceola" reminded the "Women of Texas" of their "sacred obligation" to provide succor to displaced soldiers' families. As fellow "country-women," she declared, "we are bestowing no charity when we do so" but fulfilling the highest expectations of Confederate womanhood.[21]

After enduring nearly three years of guerilla warfare in Fayetteville, Arkansas, and facing imminent Federal reoccupation in 1864, Francena Martin Sutton began conducting "councils of war" with fellow soldiers' wives to decide "who could, or who would, or who should go" south to Texas. Although the journey proved to be "as faith-testing as was that of Noah when he launched the Ark," Sutton declared that she enjoyed a "happy-go-lucky sort of life" among residents of Paris, Texas. The wife of another Confederate soldier, Missourian Partheny Horn, found herself "persuasion bound for Texas" following the 1863 issue of US Gen. Thomas Ewing Jr.'s General Order No. 11. Upon reaching Texas, Horn recalled in her memoir, Bonham residents extended "a warm welcome" and "upon there [*sic*] generous invitation we spent the night with them." While many Texans believed the sacrifices of common soldiers' wives entitled them to protection and veneration, some also believed elite refugee women deserved no such esteem.[22]

Seven months after the fall of Vicksburg, Texas minister B. L. Peel hotly addressed the "frequent remarks heard and read about the refugees" in a letter to the *Galveston Tri Weekly News*. Condemning the "insinuations" that planter-class refugees behaved as self-interested "cowards," Peel declared such charges resulted from "ignorance of the character of...the people who have come among us." Calling for an end to "low selfish slang," Peel urged Texans to "receive them with open arms." Writers to the *Tyler Journal* concurred with Peel's censure, scolding Texans in 1865 for using the label "refugee...as a term of reproach" to "our unfortunate brothers and sisters of Missouri, Ark., La., Mississippi and Kentucky...."[23]

While some Southern newspapers used the terms interchangeably, *refugee* frequently appeared in conjunction with planter-class slaveholders, while *exile* often described soldiers' families and plain folk. Although civilian use of *refugee* carried connotations of selfishness and cowardice, ascription of the label "renegade" to elites appears to have possessed even more dire implications. Upon her family's arrival in Tyler, Texas, in 1863 Kate Stone expressed bewilderment at many native Texans' overt contempt, reporting that Tyler citizens labeled the Stones and their fellow planter-class refugees "renegades." Throughout the Civil War, Texas newspapers regularly published accounts of Confederate recruiting officers' pursuits, captures, and imprisonments of Southern men who attempted to avoid military service or joined the Union Army. The reports condemned those men as "deserters," "traitors," and "desperato(s) [*sic*]" and even more frequently and nearly universally, "renegades." One prominent and well-known "miscreant," former Texas judge Edmund Jackson "E. J." Davis, garnered extensive publicity and widespread condemnation following his 1863 escape to Mexico and subsequent appointment as a colonel in the US Army. Texas newspapers repeatedly denounced Davis, most frequently characterizing him as a "renegade." Thus, Tyler citizens' application of the term "renegades" to elite refugees carried specific connotations as to the character and conduct of such persons.[24]

Indeed, elite refugees' conduct in Texas communities often exacerbated civilians' feelings of hostility toward those they viewed as having placed self-interest over the Confederate cause by virtue of voluntary flight. Expectations of privilege and expressions of obvious disdain often served to further alienate native citizens. A few miles outside Beaumont, Texas, a plain folk family allowed Louisiana refugee Eliza McHatton Ripley and her husband to shelter in their home overnight. Ripley declared that the dwelling housed pigs and chickens alongside the human occupants; as for the bed they were given, "I think there were a million of *cimices lectuarii* [bedbugs] in it," she sniffed. [25]

In addition to boasting some of the largest and wealthiest slaveholders in the antebellum South, some members of Louisiana's planter aristocracy possessed some of the region's most opulent homes, displayed lavish lifestyles, and generally believed themselves to be of a superior, cultured, genteel society. On the whole, however, Texas's elite slaveholders exhibited far less extravagance, and the vast majority of Texas citizens fell well below the planter class socially and economically. After sending his young daughter to Texas for her protection, one refugee father lamented her exposure to the state's "inferior" society, declaring there existed no person above the social standing of a Comanche in the entire region. Kate Stone described "swarms of ugly, rough" Texans and related her amusement at encountering women wearing hoopskirts with no shoes. Some elite refugees made little effort to forgo antebellum class prejudices in favor of the united cause, seeming to remain unaware of the demise of the old order. When a group of elite refugees attended a Tyler, Texas, Masonic function, Amanda Stone commented on the likelihood of witnessing "the animals at feed"; fellow Louisiana refugee Mr. Michele refused to allow the group to partake of the barbeque on grounds that it was "not clean," asking "Why should we dine with plebeians?" Lamenting the "strange...prejudice that exists all through the state against refugees," Kate Stone wrote that she felt sure Tylerites suffered from "pure envy" because "refugees are a nicer and more refined people."[26]

While elite women often expressed revulsion toward Texan lifestyles and society, native citizens of the state frequently viewed those expressions as further evidence of the decadence, moral deterioration, and selfishness of the planter aristocracy. The Stone family filled trunks with "a quantity of beautiful clothes, laces, silks, velvets, and so on" in preparation for the journey to Texas. Sarah Lois Wadley's family loaded several wagons with personal belongings prior to their own flight, including Wadley's piano and all the books the family owned. Voluntarily fleeing with enslaved persons and the trappings of their former status rather than remaining to defend home communities violated the Southern honor code and the requirements of authentic Confederate patriotism. Plain folk condemned the apparent self-interest of elite refugees arriving in Texas communities with expensive and excessive accouterments and even charged Southern Ladies with jeopardizing the war effort. In her address in a Houston newspaper, "Ceceola" urged the "gay, the thoughtless...the wives and daughters of inglorious ease...the votaries of pleasure and fashion," to set aside personal comforts for the cause and to "forget for a time the elegances of the toilet, and the enervating luxuries of pampered pride." Failure to do so, she implied, indicated an "indifference and inactivity" that could lead to Confederate defeat.[27]

Texans' responses often reiterated the loss of elite women's entitlement to luxury and ease on the basis of Ladyhood. In June 1863 Sarah Lois Wadley wrote from her family's plantation in Ouachita Parish, Louisiana, of the Stone family's unhappy departure for Texas. Declaring they had "nothing but uncertainty and discomfort" ahead, Wadley reported that "Miss Kate went away with tears as they all did," and confessed that "I hope we may never have to move to Texas." To Kate Stone, Wadley's fears seemed to be confirmed by the family's experiences in Tyler. Stone lamented that although "we have plenty of servants to do our bidding... that is about all we *do* have." The loss of material comforts in an unfamiliar environment undeniably caused elites discomfort and emphasized the stark reality they could expect from life without status privileges. The *Dallas Herald*'s editors scolded those who complained about "hard times," declaring that only when "a people can get nothing to eat and really 'nothing to wear,'" could they "grumble." "Everalline" in Brownsville, Texas, took a much harsher tone in her 1865 letter to the *Galveston Weekly News*. In her identification of "three classes of ladies" who in her estimation had earned "as much censure as any of the shirkers," she declared the worst possessed "no greater ideas of patriotism than a pig," and cared not for "who fights...as long as their wants are gratified and they are allowed uninterrupted indolence...."[28]

The blatant condescension of planter-class women often further convinced plain folk that Confederate kinship excluded elite refugees, and some contended that the pretentiousness of planter exiles contaminated their communities. In Marshall, Texas, Jennie Adkins wrote to her soldier fiancée that her hometown had been "filling up with strangers," causing a "decay" in the social environment. According to Kate Stone, Tyler residents accused elite refugees of cowardice and lack of patriotism, taunting them with the "base fabrication" that the state of Louisiana had applied for readmittance to the Union. Stone also declared that the reception of native citizens caused her to forgo even church attendance in Tyler as "a battery of hostile eyes" greeted her on her first visit. In a letter to her soldier husband, Martha Ingram of Hill County, Texas, expressed her feelings rather simply concerning an elite refugee family staying near her home with their "larg [*sic*] gang of Negros," remarking "I think they are too mutch [*sic*] on the high feluting [*sic*] order for this country." Conveying her own interpretation of elites' circumstances in Texas, Stone mused "the refugees remind me of...the nobility of France during the days of the French Revolution."[29]

In an 1863 address to citizens in Huntsville, Texas, State Legislator and Judge Peter W. Gray entreated those present to consider "whose family circles have been made desolate by Yankee bullets." "As between the rich and the poor," Gray avowed, "this war has levelled [*sic*] all distinction. ...." As is evidenced by common perceptions of planter-class refugees, many Texans embraced the wartime societal order that measured a woman's value by the extent of her sacrifices for the Confederate cause, refusing to adhere to antebellum cultural prescriptions that afforded elite Ladies superior status. As did Judge Gray, however, others appealed for Confederate unity by invoking the purportedly egalitarian quality of kindred suffering, chastising Texans for their poor treatment of elites. Interestingly, however, some of those exhortations unintentionally revealed the continuing influence of antebellum status constructions that upheld notions of elites' moral and social superiority. While the authors of a March 1865 item in the *Tyler Journal* defended "our unfortunate brothers and sisters," declaring that the "refugees...are even handed [*sic*] with our older citizens in all the work of charity, benevolence, and patriotism," they also imperiously reminded Tylerites that the presence of such "intelligent, enterprising families" benefited Texas communities as "where they go; society is improved in morals and manners." A Houston minister's 1865 letter to the *Galveston Weekly News* conveyed his concern for educational opportunities in Texas and described a "noble spectacle" he recently witnessed. Describing the "elegant and accomplished ladies, refugees, accustomed to all the refinements...of genteel life" he observed serving as tutors for some Texas children, Thomas Castleton wondered "Will not Texas ladies enter this work?" In his own letter to the same publication, B. L. Peel reminded readers that elite refugees were "not cagens [*sic*], low, or even ordinary people...they were the cream of Louisiana and no State can boast of a better class." Therefore, Peel ironically cautioned, "we should be extremely careful about stirring up sectional feeling among us."[30]

In this bitterly contentious environment, planter-class refugees often banded closely together in attempts to recreate the security of antebellum communities and the privileges afforded them there. As community and kinship constituted a fundamental aspect of aristocratic life, isolation and homesickness emphasized both elites' reliance upon peer relationships and social differences from plain folk. In Tyler the Stone family happily accepted a former Louisiana neighbor's offer to share a residence although they found the home to be uncomfortably crowded. Shortly thereafter, having received no visitors for weeks, Kate Stone commenced a "refugee hunt" rather than associate with Tylerites. Furthermore, many refugees clung to the vestiges of aloof superiority that characterized their interactions with common Southerners before the war. After at last befriending a Tyler resident, poetess Mollie Moore, Stone remarked upon the contemptuousness of some of her fellow elites, declaring "the other refugees can laugh at us if they like." Interestingly, just three weeks later, she reported that two of her mother's closest friends from the old neighborhood in Louisiana had suddenly become "cold toward us, and we do not know what is wrong."[31]

As Confederate defeat began to appear inevitable, some elite refugee women existed in a suspended state in which, as Stone declared, "we cannot bear to think about the past and so dread the future." In a July 1865 letter to her mother, Louisiana refugee Ann Mathilda Stirling Lobdell confessed her fears concerning the "reverses" her family had suffered as a result of the war, adding "I feel anxious dear Mother to know how you stand them." Going on to express her hopes for the safe return of two brothers from Confederate military service, Lobdell mused that while the "young men" could still provide "happy and comfortable homes for themselves and families...they can never again talk of Southern chivalry." For elite Southern Ladies, material wealth, family members, and social prestige were not the only casualties of war. The ideologies upon which Ladies based their identities and superior status nearly instantly fell to new Confederate ideologies.[32]

The Civil War changed the Southern ruling class's requirements of elite white women, toppling them from the protected pedestal of Ladyhood and enthroning a new female paragon in the Confederate Woman. Moreover, the refugee experience ripped planter-class Ladies from the moorings of home communities that reinforced their superiority and self-worth. In addition to finding themselves in unfamiliar, often physically uncomfortable environments, many elite refugee women encountered a wartime society that questioned their possession of what had become the preeminent characteristic of a Southern woman: patriotism. While antebellum Southern culture had extolled the virtues of Ladyhood, rewarding those who fulfilled its prescriptions with moral and social authority, war destroyed the carefully ordered society that employed race, gender, and class constructions to define both place and inherent value. By redefining the ideological requirements for true womanhood and elevating the Confederate Woman to near-saintly status, wartime Southern society invalidated the fundamental tenets of Ladyhood, allowing plain folk women to transcend traditional class barriers and entitling them to venerated standing in wartime society.

While many Southerners unquestionably rendered aid and extended kindnesses and hospitality to elite refugees and displaced persons alike, planter-class women across the Confederacy overwhelmingly encountered a scornful civilian populace after fleeing their homes and communities. Distinguishing between "refugees" and "displaced persons," many Southerners questioned elites' patriotism and accused upper class magnates of forcing the less privileged to shoulder the burdens of war. Elite refugee women in Texas found that the very qualities that rewarded them before the war now marked them as "cowardly," "selfish," and "unpatriotic." However, many could not dispossess themselves of the mantle of ideal Ladyhood, and their expectations of privilege and deference intensified plain folks' resentment. While soldiers' wives and plain folk seeking sanctuary in Texas received assistance and validation of their sacrifices for the nation, elite refugee women frequently met with criticism and hostility. After receiving "many...painful accounts" of Texans' less-than-welcoming reception of elite refugees from his state, in 1863 Louisiana Governor Thomas Overton Moore expressed his belief that "the citizens of Texas and Louisiana have every inducement to cultivate mutual respect, confidence and amity." In spite of such pronouncements and promotion of a unified Southern home front, it seems that in Texas, Southern Ladyhood precluded Confederate Womanhood.[33]

Notes

1. Col. C. J. Forshey, "The Exodus," *Galveston Weekly News*, August 19, 1863. *Newspaper Research, 1861-1865*, accessed November 20, 2012, www.uttyler.edu/vbetts/galveston_new_pt.2.htm; Forshey's readers would likely have understood the implications of his reference to the works of celebrated English-born satirist William Hogarth. Hogarth's social critiques, including his 1735 series of paintings *A Rake's Progress*, depicted the ruinous consequences of British elites' pretensions and extravagances. See "William Hogarth 1697–1764," Tate UK, accessed October 1, 2013, www.tate.org.uk/art/artists/william-hogarth-265.
2. J. W. Johnson, letter to the editor, *Tri-Weekly Telegraph* (Houston, TX), November 16, 1863, accessed September 21, 2013, in *Newspaper Research, 1861-1865*, www.uttyler.edu/vbetts/houston%20tri-w%20telegraph%201863.htm.
3. Yael A. Sternhell, *Routes of War: The World of Movement in the Confederate South* (Cambridge, MA: Harvard University Press, 2012), 140; B. L. Peel, letter to the editor, *Galveston Tri- Weekly News*, December 13, 1863, accessed October 1, 2013, AccessNewspaperARCHIVE.com.
4. For purposes of clarity, I have capitalized the term "Lady" throughout to reference women of the planter aristocracy who occupied superior social positions due to fulfillment of Southern racial, gender, and class constructions that purportedly characterized the antebellum feminine ideal.
5. Sternhell, *Routes of War*, 7, 15.
6. Sir Arthur James Lyon Fremantle, *Three Months in the Southern States: April, June, 1863* (Mobile, AL: S. H. Goetzel, 1864), 34, in Documenting the American South, University Library, The University of North Carolina at Chapel Hill, accessed October 25, 2013, docsouth.unc.edu/imls/fremantle/fremantle.html; US Bureau of the Census, *Population of the United States 1860, Compiled from the Original Returns of the Eighth Census* (Washington, DC: Government Printing Office, 1864), in The Civil War Homepage, under "Census Data," accessed December 8, 2012, www.civil-war.net/pages/1860_census.html; Paul D. Escott,

"The Failure of Confederate Nationalism: The Old South's Class System in the Crucible of the Civil War," in *The Old South in the Crucible of the Civil War*, ed. Harry P. Owens and James J. Cooke (Jackson: University Press of Mississippi, 1983), 21; Frank Lawrence Owsley, *Plain Folk of the Old South* (Baton Rouge: Louisiana State University Press, 1949), 9. In his influential work, Owsley identified yeomen, the class of landowners who ranked socially and economically below planters and above landless poor whites, as "plain folk." However, conceptions of the group known as plain folk vary among scholars. In her important study of South Carolina yeomen, Stephanie McCurry used the term "self-working farmers" for those smaller slaveholders and non-slaveholders who engaged in the physical labor of farming. See Stephanie McCurry, *Masters of Small Worlds: Yeoman Households, Gender Relations, and the Political Culture of the Antebellum South Carolina Low Country* (New York: Oxford University Press, 1995), 47-48. In order to emphasize the ideological differences between elite slaveholders and all small slaveholders and non-slaveholders ranking below the planter class in the Southern social hierarchy, I have chosen to follow the example of David Williams, Teresa Crisp Williams, and David Carlson in their *Plain Folk in a Rich Man's War: Class and Dissent in Confederate Georgia* (Gainesville: University Press of Florida, 2002); references to "plain folk" include all yeomen and poor white Southerners.

7. Joel Williamson, *The Crucible of Race: Black-White Relations in the American South Since Emancipation* (New York: Oxford University Press, 1984), 24-25; Catherine Clinton, *The Plantation Mistress: Woman's World in the Old South* (New York: Pantheon Books, 1982), xv; Williamson, *The Crucible of Race*, 27.

8. Drew Gilpin Faust, *Mothers of Invention: Women of the Slaveholding South in the American Civil War* (Chapel Hill: The University of North Carolina Press, 1996), 43, 59, 56; Anne Firor Scott, "Women's Perspective on the Patriarchy in the 1850s," *The Journal of American History* 61, no. 1 (June 1974): 52, accessed June 2013, dx.doi.org/10.2307/1918253. For more discussion of the Civil War's effects on gender ideologies, see Mary Elizabeth Massey's classic work *Refugee Life in the Confederacy* (Baton Rouge: Louisiana State University Press, 1964); Elizabeth Fox-Genovese, *Within the Plantation Household: Black and White Women of the Old South* (Chapel Hill: University

of North Carolina Press, 1988); George C. Rable, *Civil Wars: Women and the Crisis of Southern Nationalism* (Urbana: University of Illinois Press), 1989; Anya Jabour, *Scarlett's Sisters: Young Women in the Old South* (Chapel Hill: University of North Carolina Press, 2007). See LeeAnn Whites, *The Civil War as a Crisis in Gender: Augusta, Georgia, 1860-1890* (Athens: University of Georgia Press, 1995) for a more localized study.

9. Whites, *The Civil War As a Crisis in Gender,* 18; James M. McPherson, *For Cause and Comrades: Why Men Fought in the Civil War* (New York: Oxford University Press, 1998), 104; Alexander H. Stephens, transcript of "Cornerstone Address," March 21, 1861 in *The Rebellion Record: A Diary of American Events with Documents, Narratives, Illustrative Incidents, Poetry, etc.,* vol. 1, ed. Frank Moore (New York: O.P. Putnam, 1862), 44-46, in Internet Modern History Sourcebook, Internet History Sourcebooks Project, Fordham University, Bronx, New York, accessed June 10, 2015, legacy.fordham.edu/halsall/mod/1861stephens.asp; James M. McPherson, "American Victory, American Defeat," in *Why the Confederacy Lost,* ed. Gabor S. Boritt (New York: Oxford University Press, 1992), 30-31.
10. Bertram Wyatt-Brown, *Southern Honor: Ethics and Behavior in the Old South* (New York: Oxford University Press, 1982), xxvii, 88, 114, 234.
11. George C. Rable, "Rebels and Patriots in the Confederate Revolution," in *In the Cause of Liberty: How the Civil War Redefined American Ideals,* ed. William J. Cooper and John M. McCardell (Baton Rouge: Louisiana State University Press, 2009), 65; Margaret Ann Meta Morris Grimball, Journal of Meta Morris Grimball: December 1860-February 1866, 48, transcript of Manuscript #975-z, Southern Historical Collection, Wilson Library, University of North Carolina at Chapel Hill, in Documenting the American South, University Library, The University of North Carolina at Chapel Hill, accessed May 25, 2013, docsouth.unc.edu/fpn/grimball/grimball.html; "Ziola," "Our Vocation," *Southern Confederacy* (Atlanta, GA), April 27, 1861, in *Newspaper Research, 1861-1865,* accessed January 2, 2014, www.uttyler.edu/vbetts/southern_confederacy.htm.
12. Faust, *Mothers of Invention,* 18; "Organization and Departure of the W. P. Lane Rangers," *Texas Republican* (Marshall, TX), April 22, 1861, in *Newspaper Research, 1861-1865,* accessed June 5, 2015, www.uttyler.edu/vbetts/texas_women_public_voices.htm; Sallie O.

Smith, "Address," *Texas Republican*, April 27, 1861, in *Newspaper Research, 1861-1865*, accessed June 5, 2015, www.uttyler.edu/vbetts/texas_women_public_voices.htm. In her address, Smith equated the legendary courage and heroic efforts of Penthesileia, *Boadicea*, and Pallas to defend their homes and peoples to that of Confederate women. According to Greek mythology, Penthesileia, warrior queen of the Amazons and daughter of Ares, god of war, engaged in battle with Achilles. *Boadicea*, warrior queen of the Iceni tribe of East Anglia, led Britons in battle against invading Romans and ingested poison rather than allow the Roman Army to capture her. Pallas (also known as Athena), warrior maiden and daughter of Zeus, sprang full-grown from Zeus, dressed in battle armor and brandishing a sword. See H. J. Rose, *A Handbook of Greek Mythology*, 6th ed. (London: Routledge, 2014); Ben Johnson, "Boudica," accessed June 6, 2015, www.historic-uk.com/HistoryUK/HistoryofEngland/Boudica/; Michael Delahoyde "The Greek Gods," accessed June 6, 2015, public.wsu.edu/~delahoyd/mythology/greek.gods.html.

13. "Ladies of Southern Bexar to Ladies of San Antonio," *Northern Standard* (Clarkesville, TX) February 8, 1862, in *Newspaper Research, 1861-1865*, accessed June 5, 2015, www.uttyler.edu/vbetts/texas_women_public_voices.htm; "Flag Presentation," *The Ranchero* (Corpus Christi, TX), June 15, 1861, in *Newspaper Research, 1861-1865*, accessed June 15, 2015, www.uttyler.edu/vbetts/texas_women_public_voices.htm; Mary B. Breeding, "Address," *Belleville Countryman*, June 5, 1861, in *Newspaper Research, 1861-1865*, accessed June 6, 2015, www.uttyler.edu/vbetts/bellville.htm.
14. "A Lady with the Right Spirit," *Southern Confederacy*, August 10, 1861, in *Newspaper Research, 1861-1865*, accessed June 10, 2015, www.uttyler.edu/vbetts/southern_confederacy.htm.
15. Grimball, Journal of Meta Morris Grimball: December 1860-February 1866, 50, transcript of Manuscript #975-z, accessed May 25, 2013, docsouth.unc.edu/fpn/grimball/grimball.html.
16. John Q. Anderson, introduction to *Brokenburn: The Journal of Kate Stone, 1861-1868*, by Kate Stone, ed. John Q. Anderson (1955; repr., Baton Rouge: Louisiana State University Press, 1972), xii; William L. Shea and Terrence J. Winschel, *Vicksburg Is the Key: The Struggle for the Mississippi River* (Lincoln: University of Nebraska Press, 2003), 7, 8, 15; Kate Stone, *Brokenburn: The Journal of Kate Stone, 1861-1868*, ed.

John Q. Anderson (1955; repr., Baton Rouge: Louisiana State University Press, 1972), 127.

17. "To be or not to be—a Refugee," *Southern Banner* (Athens, GA), July 13, 1864, in *Newspaper Research, 1861-1865*, accessed October 1, 2013, www.uttyler.edu/vbetts/southern_banner.htm; Faust, *Mothers of Invention*, 40.

18. Letter to Maj. DeMorse, *Northern Standard*, Oct. 26, 1861, in *Newspaper Research, 1861-1865*, www.uttyler.edu/vbetts/clarksville_standard_1861.htm; Dale Baum, "Slaves Taken to Texas for Safekeeping During the Civil War," in *The Fate of Texas*, ed. Charles D. Grear (Fayetteville: The University of Arkansas Press, 2008), 91-92; John M. Weidemeyer, *John M. Weidemeyer Journal:1860-1863*, 52, in Missouri Digital Heritage Collections, The Springfield-Greene County Library District, Springfield, Missouri, accessed August 25, 2013, www.ozarkscivilwar.org/archives/4703.

19. Baum, "Slaves Taken to Texas for Safekeeping During the Civil War," 84-85; Eliza Moore Chinn McHatton Ripley, *From Flag to Flag: A Woman's Adventures and Experiences in the South during the War, in Mexico, and in Cuba* (New York: D. Appleton and Company, 1888) 66, in Documenting the American South, University Library, The University of North Carolina at Chapel Hill, 1998, accessed July 24, 2013, docsouth.unc.edu/fpn/ripleyflag/ripley.html; Stone, *Brokenburn*, 125. For the McHattons, Texas did indeed provide them a safe route to deliver cotton and supplies into Mexico, where they remained until escaping to Cuba after the war's end to set up a successful sugar plantation. For more on the wartime Confederate cotton trade in Texas, see Judy Gentry, "Confederates and Cotton in East Texas," *East Texas Historical Journal* 48, no. 1 (Winter 2010): 20-39; and Stephen A. Townsend, *The Yankee Invasion of Texas* (College Station: Texas A&M University Press, 2006).

20. Stone, *Brokenburn*, 168, 236-237, 242.

21. *Confederacy* (Macon, GA), "Exiles," reprinted in *Weekly Standard* (Raleigh, NC), September 28, 1863, accessed October 2, 2013, AccessNewspaperARCHIVE; Ceceola, "To the Women of Texas," *Tri-Weekly Telegraph*, October 17, 1863, in *Newspaper Research, 1861-1865*, www.uttyler.edu/vbetts/houston%20tri-w%20telegraph%201863.htm.

22. Francena Martin Sutton, "A Civil War Experience of Some Arkansas Women," 6, 11, box 2R203, Francena Martin Sutton Narrative [ca. 1914], Dolph Briscoe Center for American History, The University of Texas at Austin, Austin, Texas; Partheny Horn, *Memoir* [ca. 1919], 18, 20, in Missouri Digital Heritage Collections, The Springfield-Greene County Library District, Springfield, Missouri, accessed May 28, 2013, www.ozarkscivilwar.org/archives/2699. In an effort to subdue guerrillas in Missouri and Kansas, Ewing issued General Order No. 11 on August 25, 1863, effectively evicting more than 20,000 Missourians along the state's border with Kansas. See Jeremy Neely, s.v. "General Order No. 11," accessed October 2, 2013, www.civilwaronthewesternborder.org/content/general-order-no-11.

23. B. L. Peel, letter to the editor, *Galveston Tri Weekly News*, December 13, 1863, accessed October 1, 2013, AccessNewspaperARCHIVE.com; *Tyler Journal*, "Refugees," reprinted in *Bellville Countryman*, March 7, 1865, accessed November 12, 2012, in *Newspaper Research, 1861-1865*, www.uttyler.edu/vbetts/bellville.htm.

24. Stone, *Brokenburn*, 188; "Surrender of Judge Davis," *Galveston Weekly News*, April 8, 1863, accessed October 13, 2013, NewspaperARCHIVE.com; see also Tri-Weekly News, October 21, 1862, accessed October 30, 2013, NewspaperARCHIVE.com.

25. Ripley, *From Flag to Flag*, 67, 69, accessed July 2, 2013, docsouth.unc.edu/fpn/ripleyflag/ripley.html.

26. William Kaufman Scarborough, *Masters of the Big House: Elite Slaveholders of the Mid-Nineteenth-Century South* (Baton Rouge: Louisiana State University Press, 2003), 6; Giselle Roberts, *The Confederate Belle* (Columbia, MO: University of Missouri Press, 2003), 9; Ralph A. Wooster, "Notes on Texas' Largest Slaveholders, 1860," *The Southwestern Historical Quarterly* 65, no. 1 (July 1961):7; Randolph B. Campbell *Gone to Texas: A History of the Lone Star State* (New York: Oxford University Press, 2003), 214; Mary Elizabeth Mitchell Journal, 1838-1870, MS in Southern Historical Collection, University of North Carolina. Quoted in Massey, *Refugee Life in the Confederacy*, 124; Stone, *Brokenburn*, 224, 250-252, 258-259. According to Giselle Roberts, in older states such as Virginia and South Carolina, family lineage weighed significantly in demonstrating gentility and status among the planter class. Because the Lower Mississippi Valley plantation system emerged later and was regarded as a region of "promise and fortune,"

tangible displays of extravagant wealth served in part as evidence of superior social status (*The Confederate Belle*, 9, 15). Additionally, according to Randolph B. Campbell, only 3 percent of Texans held upwards of twenty enslaved persons. Furthermore, the Texas planter class placed less emphasis on the appearance of great luxury than did planter "aristocrats" in Deep South states (*Gone to Texas*, 214-216).

27. Stone, *Brokenburn*, 203; Sarah Lois Wadley, *Diary: August 8, 1859-May 15 1865*, 50, transcript of the manuscript in the Sarah Lois Wadley Papers #1258, Southern Historical Collection, The Wilson Library, University of North Carolina at Chapel Hill, in Documenting the American South, University Library, The University of North Carolina at Chapel Hill, accessed June 3, 2015, docsouth.unc.edu/imls/wadley/wadley.html; Ceceola, "To The Women of Texas," accessed June 5, 2015, www.uttyler.edu/vbetts/houston%20tri-w%20telegraph%201863.htm.

28. Ripley, *From Flag to Flag*, 67, 69 in Documenting the American South, accessed July 23, 2013, docsouth.unc.edu/fpn/ripleyflag/ripley.html; Sarah Lois Wadley, *Diary: August 8, 1859-May 15 1865*, 13, accessed September 1, 2013, docsouth.unc.edu/imls/wadley/wadley.html; Stone, *Brokenburn*, 258-59, 321; *Dallas Herald*, December 25, 1861, in *Newspaper Research, 1861-1865*, www.uttyler.edu/vbetts/dallas_herald.htm; "Everalline," letter to the editor, April 5, 1865, *Galveston Weekly News*, in *Newspaper Research, 1861-1865*, http://www.uttyler.edu/vbetts/galveston_news_pt.4.htm.

29. Virginia Eliza "Jennie" to Coleman John Nathan Adkins, December 6, 1864, transcript of the letters of John Nathan and Virginia Eliza "Jennie" Adkins Coleman, in Baylor University Libraries Digital Collections, Texas Collection, Baylor University, Waco, Texas, accessed October 1, 2013, digitalcollections.baylor.edu/cdm/landingpage/collection/tx-colm; Stone, *Brokenburn*, 239, 254, 293; Martha F. Ingram to George W. Ingram, August 30, 1863, *Civil War Letters of George W. and Martha F. Ingram, 1861-1865*, compiled by Henry L. Ingram (College Station: Texas A&M University Press, 1973), 62.

30. "One Present," letter to the editor, *Tri-Weekly Telegraph*, July 8, 1863, The Portal to Texas History, crediting Dolph Briscoe Center for American History, Austin, Texas., texashistory.unt.edu/ark:/67531/metapth236543/m1/2/zoom/?q=%22rich%20man%27s%20war%22%20date:1862-1865; See also

Thomas W. Cutrer, "Gray, Peter W.," *Handbook of Texas Online,* accessed December 03, 2013, www.tshaonline.org/handbook/online/articles/fgr25; *Tyler Journal,* "Refugees," reprinted in *Bellville Countryman,* March 7, 1865, in *Newspaper Research, 1861-1865,* accessed November 12, 2012, www.uttyler.edu/vbetts/bellville.htm; Thomas Castleton, letter to the editor, *Galveston Weekly News,* January 4, 1865, www.uttyler.edu/vbetts/galveston_news_pt.4.htm; B. L. Peel, letter to the editor, *Galveston Tri Weekly News,* December 13, 1863, accessed October 1, 2013, AccessNewspaperARCHIVE.com; *Tyler Journal,* "Refugees," reprinted in *Bellville Countryman,* March 7, 1865, accessed November 12, 2012, in *Newspaper Research, 1861-1865,* www.uttyler.edu/vbetts/bellville.htm.

31. Jean E. Friedman, *The Enclosed Garden: Women and Community in the Evangelical South, 1830-1900* (Chapel Hill: The University of North Carolina Press, 1985), xi; See also Joan E. Cashin, *Our Common Affairs: Texts from Women in the Old South* (Baltimore: The Johns Hopkins University Press, 1996); Stone, *Brokenburn,* 254, 293, 321.

32. Ann Matilda Stirling Lobdell to Sarah Turnbull Stirling, July 9 1865, Stirling (Lewis and family) Papers, Louisiana State University Archives, Baton Rouge, L.A. Author's note: I am indebted to Vicki Betts of The University of Texas at Tyler for generously directing my attention to the Lobdell letters and for allowing me to make use of her transcriptions. I am also inexpressibly grateful for Ms. Betts's tremendous contribution in transcribing her *Newspaper Research* and in making it available for online research.

33. *Galveston Weekly News,* February 3, 1864, in *Newspaper Research, 1861-1865,* www.uttyler.edu/vbetts/galveston_news_pt.3.htm.

Image 20. *Presenting the Flag, Fort Davis.*

Courtesy of Collection of the Old Jail Art Center, Albany, Texas.

Miss Almira "Myra" Sutherlin presenting the homespun flag to Samuel P. Newcomb on March 2, 1865. This image was painted by Alice Reynolds, 1941.

Chapter 11

Not Your Typical Southern Belles

Women on the Western Frontier of Civil War Texas

Deborah M. Liles

On October 13, 1864, a group of Kiowa and Comanche Indians attacked the ranch home of Elizabeth FitzPatrick, a frontier woman in her mid-thirties living in Young County, Texas. During the assault, Elizabeth's grown daughter, Susan Durgan, did what she could to protect her mother and her two small children. As she stood on the front porch and repeatedly fired a shotgun, one of the Indians warned her to stop. Standing steadfast, she continued to fight for the lives of those she loved until she was killed by a tomahawk blow to her head. When she died, any chance of resisting the Indians' attack ended. Elizabeth, her thirteen-year-old son Elijah, and her two motherless granddaughters, Lottie and Millie, were snatched up. Along with them, the Indians also took Mary Johnson and her children. Mary was the pregnant wife of Britt Johnson, a slave owned by Moses Johnson on the neighboring ranch.[1]

The journey to the Indian camp, which was somewhere past the Canadian River, took several weeks. As they retreated with the women and children, the Indians set hundreds of small fires in their wake to convince settlers that they could still attack. Just two days into the journey Elizabeth's son, Elijah, became ill and weak from drinking contaminated water, and could not keep up with the retreating party. Elizabeth was beaten, pierced with lances to prop her upright, and made to watch in horror as the Indians built a bonfire, threw poor Elijah in it, and burned him alive. It took eight months before Britt Johnson's family was rescued, and six more before Elizabeth and her family, except Millie whom the Indians would not relinquish, were freed from the Indian camp.[2]

Known as the Elm Creek Raid, this incident is still cited as one of the worst Indian attacks in the region, but it is much more than that. It is the story of many women's lives along the Texas frontier during the Civil War; it is the story of women who had to deal with the constant threat of invasion, when others in the state did not; and it is the story of women adapting to survive when resources were stretched to their limits. It is also an example of an attack that would be used to increase frontier security for those with property in a time when resources were limited. With all that said, it was only one of the unique conditions along the frontier.

The frontier region addressed in this chapter is comprised of counties that contain land west of the 98th meridian, but not those along the Rio Grande region (see chapter 7 for this). Many of these counties were formed during the 1850s and, because of this, the communities were small and conditions during the war were primitive. As in regions that were well populated, paper was scarce and expensive and few written accounts survive. There are several journals from women who purportedly lived on the frontier, but a closer examination shows they actually lived on the cotton frontier of the South, not the westernmost frontier of Texas. Hundreds of miles from where Elizabeth Neblett, Henrietta and Tennessee Embree, and Sallie McNeill lived, were Sarah Harkley Hall and her family in San Saba County. Her *Surviving on the Texas Frontier: The Journal of a Frontier Orphan Girl in San Saba County, 1852-1907* tells the stark difference between the locations.[3]

Hall and hundreds of other nameless women lived on the cattle frontier, which was an entirely different life from those located in the interior counties of Bell, Brazoria, Grimes, and others. Many lived in isolated conditions with very little access to supplies and limited contact with other people. Women on the cattle frontier are seldom mentioned unless it relates to being kidnapped or killed by Indians. Worse still they are often referred to as "disreputable women...[or] dismissed as 'women unworthy of the name of woman' or as 'women of easy virtue.'"[4] These less-than-kind descriptions give no credit, or respect, to the many women who lived in this region, and do not recognize the travails frontier women endured throughout the war years.

To understand the full story of FitzPatrick and the many other women who faced the dangers of Indians, it is first important to know why the Indians were raiding. Long before the Civil War began, settlers moved to the frontier in order to capitalize on the abundant supply of livestock. Many drove herds of cattle, horses, and even sheep to California during the 1850s to feed the thousands of prospectors living where local stock had quickly been depleted, and up to Missouri where people bound for the far west stocked their provisions for the trip. When the demand in California slowed, gold was discovered in Colorado, which provided a new market for livestock. Millions of dollars' worth of animals were driven across country to fill the needs. When new settlers moved onto former Indian lands, they gathered and amassed large holdings of wild horses and cattle.[5]

As the Indians had no say in where the white settlers could live, the only thing they could do was raid the settlers in an attempt to reclaim stock. Indian participation in the cattle and horse industry was equally as important to them as it was to those living along the frontier. This was a time when buffalo were in serious decline due to overhunting and a drought that had lasted over a decade. Like the white settlers, Indians collected livestock in their old hunting grounds, which just happened to be along the edge of white settlement in Texas. When the war began, and Federal forces pulled out of Texas and Indian Territory, many men in the frontier communities also left to fight, leaving small communities without protection. Additionally, Union and Confederate forces alike helped themselves to large herds of livestock in Indian Territory, which led to increased raids into Texas to replace their stolen stock. Conflict was inevitable.

Throughout the war pleas to protect the women and children on the frontier appeared in the newspapers, in letters to the authorities, and in public forums. Regular contributors, such as "Gray Rover" and "Rifle" fueled the fire with editorials about Indians and their frequent atrocities.[6] A letter to the editor of the *Dallas Weekly News* begged for forces to fight off Indians, "headed by black republicans" who they believed would destroy everything, as well as torture and kill women and children in the region. Letters to the governor constantly begged for help, such as that of Richard Gano from Tarrant County, who wrote how a "mother was killed, & four children carried off...[and] in another family the wife & two children killed & two children seriously if not mortally wounded." The results could be seen miles away in Houston, where a call to fight against the Union forces who "incite the wild savage to murder our women and children on our own Texas frontier" was used to persuade men to enlist in the Confederate Army.[7] Indeed there were so many calls for frontier protection that in March 1864, the new governor Pendleton Murrah issued a proclamation "forbidding the immigration to, and settlement in, any of the unorganized counties of this State," and promised conscription to anyone who did not follow this order.[8]

Not all of the reports were true; indeed some reports even admitted to using exaggerations of events and what *could* happen without added forces to protect settlers. In more cases than not, those who screamed the loudest about the dangers women and children faced were ranchers in the region. In short they exploited authorities by using women and children as the reason to obtain protection for their stock. The bitter twist in the Elm Creek Raid is that in all probability FitzPatrick and her family experienced all the conceivable horrors the frontiersmen were prognosticating because she was a rancher who declared $10,050 worth of livestock in 1863, and $7,000 the year of the attack. Indians were not there to randomly kill and kidnap the women; they were after her livestock.[9]

Before the outbreak of the war, one quarter of the US Army was in charge of patrolling the frontier settlers as they moved westward onto Indian lands. In 1861, after secession, Federal forces left the Texas frontier and Indian Territory. In April 1861 the Confederate States government in Richmond recognized that frontier defense was its responsibility. Henry McCulloch, a seasoned Indian fighter, was put in charge of 800 to 1,000 men enrolled into Confederate service as the First Texas Mounted Rifles for the period of a year. Upon completion of that service another change was made when the Frontier Regiment was formed and given responsibility for frontier defense. This regiment was both paid for and controlled by the state and included men from the frontier counties, which kept them closer to home and exempted them from Confederate conscription laws. Then, in December 1863, the Texas Legislature created the Frontier Organization. The Frontier Organization had three objectives: defending settlers and friendly Indians from the Comanches, Kiowas, and other unfriendly Indians; arresting Confederate deserters; and supporting the Southern cause. Initially intended to provide more security, the Frontier Organization actually reduced the number of men on patrol, as only one-fourth served at one time on a rotational basis. Supplemental frontier defense was offered by militia men and units but this often led to more confusion. All in all, there were always men patrolling the area, but where they were, and whose command they were under, often led to confusion and failed attempts at keeping the settlers safe.[10]

Aside from reduced or no protection, the women had other defense challenges. When the men left, either to fight in the Confederate Army or in frontier units, records show that most of them took a rifle or shotgun, a pistol, and a horse. It is entirely plausible that when the men took their own weapons to fight, they took the most lethal they owned, leaving the women with less accurate or deadly, if any, weapons to defend themselves; it is also probable they took the best horse, as they were expected to ride unknown distances. The stories that exist about women fighting Indians during the war years reference their weapon, if they had one, as being a shotgun, not a rifle. A shotgun has an advantage of hitting a bigger area, but it has a disadvantage because it requires the target to be within closer range in order to be fatal. Thus, before anything even happened, the women were at a disadvantage. Ammunition was also difficult to obtain due to the war and, when available, they may not have been the first in line to receive it, or they may not have been able to afford it.[11]

To resolve the many problems they faced, including the stress brought on by constant reports of Indian depredations on women and children, some women chose to gather in forts in a semi-permanent manner to protect themselves and their children. In the case of Fort Belknap, in Young County, many women arrived in wagon trains. Depending on the point of origin, the trips took different periods of time. Mrs. Abner Hays and her twins, Jane and Sam, along with other women, traveled for five days in a wagon train. When they arrived at the fort they discovered other women and children who had come from the Keechi Valley in northern Palo Pinto County, and the town of Jacksboro, Jack County. Incidentally, the number of women did not go unnoticed by the men assigned to defend the region, which added extra security to the fort but in return took it away from the frontier. As reported by one of the Rangers, there were "a good many widows and pretty girls at Belknap who were more than anxious to furnish us with milk and butter...we sent out guards to stay with and protect them at night."[12]

When proper forts were not available, settlers built communal enclosures. A rare list from Montague County survives that shows how eleven women and thirty-three children temporarily gathered together for protection from an Indian raid at a hastily assembled picket fort. Forts Growl, Blair, Bragg, Greer, and Murrah were just a few of the 100 that were established along the frontier before the end of the war to provide security and stretch limited ammunition.[13]

Another secure semi-permanent location was Fort Davis in Stephens County. Built after the Elm Creek raid to protect settlers, it was situated next to the Clear Fork River where the water was sweet, not salty. Thirty families forted up together, and commenced living as normally as possible. School was taught by Samuel P. Newcomb, who had recently married sixteen-year-old Susan E. Reynolds. Both Sam and Susan kept journals while they were at the fort; unfortunately for this chapter Susan's began after the end of the war.[14]

Newcomb's journal recorded many activities at the fort, including events that directly dealt with women. He opened with the sad burial of a one-year-old child, whose procession to the graveyard was composed of mainly women. The following day he wrote, "This day will very likely be long remembered by a certain young lady in the fort. It appears from the result of things that she had been behaving very disgracefully, for about 10 o'clock A. M. she gave birth to a child, but fortunately for the child it was born dead."[15] His attitude towards the unnamed woman's behavior, and the good luck of her dead child, reflects the Southern idea of chastity. No matter that this young woman was forted up on the western frontier to protect herself from possible Indian aggression, "a strict code of purity regulated white women's behavior in the Old South."[16] While this entry suggested that at least one of the women on the frontier was of easy virtue, one paragraph later Newcomb stated that any man who would gain the trust of a woman and then abuse it was "guilty of the most heinous, blackest crime that man can commit." This suggests that moral rules did not only apply to the women.[17]

Although Fort Davis was only intended to be a temporary refuge, it was exceedingly well constructed. There were twenty or more houses built with pickets, "covered with dirt and the cracks [were] stopped with dirt," and several had glass windows. There was also an abandoned stone house that was used when danger was perceived. Despite being in what might be considered primitive conditions, civil life continued. Weddings were held, parties were given, and religious services were performed whenever possible. Women went about daily life while many of the men served in frontier units or left the fort to hunt for livestock to add to their herds. They made supplies, such as candles and soap, milked the cows and sheep, and produced all of the cloth used for clothing by carding, spinning, weaving, and sewing by hand. One of the women, Miss Almira [Myra] Sutherlin, was asked to make a flag for the fort. Other women made the cord to hoist it up the flagpole, and on March 2, 1865, Texas Independence Day, Sutherlin and a "train of ladies" presented her homespun flag to Newcomb, who proudly accepted it on behalf of the fort.[18]

As historian Ann Patton Malone explained, ideals of the times were highly influenced by the Victorian image of womanhood, but that did not generally apply to those living on the frontier. While the Southern ideal of chastity was one that Newcomb believed the women should adhere to, there was more to being a woman on the frontier besides maintaining one's virtue. These women adapted out of necessity for survival, which had little to do with Victorian ideals and standards of living. Susan G. Butruille, historian of western women, wrote that "frontier women themselves recognized the masquerade of True Womanhood—the ridiculousness of trying to be helpless and submissive when the very lives of your family depend[ed] on the swiftness of a blow, the accuracy of a gunshot...the strength to butcher a whole hog, or heft countless loads of wet wash."[19] The women were not the only ones who accepted this difference. Historian Mark M. Carroll stated that "frontier social dynamics encouraged Anglo-Texas men to adopt conceptions of women that deviated substantially from those commonly found in the rest of the South."[20] These women were adept at working alongside their husbands, as well as handling their everyday chores. This quality undoubtedly prepared them for the long periods of absence and survival without their mates when the war began, a bonus when compared to many others living further to the east.[21]

This is not to say that some women did not have the advantages of slaves and the ability to indulge in such luxuries as music, dancing, and free time, but these women numbered very few. One was Susan Loving, wife of cattleman, trader, and slave-owner, Oliver. Loving, his wife Susan, their children, and his extended family, moved to Texas from Kentucky in early 1845, and to Palo Pinto County by 1855. Loving was listed as a "trader" living in Pleasant Valley with his wife and five of their children and eight slaves in 1860.[22] Susan was often home without her husband, as he was gone driving cattle to markets in multiple locations. Aware of the fact that cattle drives attracted Indian attacks, she was surely prepared to hear bad news but probably not to hear that Oliver was being held by Union officials in Denver, Colorado, in 1861. Unwilling to let him return home to the South with payment in gold from a sale of over 1,000 head of cattle, officials kept Loving imprisoned for months. When he arrived home on August 9, 1861 (with the gold), Susan and the children were gone. Loving did not know if they were alive until he found them sheltering at his daughter's home in Weatherford, just one county to the east. Like many other women, Susan relocated to avoid trouble during the war.[23]

Like other women in the South, frontier women were concerned about their men and their participation in the war. In Llano County twenty-two men of German descent formed a militia to patrol their frontier when Federal forces left forts Mason and Martin Scott, while non-Germans organized the Llano State Guards. In February, 1862, a company of 100 men from Llano and surrounding counties signed up with Co. E, Seventeenth Texas infantry regiment, McCullough's Brigade, Walker's Division. Rather than being assigned to fight in the eastern theatres, they were stationed in Little Rock, Arkansas. What was at first a safe location soon became a death camp. Typhoid and an epidemic of measles swept through, killing over 1,500 men from Texas and Arkansas within a two month period. Without a shot being fired, wives were made widows in Llano County.[24]

The women of Llano County were by no means the only ones who lost their husbands, brothers, and fathers to disease. Elizabeth Fletcher was born in what would become Parker County on January 6, 1855. She was left with her mother and three siblings when her father, William Fletcher, died in Confederate service after an illness in Virginia. Elizabeth reported that they had sufficient food to eat, as they grew their own vegetables, raised their own chickens and milk cows, and also cultivated wheat and corn. The widow Fletcher also raised enough cotton for fabric and sheep for wool to make her family's clothing. Elizabeth's recollections of the war address the connection between the livestock and danger from Indian raids: "the settlement was surrounded with cattle ranches, and many of the settlers, especially the young men, worked more or less as cowhands on the adjacent range. Our most feared trouble was the Indians. They were a constant menace. In the vicinity of the Ash Creek settlement there were frequent Indian raids, and a number of settlers were killed during my childhood days." She and her brothers were not harmed, but the Indians stole their horses. Unfortunately her neighbors, the Hamilton and the Davis families, were not as lucky. Like others on the frontier, Elizabeth's memories of the war were of Indian, not Northern, aggression.[25]

When the women were not trying to protect themselves or their children, they went about trying to make life as normal as possible. Church activities continued throughout the course of the war in most of the counties. In Decatur, Wise County, women's influence could be seen in the establishment of the first church in 1862, which was Methodist. Methodist circuit preachers, such as Pleasant Tackitt, were frequently in both Parker and Palo Pinto counties. Baptism by immersion was conducted, even to the point of submerging one woman in the shallow, muddy waters (due to a severe drought) of the Brazos River. Another ritual in church during the war was participating as a mourner when called to do so. Public grief was one way of showing support by "sanctify[ing] the martyrdom of others," and reminding those on the home front how insignificant their own sacrifices were. Largely the responsibility of the women, as men were busy fighting for the cause, their mourning "assur[ed the men] of spiritual and political immortality," as well as "serve[d] as a comforting ratification of female subservience and compliance." Jonathan Hamilton Baker, a Palo Pinto County resident, recorded in his diary that mourners were called for weekly in church, and the women would generally be the ones to take up the task.[26]

Church life was not the only arena in which the frontier women were active. As the fighting in the war reduced the amount of cotton exports from the South, the demand for wool-cloth products rose. Seeing an opportunity to cut costs by clothing their soldiers in home-spun material instead of buying uniforms, Texas created a military board to encourage production of woolen products. They imported 40,000 pairs of wool and cotton cards and distributed them—sometimes for sale, other times given to the needy—among the different counties. The distribution of some these cards to seventeen "Mesdames" at the cost of $12.50 per set was recorded in the documents of Jack County on August 3, 1863. By July 4, 1864, a second round was distributed to eleven war widows, however this time they were gratis due to the "distressful financial conditions caused by war." Truth be told, financial conditions for the wives of soldiers would have prohibited many from purchasing cards, as their cost was more than the $12 per month that most soldiers were paid to fight in the war.[27]

Along the northern end of the frontier, "bushwackers," military deserters, outlaws, and horse and cattle thieves, frequently dealt havoc on the settlers.[28] On the southern end, reports of runaways and renegades on their way to Mexico were the concern. Maj. W. J. Alexander, Commander of the Southern Division of the Texas State Troops, noted that "deserters and renegades" often entered homes demanding food as they passed through the area of Camp Verde in Kerr County. In nearby Medina County, Mary Davenport worried about Indians coming to take her stock, but renegades, not Indians, visited Mary and her young daughter Polley multiple times during the war years. During one incident, men who were presumed to be deserters on their way to Mexico stormed into her home and demanded she prepare them something to eat. As she cooked, they looked around for anything of value. Mary was ready for such moments and had wisely hidden her prized possessions under a floorboard. Years later she related how nervous she had been when one of the men had been standing on the very plank above her valuables but mercifully did not discover them. Instead of killing or robbing her when they invaded her life and home, the men only got away with a home cooked meal.[29]

Many families suffered from food shortages due to the war, and state help was often minimal. A letter in the Dallas *Weekly Herald* as early as December 1862, pointed to the need to help the families of soldiers and how wrong it was that their families should suffer when the men were away fighting. There was a call for those who had extra food to help those who were less fortunate by pointing to the simple fact that families could not afford fifteen dollars for flour or twenty dollars for pork "out of the scanty pay of a private soldier."[30] From Camp San Saba, in present day Coleman County, Third Sgt. with Company "K" C.G. Wood pleaded for, and surprisingly received, a discharge to go to the aid of his wife and seven children. In his words, his "source of distress to my mind such as I have never known before" was due to their destitute condition. His wife and family were trying to survive with no meat, very little bread, terrible clothing, and he believed, facing constant danger from Indian attacks. Their only source of protection was their nine-year-old son, as the oldest boy had enlisted.[31]

In San Saba County, Sara Harkey Hall was one of nine children living with both of her parents during the Civil War years. In her records of daily life, she wrote about learning to knit using two pieces of straw and finding out the hard way that clothing had to last until the next season's cotton had been carded, woven, and sewn into new outfits. Luckily for Sara, both parents worked in some way to provide for the family during the war, as did everyone in the household. Sara's mother made cloth and blankets and, among other things, Sara and her siblings gathered mercifully abundant wild grapes and pecans in 1863 and 1864. The grapes were pressed and processed into wine, then bottled in quarts and sold for seventy-five cents each. The pecans were sold in Brenham for enough money to purchase 250 yards of calico, sugar, and "lincon [*sic*] coffee." Another observation young Sara made was a visit made by a Capt. Wood who stopped at their house so that Sara's father (a Union man) would write a letter for him. This recollection was actually tied to Sara's embarrassment of having to wear her father's shirt while her one dress was being washed, but it adequately sums up the lack of primary documents from the frontier region, due to the simple fact that many of those residents—permanent or temporary—did not read or write.[32]

The Texas frontier was a vast region spanning more than 400 miles of varied conditions and experiences during the war years. This chapter began in the northern portion with the story of rancher Elizabeth FitzPatrick's horrific Indian attack in Young County; it will end on the southern portion with the war experiences of Ann Raney Coleman and Sarah Jane Newman.

Ann Coleman, a divorced woman with a fascinating history before the onset of the war, lived on the coast in Matagorda in 1860. To help support herself during the war years, she did a variety of different work including taking charge of the home of a wealthier woman who had opted to relocate to Victoria with her family and slaves. To add to the various challenges Ann faced, her pregnant daughter and grandchildren moved in to her home when her son-in-law enlisted with the Confederate Army. Ann raised a large garden with half an acre of corn and other vegetables, and also had over a hundred chickens to supplement her income and provide food for the many mouths under her roof. The work was difficult and she wrote that "I would be so hot and tired that I would cry like a child, for my daughter was in a situation [pregnant] that she could not help me."[33]

Life changed when the town was invaded by the Federals on November 27, 1863. The local women were given an hour's notice to flee to avoid the bombardment by Union forces. Some fifty women and children went to the ditches to protect themselves, and then ran further up the coast when a Confederate soldier warned them of immediate danger. She initially refused to leave as she was having a cup of coffee and "was determined not to be cheated out of that, as I could not well do without it." A well-aimed shell that landed twenty or so yards away changed her mind, and she also fled to the ditch. Stubbornly refusing to block the noise with cotton in her ears, Ann listened to the shells fall all around until the women were advised to flee by a Confederate officer. She grabbed her grandson's hand and ran as fast as she could: "I was crossing a bridge when one shell passed me within a yard or two. The wind from it was so strong that it was with difficulty I kept my feet. The little boy was thrown down by the force of the wind from the ball." When they returned home the next day many of the homes were burned to the ground, and supplies were limited. She recalled having to stand in lines with other women to await rations because one of the shells had landed in her garden and ruined it.[34]

Food shortages were not the only problem the women in Nueces County faced. The town experienced a devastating fire during a particularly strong wind. When Ann's roof ignited she collected water from the cistern and handed it up to her daughter to put it out. In fear that it might reignite, they removed all of their belongings and took them to the nearby prairie for safekeeping. Firewood was always needed for heat and cooking, so planks from the damaged homes were quickly scavenged: this also included the ruins from the Baptist church when it blew down in a violent midnight storm. Ann and her daughter gathered as much of the wood as they could carry and stored it in the house. In the morning other women picked up what they could before a "little man" decided they could not have any more. Ann and the women "told him there were enough of us to whip him, so he had as well say nothing...[as we] threatened to tie him hand and foot if he should resist us." As Ann stated,

"Be assured that it was the women that protected themselves in this war and not the men."[35]

Sarah Jane Newman, who was also known as Sally Scull, also lived on the southern end of the frontier. She was known for her skills with the two pistols she carried, as a horse trader before the war, and as a freight driver during the war years. Married five times, her relationships ended a multitude of different ways: her first marriage dissolved when he divorced her, the second when she reported him dead, the third husband disappeared, she divorced the fourth, and her final husband is rumored to have killed her. Added to these tumultuous relationships, there were several reports, one from John S. "Rip" Ford, that she had shot several men at different intervals in her life, perhaps even a couple of those husbands.[36]

In the years before the Civil War, Scull had gained much experience in the horse and cattle trading industry. From her home base of Banquete on the Old Camino Real, she frequented Mexico to get herds of 150 or more wild horses, and then trailed them across Texas to the active New Orleans markets. During the years of stock trading she gained invaluable geographical knowledge, as well as a sense of business that would add to her non-typical lifestyle.[37]

During the war the Old Camino Real through southern Texas became known as the Cotton Road. The Union blockade of Galveston thwarted attempts to import and export goods via New Orleans and other port cities. As international law prohibited interference with Mexican ships, Confederate trade continued through Matamoras via the Cotton Road. Thousands of bales arrived in Alleyton, the terminus of the railroad from Houston, to be freighted overland to the Mexican markets. The formerly mentioned Ann Coleman wrote to her niece about the wharfs "full of cotton to go to Mexico and from there to England." All that was needed was someone to take it there.[38]

Image 21. Sally Scull's cotton route.

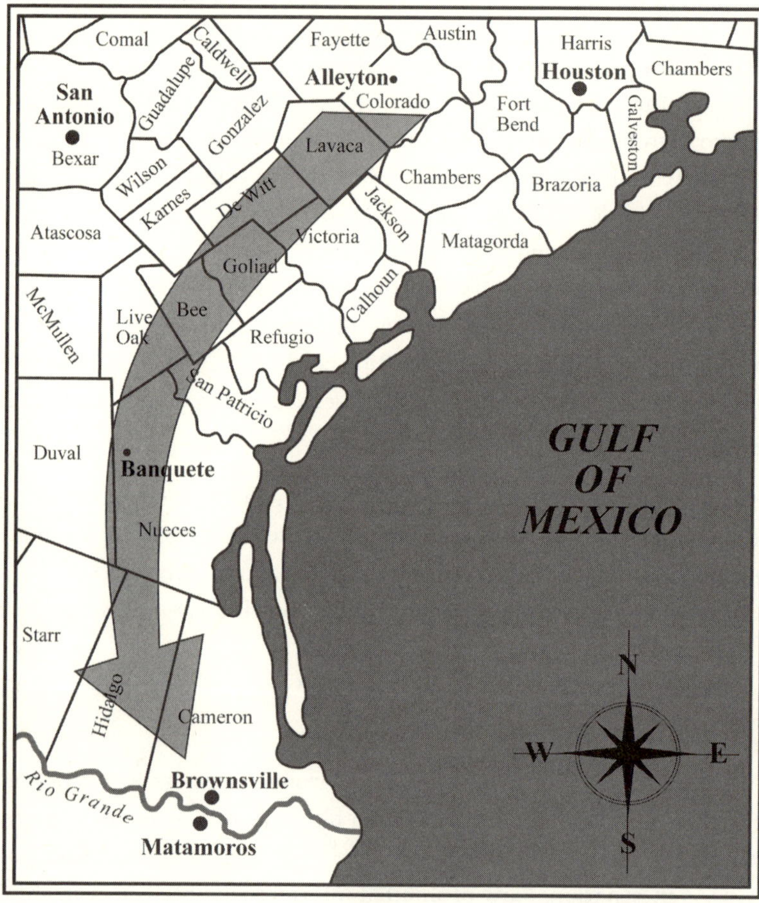

Map 4

Sally Scull transported cotton from Alleyton to Matamoros, Mexico.

Using the labor of Mexican *vaqueros*, Scull freighted ox-pulled wagon loads of cotton from Alleyton to Matamoros, Mexico, a distance close to 325 miles. Fluent in Spanish, an outstanding horsewoman, and known for her frequent use of foul language and for being difficult to get along with, she accompanied her many wagons to their destinations with her six-shooters on her side. Through her and others' efforts, Confederate cotton was sold to England. This generated needed cash flow to purchase supplies that were shipped back to Matamoras, and then transported back to Alleyton via their oxcarts. [39]

Although it was not often an ideal place to be, many women did what they had to do to survive along the Texas frontier during the Civil War. Drew Gilpin Faust wrote that white Confederate women in the path of Union soldiers were rarely assaulted, but on the western frontier Union men were generally not the threat or the concern; when they were, the women banded together and survived. Due to the large numbers of livestock in most of the frontier counties, Indian attacks, real and imaginary, were the main focus, but this was not the only problem the women faced. While they managed homes and hearths, dealt with shortages of food and supplies, confronted deserters, intruders, and countless other difficulties that accompanied life on the frontier, they contended with the fear of their men fighting in near and distant locations. Like other women in Civil War Texas, and throughout the rest of the country, the women adjusted as the situation dictated to survive and emerge from those tumultuous years.

NOTES

1. Patricia Adkins Rochette, *Bourland in North Texas and Indian Territory During the Civil War: Fort Cobb, Fort Arbuckle & the Wichita Mountains.* Volume I. *Colonel James G. Bourland Timeline and Volume II. Appendix* (n.d., n.p), 277-281. Testimonies from the grown children and another captive woman are recorded in this version of the event. Britt Johnson was instrumental in the rescue of his wife and children in June 1865; he was killed in 1871 by Kiowa Indians. See Michael E. McClellan, "Johnson, Britton," *Handbook of Texas Online,* accessed June 22, 2013, http://www.tshaonline.org/handbook/online/articles/fjo07.
2. Ibid. Millie eventually married a Kiowa. Mrs. Roland from Jack County was rescued at the same time as Elizabeth FitzPatrick.
3. The jacket of Erika L. Murr's *A Rebel Wife in Texas: The Diary and Letters of Elizabeth Scott Neblett, 1852-1864* states that "despite the frontier conditions...[Neblett] aspired to the 'cult of true womanhood.'" Neblett lived in Grimes County, located in the eastern portion of Texas, and several hundred miles from the western frontier of white settlement in 1860. In this setting women faced less threats and could focus on the "cult" to which Murr refers. Erika L. Murr, ed., *A Rebel Wife in Texas: The Diary and Letters of Elizabeth Scott Neblett, 1852-1864* (Baton Rouge: Louisiana State University Press, 2001); Amy L. Wink's *Tandem Lives: The Frontier Texas Diaries of Henrietta Baker Embree and Tennessee Keys Embree, 1856-1884* (Knoxville: The University of Tennessee Press, 2008), suggests that both Embree women also lived on the frontier, but Henrietta wrote about how far away her husband had to go to help women and children who were forted up from Indian attacks in Comanche County. Additionally, Tennessee's fondness for reading about early Indian problems in the colonies suggests she is far removed from Indians in her Bell County home, also approximately one hundred miles from the frontier (105, 125). Other work includes Angela Boswell's "The Civil War and the Lives of Texas Women" in Charles Grear's *The Fate of Texas: The Civil War and the Lone Star State* (Fayetteville: University of Arkansas Press, 2008), but this is about the women of Colorado County. Vicki Betts' "'A Sacred Charge upon Our Hands': Assisting the Families of Confederate Soldiers in Texas,

1861-1865" in Kenneth W. Howell's *The Seventh Star of the Confederacy: Texas during the Civil War* (Denton: University of North Texas Press, 2009), examines women in South Texas.

4. Margaret Walsh, "Women's Place on the American Frontier," *Journal of American Studies* 29, no. 2 (August 1995): 241-255, quotation from 243.
5. Deborah Liles, "Southern Roots, Western Foundations: The Peculiar Institution and the Livestock Industry on the Northwestern Frontier of Texas, 1846-1864" (Ph.D dissertation, University of North Texas, 2013); Lillian Schlissel, Vicki L. Ruiz, and Janice Monk, eds., *Western Women, Their Land, Their Lives* (Albuquerque: University of New Mexico Press, 1988), 100.
6. Dallas *Weekly Herald,* June 5, 1861.
7. First quotation from *Dallas Weekly,* October 18, 1861; Second quotation from Houston *Tri-weekly Telegraph,* January 18, 1864; Third quotation from Richard Montgomery Gano to Francis R. Lubbock, August 12, 1863. Records of Governor Francis R. Lubbock, Archives and Information Services Division, Texas State Library and Archives Commission.
8. Proclamation by P. Murrah, March 26, 1864, in Dorman H. Winfrey and James M. Day, eds., *The Indian Papers of Texas and the Southwest, 1825-1916,* IV (Austin: Texas State Historical Association, 1995), 80.
9. Young County tax rolls, 1857-1864 (microfilm, Willis Library, University of North Texas).
10. Arrell Morgan Gibson, "Native Americans and the Civil War," *American Indian Quarterly* 9, no. 4 (Autumn, 1985): 387; Robert Utley, *Lone Star Justice: The First Century of the Texas Rangers* (New York: Berkley Press, 2002), 124-128; John W. Gorman "Frontier Defense: Enlistment Patterns for the Texas Frontier Regiments in the Civil War," in *The Seventh Star of the Confederacy: Texas during the Civil War,* ed. Kenneth W. Howell (Denton: University of North Texas Press, 2009), 72; David Paul Smith, "Frontier Organization," *Handbook of Texas Online,* accessed march 23, 2013, http://www.tshaonline.org/handbook/online/articles/qkf02. A review of the county histories does not indicate that the women in the seven counties had friendly relations with the Indians in the area.

11. Drew Gilpin Faust, *Mothers of Invention: Women of the Slaveholding South In the American Civil War* (Chapel Hill: University of North Carolina Press, 1996), 199-200; Rochette, *Bourland in North Texas,* A236-A324; An article in the *Northern Standard* stated that Judge Gwinn in Montague County authorized paying private citizens five dollars a pound for ammunition, which was a tremendous amount (*Northern Standard,* April 28, 1863).

12. Mary Whately Clark, *The Palo Pinto Story* (Fort Worth: The Manney Company, 1956), 55-57. The white women were not the only ones who sought refuge at the fort, as there were also Indian women there from unnamed tribes. In their recollections years later, Jane and Sam recalled one of the Indian women cooking an unfortunate turtle over a fire. Whether this represented a lack of food or a difference in food preference is not mentioned; Grady William Box, "The Civil War in North Central Texas: Its Impact on Frontier Families, 1860-1874" (M.A. thesis, Texas Woman's University, 1991), 31; Barbara A. Neal Ledbetter, *Fort Belknap Frontier Saga: Indians, Negroes and Anglo-Americans on the Texas Border* (Burnet, Texas: Eakin Press, 1982), quotation from 103.

13. Mary G. Ramos, "The Pre-Civil War Frontier," accessed November 5, 2013, http://www.texasalmanac.com/topics/history/pre-civil-war-frontier; Rochette, *Bourland in North Texas,* 219.

14. Sally Reynolds Matthews, *Interwoven, A Pioneer Chronicle* (Austin: University of Texas Press, 1958), 17. Sally was Susan Reynolds Newcomb's sister.

15. Samuel P. Newcomb Diary, Briscoe Center for American History, University of Texas at Austin, (transcription). Jan. 1, 1865, first and third quotation from Jan. 2, 1865,

16. Drew Gilpin Faust, *Mothers of Invention: Women of the Slaveholding South in the American Civil War* (Chapel Hill: University of North Carolina, 1996), 126.

17. Samuel P. Newcomb Diary, Jan. 2, 1865.

18. Sally Reynolds Matthews, *Interwoven,* 19-23; Samuel P. Newcomb Diary, Jan 1 and 21, 1865; April 26, 1865, first quotation from January 1, 1865, second quotation from March 2, 1865.

19. Susan G. Butruille, *Women's Voices from the Western Frontier* (Boise: Tamarack Books, 1995), 87.

20. Mark M. Carroll, *Homesteads Ungovernable: Families, Sex, Race, and the Law in Frontier Texas, 1823-1860* (Austin: University of Texas Press, 2001), 98.

21. Walsh, "Women's Place on the American Frontier," 246; Ann Patton Malone, *Women on the Texas Frontier: A Cross-Cultural Perspective* (El Paso: Texas Western Press, 1983), 15.

22. Seymour V. Connor, *The Peters Colony of Texas: A History and Biographical Sketches of the Early Settlers* (Austin: Texas State Historical Association, 1959), 105, 316; Eighth Census of the United States, Palo Pinto County, Schedule 1 (Free Inhabitants); Eighth Census of the United States, Palo Pinto County, Schedule 2 (Slave Inhabitants).

23. Mary Kemp, Judy James, and Pam Tarpley, *Parker County Legends: Trail Bosses and Wild Hosses* (Weatherford, TX: Nebo Valley Press, 2007), 26; "Memoirs of Henry Belding," *West Texas Historical Association Year Book* 29 (October, 1953): 87-88. Loving made rings for all of the girls in the family with some of the Colorado gold. (Nancy Dozier, Presentation on Oliver Loving at the Doss Center in Weatherford, Texas, September 21, 2013).

24. Karylon Hallmark Russell, "In the Shadow of the Civil War," *Llano News,* April 27, 2011; "Camp Nelson Confederate Cemetery," accessed August 25, 2013, http://www.couchgenweb.com/civilwar/camp_nelson_cemetery.htm.

25. Elizabeth Roe interview with US Work Projects Administration, Federal Writers' Project, Folklore Project, Life Histories, 1936-39, 3-6.

26. Cliff D. Cates, *Pioneer History of Wise County: From Red Men to Railroads-Twenty Years of Intrepid History* (St. Louis, MO: Nixon-Jones, 1907), 135; Henry Smythe, *Historical Sketch of Parker County and Weatherford, Texas* (St. Louis, MO: Louis C. Lavat, 1877); Drew Gilpin Faust, "Altars of Sacrifice: Confederate Women and the Narratives of War," *Journal of American History* 76, no. 4 (March 1990): 1214; Faust, *Mothers of Invention,* quotation from 188; Jonathan Hamilton Baker Diary, Tarrant County Archives, Fort Worth, Texas, entry from September 14, 1861.

27. "Wool and Mohair Industry," *Handbook of Texas Online*, accessed November 20, 2009, http://www.tshaonline.org/handbook/online/articles/WW/asw2.html; Ida Lasater Huckabay, *Ninety-Four Years in Jack County, 1854-1948* (Waco: Texian Press, 1974), quotation from 92-93; Earnest Wallace, *Texas in Turmoil* (Austin: Steck-Vaughn, 1965), 131.
28. Box, "The Civil War in North Central Texas," 19. For more information on the Texas Troubles see Donald E. Reynolds, *Texas Troubles: The Slave Insurrection Panic of 1860 and the Secession of the Lower South* (Baton Rouge: Louisiana State University Press, 2007).
29. Florence Angermiller and Emma Kelly Davenport, *Pioneer Experiences of Mary Davenport and Nancy Kelley*, US Work Projects Administration, Federal Writers' Project, Life Histories, 1936-39, 1-2; "Under the Rebel Flag: Life in Texas During the Civil War," W. J. Alexander to Jeremiah Y. Dashiell, July 29, 1863, accessed December 13, 2013, https://www.tsl.texas.gov/exhibits/civilwar/documents/1863/wj_alexander_jul29_1863_1.html; Mary's father, Captain John Crane, and her second husband, John Davenport, had both been murdered by Indians.
30. Dallas *Weekly Herald*, December 13, 1862.
31. "Under the Rebel Flag: Life in Texas During the Civil War," C. G. Wood to James E. McCord, October 10, 1863, accessed December 18, 2013, https://www.tsl.texas.gov/exhibits/civilwar/documents/1864/cg_wood_oct13_1863_1.html.
32. Sarah Harkey Hall, *Surviving on the Texas Frontier: The Journal of an Orphan Girl in San Saba County* (Austin: Eakin Press, 1996), 13-17, quotation from 17. Lincoln coffee was generally any coffee that was made from substitute products.
33. C. Richard King, ed., *Victorian Lady on the Texas Frontier: The Journal of Ann Raney Coleman* (Norman: University of Oklahoma Press, 1971), xv, 153, 155. As was the custom, it was not mentioned that her daughter could have been pregnant but just a few pages later the newborn baby is mentioned.
34. J. Barto Arnold III, "Fort Esperanza," *Handbook of Texas Online* accessed August 11, 2013, http://www.tshaonline.org/hand-

book/online/articles/qcf02; King, *Victorian Lady on the Texas Frontier,* 155-159, first quotation from 158, second quotation from 159.

35. King, *Victorian Lady on the Texas Frontier,* 156, quotations from 154.
36. Dan Kilgore, "Scull, Sarah Jane Newman [Sally]" *Handbook of Texas Online,* accessed November 6, 2013, http://www.tshaonline.org/handbook/online/articles/fsc33.
37. Dan Kilgore, "Two Sixshooters and a Sunbonnet: The Story of Sally Skull," accessed November 6, 2013, www.tamu/faculty/ccbn/dewitt/skulllegend.html.
38. Kilgore, "Two Sixshooters and a Sunbonnet"; King, *Victorian Lady on the Texas Frontier,* 155 fn.
39. Kilgore, "Two Sixshooters and a Sunbonnet."

Notes on Contributors

Vicki Betts is a librarian at The University of Texas at Tyler. She is author of *Smith County, Texas, in the Civil War* (1977) and "'A Sacred Charge Upon Our Hands': Assisting the Families of Confederate Soldiers in Texas, 1861-1865" in *The Seventh Star of the Confederacy: Texans During the Civil War* (2009).

Angela Boswell received her Ph.D. in history from Rice University, and is professor of history at Henderson State University in Arkadelphia, Arkansas. She is the author of *Her Act and Deed: Women's Lives in a Rural Southern County, 1837-1873* (2001), which won the Liz Carpenter Award from the Texas State Historical Association, coeditor of *Women Shaping the South: Creating and Confronting Change* (2006), and coeditor of *Searching for Their Places: Women in the South Across Four Centuries* (2003).

Brittany Bounds received her Ph.D. in American History at Texas A&M in 2015, specializing in social and military/diplomatic history. She now teaches American Studies as an Assistant Professor at National Defense University in Washington, DC.

Judith Dykes-Hoffmann holds a Masters of History from Texas State University where she worked with historian Dr. Victoria Bynum, and a Ph.D. from the University of Texas at Austin. Her dissertation "On the Edge of the Balcones Escarpment: The Urban and Cultural Development of New Braunfels and San Marcos, Texas, 1845-1880" was under the direction of late famed geographer Dr. Terry Jordan-Bychkov. She currently teaches at Texas Lutheran University in Seguin, Texas.

Dorothy Ewing graduated from Texas A&M-Corpus Christi with a bachelor's degree in history and a master's degree in interdisciplinary studies. She is a member of the Texas State Historical Association, the Nueces County Historical Society, and the American Association of University Women. She has presented papers at several history conferences including a Civil War Sesquicentennial Program in Vicksburg, Mississippi.

Bruce A. Glasrud is Professor Emeritus of History, California State University, East Bay and Retired Dean, School of Arts and Sciences, Sul Ross State University. An award-winning specialist on African Americans in the South and the West, Glasrud has published over thirty books including *Free Blacks in Antebellum Texas* (2015).

Linda S. Hudson, Ph.D., received the East Texas Historical Association's Chamberlain Award for best journal article in 2009, "Uppity Women Rise Up and Have Breakfast"; the Fehrenbach Award for *Mistress of Manifest Destiny: A Biography of Jane McManus Cazneau, 1807-1878* (2001), and the Texas State Historical Association's Caldwell Award for "The Last Spanish Governor of Texas." Her latest work is a Database of Texas Supreme Court appeals involving free blacks, slaves, and former slaves, 1840-1907, available at the Portal to Texas History, University of North Texas Libraries. She is retired and lives at Comanche, Texas, where she continues writing about Texas History.

Deborah Liles received her Ph.D from the University of North Texas, where she currently teaches history. She is the author of *Will Rogers Coliseum* (2012) and several journal articles. Current projects include "Southern Roots, Western Foundations: The Livestock Industry and Slavery on the Northwestern Frontier of Texas, 1846-1865," (2017) and "Oliver Loving: Dean of the Texas Trails" (2017).

Elizabeth S. Mata received her B.A. in History and her M.A. in History and Political Thought from Texas A&M International University. A native of Laredo, she is presently an adjunct American history professor at TAMIU.

Beverly Rowe received her Ph.D. in American History from the University of North Texas in Denton in 1999. She is a tenured faculty member at Texarkana College in Texarkana, Texas, where she has been employed for the past twenty-three years.

Rebecca Sharpless is professor of history at Texas Christian University. She is the author of *Cooking in Other Women's Kitchens: Domestic Workers in the South, 1865-1960* (2010), and *Fertile Ground, Narrow Choices: Women on Texas Cotton Farms, 1900-1940* (1999). She is currently researching the impact of wheat cultivation on North Texas.

Candice N. Shockley teaches dual credit classes at Cuero High School and is an adjunct instructor at Victoria College. Her interest in Texas women's studies encouraged her to pursue a master's degree in history at Texas State University with a focus on the experiences of Army Nurse Corps veterans in the Vietnam War. Originally from Victoria, Texas, Shockley has also worked as a writing tutor and published several articles with Wiley-Blackwell.

Jerry Thompson, Regents Professor at Texas A&M International University and former president of the Texas State Historical Association, has written or edited over twenty-five books on the Civil War in the Southwest. He has received numerous awards from the Texas State Historical Association, Arizona Historical Society, and the Historical Society of New Mexico.

Index